# AFTER ANARCHY

# AFTER ANARCHY

## LEGITIMACY AND POWER IN THE UNITED NATIONS SECURITY COUNCIL

*Ian Hurd*

**PRINCETON UNIVERSITY PRESS** PRINCETON AND OXFORD

Copyright © 2007 by Princeton University Press

Published by Princeton University Press, 41 William Street,
Princeton, New Jersey 08540

In the United Kingdom: Princeton University Press, 3 Market Place,
Woodstock, Oxfordshire OX20 1SY

Library of Congress Cataloging-in-Publication Data

Hurd, Ian.
After anarchy : legitimacy and power in the United Nations Security
Council / Ian Hurd.
p. cm.
Includes bibliographical references and index.
ISBN-13: 978-0-691-12866-5 (hardcover : alk. paper)
ISBN-10: 0-691-12866-9 (hardcover : alk. paper)
1. United Nations. Security Council.   2. United Nations—
Resolutions.   3. Legitimacy of governments.   I. Title.
JZ5006.7.H87   2007
320.01'1—dc22       2006028997

British Library Cataloging-in-Publication Data is available

This book has been composed in Galliard

Printed on acid-free paper. ∞

press.princeton.edu

Printed in the United States of America

3   5   7   9   10   8   6   4   2

# Contents

# *Preface*

IN 2002, as the United States planned an attack on Iraq to remove Saddam Hussein from power, American diplomats sought political support for the mission from all quarters. They pursued bilateral negotiations for the support of foreign governments; they approached NATO to aid in the defense of Turkey; they appealed directly to publics around the world; and they brought the matter to the United Nations Security Council. The Council, famously, came to play a central role in the diplomatic drama prior to the start of the war in March 2003. It was the forum for what turned out to be perhaps the most heated diplomatic confrontation in world politics since the Cuban Missile Crisis. For its efforts, the Council earned itself scathing criticism from all sides, both supporters of the war and opponents, and the camps agreed on the key point: that the Council had "failed" a crucial test. One side believed it had failed in its responsibilities by refusing to authorize the U.S.-led war, and the other believed it had failed by being unable to stop it. As a result, the Council was revealed to be "strategically irrelevant" to the United States, "morally bankrupt," and "simply incompatible" with the new realities of world power.[1] President George W. Bush himself implied that the Council had missed its last chance "to show its relevance."[2] The vehemence of the attacks on the Council matched the energy devoted in earlier stages to lobbying the Council over the terms of its resolutions on Iraq. Both activities were pursued with great vigor, reflecting the belief that great stakes were in play.

The controversy at the Council was over the legitimacy that comes from a Council resolution. The two camps were aiming for the same goal—to appropriate that legitimacy for themselves, although they intended to use it for opposite political purposes. When Kofi Annan claimed that the UN Security Council holds "unique legitimacy"[3] to authorize military action, many states appeared to agree with him. Even the Americans apparently shared the belief that more countries would come to support the U.S. if the American position were legitimized by the Council.[4] The American diplomatic effort prior to the war was shaped by the per-

---

[1] Krauthammer 2003; Glennon 2003.

[2] Press conference, February 23, 2003, Crawford, Texas.

[3] Interview with Kofi Annan by BBC News, September 10, 2002, published at news .bbc.co.uk/2/hi/middle_east/2250948.stm.

[4] Tharoor 2003. Statements confirming the link between Council approval and third-country support for the invasion were made by Russia, Canada, most countries in the European Union, India, and many others. For a useful summary, see the *Observer* (London), January 12, 2003.

haps strategic use of those beliefs as a tool to reduce the political costs of the mission; this is what made it rational to spend energy winning Council approval in 2002. Legitimacy, therefore, carries a behavioral implication, as Annan later explained: "The legitimacy that the UN conveys can ensure that the greatest number of states are able and willing to take" collective action against collective threats.[5]

But what kind of difference does legitimacy make in international politics, and under what circumstances does it work? What kind of power is it? How can it be transferred among actors, and how can it be used by states as a tool in their own pursuit of political advantage? These are the questions pursued in this book. Along the way I show that legitimacy is central to the power of international organizations (IOs) and to world politics more generally, and also that we can use it to begin to explain some phenomena in world politics that were hitherto unaccounted for. These include perennially vexing questions in the study of international organizations regarding the relation between the power of states and the power of IOs, the sources of power for IOs, and the nature of states and their interests. The focus here is on the UN Security Council and the particular consequences of its legitimacy/illegitimacy for world politics, and therefore it is the power of the Council, including the making, use, and loss of that power, that gets the most attention. The analysis, however, has implications for the study of other international organizations.

## ACKNOWLEDGMENTS

This book would not have been possible without the support and attention of many people. Foremost among them, I thank Alexander Wendt for his attention to the project over many years. Several colleagues and friends read the entire manuscript, and for this I thank Bruce Russett, Michael Barnett, Elizabeth Shakman Hurd, Roland Paris, Alex Wendt, and the anonymous reviewers for Princeton University Press. For comments on individual chapters and helpful discussions on the cases and concepts in the book, I thank Karen Alter, Jose Alvarez, Risa Brooks, Stephen Brooks, Bruce Carruthers, Ian Clark, William Connolly, Bruce Cronin, Sam Daws, Michael Doyle, Martha Finnemore, Siba Grovogui, Terrence Halliday, Brian Job, Robert Keohane, Michael Loriaux, Robert McLaren, Louis Pauly, Daryl Press, Richard Price, Henry Shue, Christian Reus-Smit, Hendrik Spruyt, James Sutterlin, Benjamin Valentino, Erik Voeten, Jennifer Welsh, William Wohlforth, and Mark Zacher. Christopher Swarat provided excellent research assistance.

---

[5] Secretary General's statement to the Security Council, September 11, 2002, published at www.un.org/apps/sg/sgstats.asp?nid-44.

The project began as a dissertation written under the guidance of Bruce Russett and Alexander Wendt, and I owe them great thanks for their support. The dissertation was supported by grants from the Social Sciences and Humanities Research Council of Canada, the Department of National Defence of Canada, and the Yale Dissertation Fellowship. My interest in International Relations theory and institutions began at Carleton University in Ottawa, where I was lucky to be taught by Maxwell Cameron, Sharon Sutherland, and Barbara Jenkins. I am grateful to them for their early encouragement.

I wish also to thank the people and institutions who gave me opportunities to discuss aspects of this work in seminars, including Michael Doyle and Jose Alvarez and their seminar at Columbia Law School, the PIPES seminar at the University of Chicago, Steve Brooks and Bill Wohlforth at the Dickey Center at Dartmouth College, Brian Hanson and the Center for International and Comparative Studies at Northwestern University, Erik Voeten and Martha Finnemore at George Washington University, Ian Clark and Christian Reus-Smit and the Australian National University, Jennifer Welsh and Sir Adam Roberts at the Center for International Studies at the University of Oxford, Jan Wouters and Bart Kerremans at the Katholieke Universiteit Leuven, Johan Meeusen and Peter Bursens at Universiteit Antwerpen, and Carola Weil and Stacie Goddard at the Center for International Studies at the University of Southern California.

Parts of chapter 2 appeared in "Legitimacy and Authority in International Politics," *International Organization* 53, no. 2 (spring 1999): 379–408, © 1999 by the IO Foundation and the Massachusetts Institute of Technology, used with permission. Some material from chapter 5 is based on the article "Legitimacy, Power, and the Symbolic Life of the Security Council," *Global Governance* 8, no. 1 (January–March 2002): 35–51, © 2002 by Lynne Rienner Publishers, used with permission. A version of chapter 6 appeared as "The Strategic Use of Liberal Internationalism: Libya and the UN Sanctions, 1992–2003," *International Organization* 59, no. 3 (July 2005): 495–526, © 2005 by the IO Foundation, where it won the Robert O. Keohane award for the best article in *International Organization* by an untenured scholar for 2005. It is reprinted with the permission of Cambridge University Press.

Finally, I am endlessly indebted to Beth Hurd for her encouragement and insight in this project and in everything else. This book is dedicated, with love, to her and to our daughters, Ally and Sophie.

# AFTER ANARCHY

# CHAPTER 1

# Introduction

THUCYDIDES' ACCOUNT of the negotiation between Athens and the Melians is one of the earliest known statements of the connection between legitimacy and power. Resisting an ultimatum from Athens, the Melians suggest that might does not make right: "in our view it is at any rate useful that you should not destroy a principle that is to the general good of all men—namely, that in the case of all who fall into danger there should be such a thing as fair play and just dealing."[1] The Melians put forward a case which differentiates between the justice that comes from superior power and the justice that comes from general rules and morals, arguing that these latter should be valued for both instrumental and normative reasons by the weak and strong alike. Some rules of war and diplomacy, they say, are legitimate and should be respected. They lose the argument, of course, and ultimately pay a high price for it, but in the process the Melians play their part in launching a long debate over the relationship between legitimacy, authority, and power. The debate has been continued in philosophic and sociological settings, carried forward by Aristotle to Machiavelli, Locke, and Rousseau, and on to Marx and the twentieth-century philosophers of modernity such as Weber. But although there is plenty of evidence that practitioners of international relations (IR) take seriously the power of international legitimacy and that academics make frequent reference to it in an ad hoc way, the concept itself only rarely receives sustained attention in analyses of the international system.

This book works on two levels. It raises important conceptual issues from the leading edge of IR theory and applies them to an understanding of the practical day-to-day operation of the UN Security Council. It can therefore be read as a work on IR theory or as a document of UN studies, as advancing theory or empirics. Better still, it might be seen as doing all of the above.

The central purpose of the book is to introduce a workable concept of legitimacy to the study of International Relations. Although the use of the term "legitimacy" is common in International Relations, very little attention is given to what it means or how it works. There is no available model of legitimacy for use in international relations that would allow serious inquiry into its causes, consequences, and implications. My first goal here is

[1] Thucydides 1954, 402.

to provide such a model and show its worth by using it to explain empirical phenomena in world politics. The model itself, developed by borrowing from sociology, psychology, and management studies, fills a gap in International Relations that has been widening since the rise of constructivism in the late 1980s. Absent an account of legitimacy, much of constructivism's empirical work on the "logic of appropriateness" remains ungrounded; legitimacy is inherent in the constructivist approach, and yet to date there has not been a full-fledged exploration of the concept and its operation.

The theory of legitimacy, then, contributes in two ways: first, by opening up the empirical study of the Security Council in ways previously not possible; and, second, by providing a bridge between rationalist and constructivist approaches. On the empirical contribution, my interpretation shows the importance of beginning with considerations about legitimacy and legitimation when trying to understand either the history or the current practice of the Council. From the earliest debates over the veto in 1945, to the current controversies over peace missions, new members, and the 2003 Iraq crisis, and into the future of Council reform, we can see the fundamental role played by the processes of legitimation and delegitimation in all that the Council does. It is not too much to say that the Council has power when it is seen as legitimate and loses power as that perception recedes. All Council decisions contain at least some concern for how the choices will help or hurt its legitimacy to various audiences. In some moments, as with the endgame of the Libyan sanctions in the 1990s, legitimacy concerns can come to dominate other considerations in the decision-making calculus of even the Great Powers at the Council. At such times the central role of legitimacy is made clearest; but it remains important even in the more mundane politics of day-to-day Council operation. The empirical cases in the book draw from both the moments of high-politics drama and the more commonplace "normal politics" of the Council.

The essential role legitimacy plays in international politics complicates the academic study of International Relations, because it means that at least some part of outcomes are influenced by this shifty, intersubjective quality which is only indirectly available for empirical study. The power of legitimacy to define actors' goals and interests, as well as to construct what actors take for granted, means that observers of the international field need some way to monitor and decipher actors' senses of the legitimate and illegitimate.[2] To read international politics without paying attention to the competition over legitimacy would leave one with no way to understand such common acts as saving face, offering justifications, using

---

[2] See Hurd 1999 for some of the theoretical foundations to the study of legitimacy in IR.

symbols, and being in a position of authority. One cannot be offended by another's rejection of protocol, or by a rival being well treated by a third party, unless one shares a common definition of what appropriate protocol requires and what constitutes a step up or down on the ladder of status. Such acts make up a large proportion of the stuff of foreign policy and international politics, just as they are common in domestic and interpersonal politics, but they cannot be decoded without a prior sense on the part of the observer of what the actors accept as legitimate and what they define as illegitimate.

An institution that exercises legitimated power is in a position of authority.[3] In international relations, this means that a legitimated international organization possesses sovereign authority. Sovereignty, understood as the "right to exercise final authority" over a people and territory, is distributed among various types of actors in the international system.[4] This includes states, of course, but also, as is shown in the following chapters, any international institutions such as the Security Council which exercise legitimated power over states. The presence of sovereign authority in nonstate actors suggests that the common understanding of the term "international anarchy" is misleading. The international system comprises diverse actors with legitimated power and so has diverse locations of sovereign authority. State interactions occur in a social space that contains authoritative institutions like the Council, and this contradicts the "anarchic" premise of much contemporary IR scholarship.

This book explores these issues through the practical workings of the Security Council. It examines how the members of the United Nations approach the Council and how the Council responds in its daily operations. The practical role of the Council in international relations is not well understood, despite the great deal of reporting and analysis on its actions since 1945. Even simple questions about the behavior of the Council and its effects on states and on the international system have complicated answers. This complexity, I suggest, is due in part to an underappreciation of the role of legitimacy and legitimation in the routine business of the Council. Without understanding the peculiar nature of power based on legitimacy, one cannot understand the behavior and effects of the Council.

Consider, for example, what appears to be a simple question: What power does the Council have in international politics? Its most tangible products are its formal resolutions: the Council issued approximately 1,675 official resolutions as of May 1, 2006, as well as many hundreds of Presidential Statements. These are all carefully negotiated statements of

---

[3] Barnett 2001; Voeten 2005.
[4] The definition comes from Biersteker and Weber 1996, 2.

intent, resolve, concern, or action, and together they make up the Council's most tangible contributions to world politics. Each is drafted, discussed, debated, and duly promulgated, after which it is published, publicized, and sent to research libraries worldwide. It is not entirely clear what happens after that. Some resolutions become famous because they relate to conflicts that are in the public consciousness, for instance, Resolutions 242 and 425 on the Israeli-Palestinian conflict and 660 and 678 on the Iraq-Gulf War. Most, however, do not. Moreover, the real impact on the world of even the "famous" resolutions is not easy to trace. They are generally seen as important documents in international politics, but this certainly does not mean they are automatically followed. Despite the legal obligations they might create, Council resolutions clearly do not necessarily elicit full and complete compliance by nation-states. States still seem to "pick and choose" from Council decisions those elements they respect while pretending other elements do not exist.

This obvious fact of international politics leads to a conundrum: if the most visible products of the work of the Security Council cannot be judged as clearly successful in shifting the policies of member states, then does the body really have the power it was intended to have under the UN Charter? Indeed, what actually is the power of the Security Council, and where does it come from? More broadly, where does any international organization get its power? In a world of formally independent nation-states, the answers to these questions are intrinsic to the claim that international organizations matter at all in the international system.

If we see states as sovereign bodies, legally free to make their own decisions, and international organizations as constraints on state freedom, then there is a contradiction at the heart of the most powerful organizations in international relations. The founding documents of many international organizations give them broad powers to supervise, regulate, and enforce activities throughout international politics and economics, and yet the rights of sovereign states are supposed to protect them from outside interference, including that of international organizations. States are supposed to be sovereign, and yet an effective international organization must, in some way, infringe on the freedom of states. Hardt and Negri describe the contradiction:

> On the one hand, the entire U.N. conceptual structure is predicated on the recognition and legitimation of the sovereignty of individual states, and it is thus planted squarely within the old framework of international rights defined by pacts and treaties. On the other hand, however, this process of legitimation is effective only insofar as it transfers sovereign right to a real *supranational* center.[5]

[5] Hardt and Negri 2000, 4–5.

Perhaps nowhere is this paradox more clearly exhibited than with respect to the UN Security Council. The Council is endowed with tremendous formal power by the UN Charter and with primary authority in the international system over questions of international peace and security. And yet it is apparent in the post–Cold War world that attempts by the Council to use that power generate enormous controversy. The Council's power is spelled out explicitly in the Charter, but in practice its use is always problematic.

This contradiction between international commitment and state sovereignty is traditionally resolved in academic texts by noting that international obligations are generally binding only when a state *chooses* to be bound. A state could so choose either by joining an organization like the United Nations, and thus consenting to the authority of the Security Council as defined by the UN Charter,[6] or by complying with or ignoring a particular decision of the Council on a case-by-case basis.[7] Either way, the power of the Security Council and its decisions perpetually depends on the consent of states, either prior (when the state joined the UN) or contemporary (when the state responds to a particular requirement). In this way the institution can be seen as entirely consistent with, and indeed subordinate to, the independent desires of sovereign states.[8]

The "consent" approach to resolving the contradiction is convenient but at odds with certain evidence about state behavior toward international rules.[9] On the one hand, state decision makers often seem to take at least some international obligations extremely seriously, even when they might prefer to ignore them. National governments expend a great deal of energy in managing and interpreting international obligations, while also trying to influence what international organizations say and do. On the other hand, even when states violate international commitments, that violation is usually accompanied by an effort on the part of the state to present the violation as consistent with its obligations. In both cases, the free choice of states seems at least partially constrained by the existence of the organizations, even when they do not wish to be constrained and even when they choose

---

[6] This is generally the attitude taken regarding consent in the field of International Law. The capacity to conclude treaties, and so be bound by them, is enshrined in the *Vienna Convention on the Law of Treaties (1969)* as a right possessed by every state. See Harris 1991, chap. 10.

[7] Realists and neorealists in IR theory tend to take this view of consent. International organizations are, in this tradition, the *reflections* of autonomous state decisions rather than independent actors in their own right. See Grieco 1993 and Mearsheimer 1994/95. For further discussion of consent in state commitments, see March and Olsen 1998; Martin and Simmons 1998; and Kahler 1998.

[8] Van Oudenaren (2003) suggests that the legitimacy of an international rule is gauged by the degree to which it approaches universal consent among states. I define legitimacy in non-choice terms below.

[9] See also Williams's critique of the contractual model of IR (2005, 204–210).

to maneuver around an international obligation. States generally try to *manage* their relations with international organizations such as the UN and to influence their development rather than ignore them or pretend they do not exist. That some international organizations are taken for granted is important, for it means that the organization is in a position of power in international society, even if states sometimes choose not to comply.

In a notable article published in 1966, Inis L. Claude Jr. suggested a more satisfying way to resolve the conceptual conflict between state autonomy and international obligation.[10] Claude argued that states sometimes perceive international organizations as legitimate and therefore view the obligations they embody as acceptable and correct. Singling out the Security Council, Claude pointed to the apparent power of some organizations to confer and withhold legitimacy from actors and decisions. The Security Council of the 1960s had power, he noted, because its statements and resolutions were recognized as representing the views of a large segment of the world's states. The Council was authorized to speak and act on behalf of the "global community," and thus its utterances and behavior carried more force than had they been carried out by individual Council members.[11] Claude's aim was to rebut those critics of the Security Council who saw it as "merely" a talking-shop not constituted to take meaningful action. He recognized that the Security Council was powerful precisely because its actions and pronouncements represented the collective sentiment of some respected part of the international community. This power of "collective legitimation" is one potential source of the Council's influence over international relations which, significantly, does not rely on the choice or consent of individual states; its effects do not come from states *choosing* to recognize them.[12] Rather, they come from processes of socialization and symbolism which operate on a different level than instrumental decision making.

In the decades since Claude's contribution the field of International Relations as an academic discipline has changed dramatically, with a greater emphasis today on social phenomena of all kinds. His provocative thoughts on the UN Security Council's powers of "collective legitimation" would seem to fit more comfortably in today's IR universe, but the link between the new social theories of international relations and the question of the legitimacy of international organizations has not yet been drawn. The real world of international politics has also changed, with activity in

[10] The original article appeared in *International Organization* 20 (1966): 367–379. It is expanded and reprinted in Claude 1967.

[11] On the connection between legitimacy and community, see also Clark 2005.

[12] Slater's (1969) response to Claude highlights the fact that states may grow "disenchanted" with IOs that associate themselves with positions the states are opposed to, and Slater treats this as "delegitimation."

and around the Council greatly increased. The new atmosphere of cooperation among the Council's permanent members since the late 1980s has meant that the body is better able to take meaningful action on a range of issues, including sanctions, enforcement, and "peace building." These new possibilities for action in turn have caused an increase in political contestation at the Council, as states compete to use its power to serve their own strategic interests. The limits of this new freedom were made clear when the Great Powers presented competing versions of international legitimacy claims over the U.S.-Iraq issue in 2002 and 2003. At such moments the power of the Council is called into question by contests among the powerful states regarding how legitimacy should be interpreted. Yet these contests help to clarify the central place of legitimation in the politics of the Security Council.

## LEGITIMACY

"Legitimacy," as I use the term, refers to an actor's normative belief that a rule or institution ought to be obeyed.[13] It is a subjective quality, relational between actor and institution, and is defined by the actor's *perception* of the institution. The actor's perception may come from the substance of the rule or from the procedure or source by which it was constituted. Such a perception affects behavior, because it is internalized by the actor and comes to help define how the actor sees its interests. Once widely shared in society, this belief changes the decision environment for all actors, even those who have not been socialized to the rule, because it affects everyone's expectations about the likely behavior of other players. I make no moral claim about the universal legitimacy, or, even less, the moral worth, of any particular international rule; I am interested strictly in the subjective feeling by a particular actor or set of actors that some rule is legitimate.[14] In this sense, saying that a rule is accepted as legitimate by some actor says nothing about its justice in the eyes of an outside observer.[15] Further, an actor's belief in the legitimacy of a norm,

---

[13] The literature on legitimacy in political theory is large. Good introductions include Flathman 1993 and Beetham 1991. From the psychology literature, see the reviews in Tyler 2006 and Zelditch 2001.

[14] Thus I am also making the working assumption that we can treat states as unitary actors with corporate identity and the capacity to "feel" the pull of a legitimate rule. This is a contentious assumption that glosses over many angles of social life, but I think it is appropriate for the present purposes.

[15] Franck 1990; Buchanan 2003. How perceptions of legitimacy and justice are related within the individual remains an open question. Rawls (1971) and the contractarians generally make these one and the same.

and thus its following of that norm, need not correlate to the actor being "law-abiding" or submissive to official regulations. Often, precisely the opposite is true: a normative conviction about legitimacy might lead to *non*compliance with laws when laws are seen as conflicting with the conviction. For instance, Nicholas Kittrie presents strong evidence and wide empirical illustration of the fact that people whom he calls "political offenders" are motivated to break laws in order to comply with their own normative (legitimate) convictions.[16] Only when invested in the laws of the state does legitimacy contribute to state-supporting "law and order."[17]

Legitimacy is a difficult concept to study. It is a phenomenon that is both internal to actors and intersubjective. Either way, it is not readily accessible to outside observers (or even to the actor itself); it is complicated and entangled in many other concepts, such as interests, habits, and cultural practices. It can also be contradictory in that it is entirely possible for an actor to feel a "compliance pull" of several competing and irreconcilable legitimate rules or institutions all at once. For this reason, I do not follow Habermas, among others, down the path of trying to discern whether individuals' belief in the legitimacy of an institution is well founded.[18] We lack the adequate tools, in my opinion, to make much progress on that road. Those who do go this way tend to end up relying on strong assumptions about the "true" interests and sentiments of others. This, I believe, leads to an unfortunate discrediting of studies of legitimacy in general, and thus even greater problems when one wants to explore the phenomenon and its consequences. None of these epistemological difficulties, however, should prevent a discussion of legitimacy; it is central to social life and needs to be taken seriously by International Relations. The absence of strictly satisfying methodological techniques for isolating and measuring the phenomenon means only that we need to be more creative and curious in how we approach it.

The question of legitimacy in a social system comes to the fore only when the system is accepted as "conventional" or "arbitrary" in the sense of being one possibility among many, rather than as natural or pre-given or inevitable.[19] In European society the transition to "arbitrary" authority is generally seen as marking the shift to a "modern" mode of thought and authority, where political dominance came to be justified on grounds other

---

[16] Kittrie 2000.

[17] Tom Tyler's (1990) study of legitimacy and domestic laws emphasizes the contribution legitimacy makes to compliance rates. This is possible because his subjects agree that the laws are legitimate.

[18] Habermas 1984.

[19] Pierre Bourdieu (1991) provides an excellent discussion of the concept of "arbitrariness" in social institutions.

than as God-given.[20] The "arbitrariness" of political authority in an increasingly secular European world had to be justified, and this led to various
contractarian, nationalist, and utilitarian theories of government that have
competed for popular support and empirical justification since the Enlight-
enment.[21] The consequent shift in international relations has been later in
coming, but the same problem exists there also. Several recent works try to
establish what might be called the moral foundations of international relations, either attempting to justify the existence of separate states or proposing an alternate model.[22] In international relations, an emphasis on questions of legitimacy in international institutions is growing as the belief in
the inevitability of a state-centered balance of power is in decline.

Legitimacy is a quality that might become attached to a formal organization, an informal institution or practice, or a particular rule or individual. It is worth exploring in all these manifestations. However, in looking
at the legitimacy of the Security Council, the present project is primarily
concerned with a single formal organization and its complex of symbols,
authority, and history, rather than with the legitimacy of particular decisions, processes, or individuals. The distinction between institution and
organization is a tenuous one, and the category of institution, broadly
understood, probably encompasses the category of formal organization.[23]
Moreover, I deal with the legitimacy of the Council *among states*, rather
than its legitimacy in the eyes of the *citizens* of those states.[24] Many interesting questions are thereby missed, including questions about the popular legitimacy of the UN (and its opposite: the belief in the threat from
the UN's "black helicopters"), and the "domestic effect" of governments
using the UN's symbols to win gains with domestic constituencies. The
issue of the Council in domestic politics is important[25]—and I allude to
it briefly in chapter 5—but I am largely concerned with the ways that the
legitimacy of the Council affects interstate politics.

Many scholars make use of the concept of legitimacy to explain international outcomes, though few have provided an account of how legitimation produces its effects. In fact, most traditions in IR theory find legiti-

[20] Connolly 1984. On secular political authority in IR, see E. S. Hurd 2004.

[21] A penetrating view of the complications to which such justifications lead is provided by
Jacques Derrida (1986).

[22] See, for instance, Beitz 1979; Held 1995; Walzer 1977; and Buchanan 2003.

[23] One could draw the distinction the other way around and see institutions as the practices and rules that are derived from a given (formal) organization. I prefer to rest the distinction on the formal nature of organizations and the broader, informal nature of institutions. See Young 1994; and Powell and DiMaggio 1991.

[24] For public opinion about international organizations, see, for instance, Gibson and
Caldeira 1998.

[25] This issue is fought over in the United States by writers such as Jesse Helms (1996)
and Edward Luck (1999).

macy to be relevant to the central questions in their research programs. For instance, international lawyers have displayed an interest in what legitimacy might add to legality when considering the compliance pull of rules and institutions. Foremost among these writers is Thomas Franck, who, in a series of works on "the power of legitimacy among nations," identifies the characteristics of international law that increase its compliance pull. He finds legitimacy to be one of these.[26] Murphy and Weston each examine the legitimacy of individual acts of foreign policy and consider how this relates to their legality.[27]

Realists and liberals often find that legitimacy claims are useful as states attempt to defend their interests against opponents. Stephen Krasner in his history of Westphalia finds that "the idea of sovereignty was used to legitimate the right of the sovereign to collect taxes, and thereby to strengthen the position of the state," and Goldstein and Keohane discuss more generally the view that powerful actors use ideas "to legitimize their interests."[28] E. H. Carr's classic dissection of liberal "idealism" stands in part on the premise that a strong state can advance its interests by "so eagerly cloak[ing] itself in ideologies of a professedly international character."[29] Ikenberry notes that Great Powers have an "incentive to create a legitimate order after [major wars]," both to reduce enforcement costs and to lock in their favorable positions, and Keohane and Nye define a kind of "normal politics" that takes place within an "international regime [that] is accepted as legitimate."[30] In this tradition, scholars generally assume that state consent is the source of the legitimacy of international rules. Brilmayer asks, "How legitimate is international hegemony?" and answers that it is legitimate "so long as political arrangements are based on state consent."[31] Christopher Gelpi finds that interstate agreements have a greater effect on future behavior when parties view them as legitimate, and the distinguishing feature that lets us know they are seen as legitimate is explicit state consent.[32]

---

[26] Franck 1990, 1992, 1995. Applying Franck's framework, Fassbender (1998, 317) asks whether it might be used to predict how the Security Council should be reformed—and he answers no, concluding that "the concept of legitimacy adds nothing to what has already been considered."

[27] Murphy 1994; Weston 1991. That legitimacy should get more of a hearing from lawyers than from many IR scholars is curious, since the lawyers all begin by distinguishing between legitimacy and legality, and therefore immediately concede that by considering the effect of legitimacy they are operating outside the province of law itself.

[28] Krasner 1993, 238; Goldstein and Keohane 1993, 4.

[29] Carr 1946, 145. Among realists, see also, for instance, Kissinger 1964; Morgenthau 1960, chap. 32.

[30] Ikenberry 2001, 53; Keohane and Nye 2001, 120.

[31] Brilmayer 1994, 14, 193.

[32] Gelpi 2003.

Among the interpretivist branches of IR theory, legitimacy is often connected to the existence of international society. Where scholars inquire into the constitution of states and their interests, attention is naturally drawn to the effects of legitimated ideas and institutions. The English School is a natural home for the study of legitimacy in that it sees the state as embedded in a social context.[33] In Ian Clark's book, legitimacy and international society are deeply related, and he traces the evolution of European ideas about "rightful membership" in that society developing alongside ideas about the legitimate behavior of modern states.[34] Something similar is at work in the democratic peace literature, where the empirical regularity central to that research project is often explained as the result of democracies taking into account their views on the legitimacy of their rivals' domestic constitutions before deciding to use force.[35] Constructivism is equally amenable to studying the effects of legitimation, and Bukovansky, for instance, sees the power of legitimated international ideas on domestic would-be revolutionaries. She shows that internationally legitimated discourses, such as republicanism or absolute monarchy, can be important resources for groups attempting to redefine the nature of the sovereign state from the inside, as it were.[36]

These references point to an enduring place for legitimacy in studies of international relations but at the same time a marginal one. Except for the recent interpretive literature, very few of the references to legitimacy as a cause of international outcomes include an explanation of how it functions. This leaves open a potentially productive research opportunity, since, as Thomas Franck suggests, the international system should be the *best* social system in which to observe a "normative" (i.e., legitimated) social order in its pure form precisely because of the absence of an international government to enforce international laws and contracts.[37] The evidence of a recent turn toward "legitimacy language" in International Relations is valuable, but so far it lacks a discussion of how and why legitimacy operates among international institutions and organizations and what its implications are.

One might go about making this connection in many ways. The path I pursue here investigates the issue of the legitimacy of social institutions through a historical examination of the United Nations Security Council. The Security Council is a highly suggestive location in which to observe

---

[33] For instance, Bull 1995.

[34] Clark 2005.

[35] Russett and Oneal 2001.

[36] Bukovansky 2002. See also Barnett 1997; Ruggie 1998, esp. chaps. 1 and 2; and Knight 1998. For a view from French political theory, see Coicaud's (2002) theoretical introduction to legitimacy and his application to international organizations (2001).

[37] Franck 1990.

the workings of legitimacy for the very reason that the Council ostensibly has at its disposal the greatest material power of any international organization in history and yet has great difficulty deploying that power. Two broad categories of research are presented: first, from the earliest efforts at legitimating the UN through (and before) the UN Conference at San Francisco in 1945; and, second, from states' later efforts to benefit from and contest that legitimacy. We will see that legitimacy matters to social institutions (formal or informal, international or otherwise) because it affects the decision calculus of actors with respect to compliance; it empowers the symbols of the institution, which become political resources that can be appropriated by actors for their own purposes; and it is key to their being recognized by actors as "authoritative." The possibility of international authority in international organizations (as opposed to that authority in the traditional form of the nation-state that we are accustomed to) creates a problem for theories of IR that start with the premise of "anarchy."

## THE SECURITY COUNCIL

The Council is potentially the most powerful international organization ever known to the world of states, which makes it a crucial test case for the operation of legitimacy in the international system: its peculiar combination of extensive powers and political limitations means that its effectiveness depends on its legitimation. This section gives a brief overview of the Security Council and explains why the institution is a useful place to see behavioral consequences from strategies of legitimation in international relations.

The Council is composed of fifteen member states, five of them permanent members and specified by name in the Charter. These are the United States, Russia (replacing the Soviet Union in 1991), China, the United Kingdom, and France. The rest are elected for two-year terms out of the general population of the UN General Assembly under a formula that ensures representation to five "regions" of the world.[38] The Security Council

---

[38] These are Africa, Asia, Eastern Europe, Latin America, and "Western Europe and other." Calling them "regions" is somewhat problematic, given the nongeographic character of this last category. The "Western Europe and other" category grew out of the "British Empire" category of earlier times, and recently saw the addition of Israel. It might be better to call these "groups of nations" rather than "regions." Each group determines for itself which of its members will occupy a nonpermanent seat in the Council. The Secretary General's High-Level Panel in 2004 recommended a new four-group regional system for Council elections. See http://www.un.org/secureworld/.

is the executive agency of the UN on matters of "international peace and security"; thus concentrating my examination on the Council rather than any other element of the UN system (or on the UN system as a whole) provides a manageably sized subject of great consequence.[39] The Charter grants the Council wide latitude to "determine the existence of any threat to the peace, breach of the peace, or act of aggression" (Art. 39) and the authority to *require*—not merely allow or recommend—all kinds of supporting action from the member states when such an international threat, breach, or act has been found (Arts. 40, 41, 42, 36).[40] These determinations and requirements are made by the Council on behalf of the entire organization and all its members (Art. 24). Council decisions are legally binding on all 191 member states, they trump any conflicting domestic law or treaty passed by member governments (Arts. 25, 103), and there is little room for any kind of appeal from its decisions.[41] The Charter may in theory put all the resources of the member states at the disposal of the Council in the enforcement of its decisions (Arts. 43, 45). This ability to mobilize massive coercive resources is unprecedented among international organizations, and almost all states in the system have consented to it in a highly public way.

Compare this to the security provisions of the League of Nations. Under the covenant of the League, as described by Bowett:

> A state resorting to war in violation of its undertaking with regard to pacific settlement was deemed to have committed an act of war against all members. Yet it was left to each member to decide whether a breach had occurred or an act of war had been committed, so that even the obligation to apply economic sanctions under Article 16 (1) [of the Covenant of the League] was dependent on the member's own view of the situation. Military sanctions could be recommended by the Council [of the League], but the decision on whether to apply them rested with each member.[42]

In law, and probably also in practice, this left the League Council with significantly less capacity to act effectively compared to the UN Council.

---

[39] Trying to make generalizations about the entire UN system, as Rosenau (1992) ambitiously does, is problematic because of the immense and highly varied character of the processes and institutions that comprise the system.

[40] Some of these provisions are moribund, because they depend on the prior negotiation of military contribution agreements between the UN and individual states under Art. 43, none of which have been made. See Harris 1991, 881–82.

[41] On the issue of appeal to the International Court of Justice (ICJ), see Caron 1993, n. 35; and Bothe 1993, 80. The responsibilities of states to the international organizations of which they are members are restated clearly in the *Reparation for Injuries* case at the ICJ.

[42] Bowett 1982.

Despite the impressive formal powers of the UN Charter, clearly, as Michael Barnett says, "the UN's power derives primarily from its ability to persuade rather than its ability to coerce."[43] Joseph Nye makes a similar point by linking the UN to his view of "soft power":

> The UN has a great deal of soft power of its own. In other words, it is attractive and that gives it a certain amount of power. What the UN can convey that is particularly important is legitimacy, an important part of soft power. Other countries, including the United States, should find it in their self-interest to work with and through the UN, because they need that legitimacy for their own soft power.[44]

The scope of the Council's official powers in the Charter is less relevant than the domain of its practical capacity to persuade, which is in part a function of states' beliefs about its legitimacy. Even with both the formal powers granted to the Council in the Charter and the explicit consent of the UN membership, the Council has acted to the full extent of its coercive capability relatively infrequently, and, when it has, it has generally been criticized for acting illegitimately by some of the leading writers on international law. For instance, Burns Weston argues that several of the key resolutions around the 1990–91 Gulf War were illegitimate and thus should have been arranged differently, even though he agrees they were legally taken and probably directed toward an appropriate goal.[45] Similarly Jose Alvarez lists several Security Council actions (on Iraq, Libya, and Haiti, among others) which he says failed to follow legitimate procedures and thus seriously threaten the Council's credibility.[46] The Council is charged with illegitimacy much more frequently than with illegality, indicating that what is at stake is not whether the Council is acting within the letter of the Charter (partly because the Charter is so broad and vague as to the limits of the Council's powers) but something else. Being seen as illegitimate has a cost. Russett and Sutterlin make the point explicitly, concluding, with reference to the process the United States and the Security Council used in the Gulf War, that "the manner in which the gulf military action was executed by the United States and its coalition partners will likely limit the willingness of Council members to follow a similar procedure in the future."[47] These authors imply that repeated actions

---

[43] Barnett 1995, 429.
[44] Nye 2004.
[45] Weston 1991.
[46] Alvarez 1995. Caron (1993) also gives a list of the Council's claims of illegitimacy, and Reisman (1993) makes a similar argument regarding the Libyan affair.
[47] Russett and Sutterlin 1991, 83.

which appear illegitimate will ultimately impair whatever ability the Council might have to take credible action.

Those who worry that the Council acts in ways that are illegitimate are presuming, as a start, that the Council needs to be seen as legitimate to act effectively and that can squander that store by ill-considered decisions. Inis Claude, for his part, highlights the other side of the equation: that with legitimacy the Council has power. Both positions depend on an unstated theory of what legitimacy is and how it is created, used, and lost. If the credibility and power of the Council are functions of legitimacy, then this suggests a need to examine directly the workings and history of its legitimation. States' recognition that the Security Council is legitimate is the product of a historical process that began with the conferences prior to the end of World War II and has continued in various ways through the recent spate of reform proposals motivated by the fiftieth anniversary of the UN and on into the U.S.-Iraq crisis of 2003. This book seeks to provide an answer to the questions about legitimacy that underlie these positions. First, if wasting the organization's "capital" of legitimacy makes action more difficult, how does the presence of legitimacy make action easier? Loss of legitimacy is of concern to organizations because the *presence* of legitimacy afforded power. But what kind of power? Claude said that legitimacy is power, but he did not address how or why that power works. Second, how is legitimacy used in the specific context of international organizations? What are the limits of legitimacy as an instrument of power? Finally, how can the power of legitimacy be challenged? The capacity of legitimacy to provide order is inherently conservative, as it encourages behavior which reinforces existing structures. How can delegitimization be achieved by those pursuing change rather than the maintenance of the status quo?

The following chapters offer provisional answers to these questions. Case studies of aspects of the life of the Council are examined, illustrating the operation of legitimation and delegitimation, and showing that legitimacy affects all kinds of states, although these effects differ among audiences. Chapter 3 discusses the San Francisco Conference of 1945 and looks at the Council's legitimation with regard to small and medium states; chapters 4 and 6 examine how strong states find their decision environments changed by legitimation of the Council; and chapter 5 explores how legitimation affects the strategic decisions of a country like Libya which, in the early 1990s, was considered by many to be outside the international community. These four empirical chapters, taken together, will enable us to draw generalizations about legitimacy and the Council in the conclusion of the book.

## IMPORTANCE OF THE ARGUMENT

This book contributes to two of the leading controversies in IR theory: the relationship between constructivism and rational choice, and the relationship between states and international institutions. Much of the energy in IR theory today stems from the parallel rise of rationalism and constructivism and their ongoing conversation with each other and with their critics. Presented originally as two distinct answers to the problems and limits of neorealism, rationalism and constructivism increasingly turned their attention to each other through the 1990s. Their differences, both real and alleged, in the areas of methodology, ontology, and epistemology have come to define a new set of conventional debates in IR theory. This framing of the discipline was institutionalized in the fiftieth anniversary edition of the journal *International Organization* in 1998, where the editors presented a view of the field of IR based on a debate between rationalist and constructivist approaches.[48]

The present book demonstrates, by example, that the two traditions can be complementary rather than mutually exclusive.[49] My approach takes rationally calculating actors (states) as a given but places them in a socially constructed context. Legitimacy, a socially constructed phenomenon, affects the strategic calculations and self-conceptions of these actors. The payoffs sought by actors through strategic behavior might be material or symbolic, and in either case they depend significantly on sociological processes related to legitimation. A symbol is a valued good—one it makes sense to attempt to acquire—by virtue of the process of legitimation that surrounds it. Strategic actors will spend energy and money to acquire symbolic goods. Unpacking this activity requires us to use tools from both the rational-choice and constructivist toolboxes. Thus part of the theoretical payoff to the present work is showing how to combine the strengths of rationalism and constructivism. I argue, for instance, against treating the logics of consequences and appropriateness as if they were discrete and mutually exclusive models of states.[50]

This book contributes to an emerging literature that attempts to capitalize on the convergence of the two approaches, but with significant differences depending on whether the argument is coming from the constructivist or rationalist side. For instance, Bukovansky, cited above, presents a complementary argument to that given here by showing how strategic leaders sought legitimacy in the (socially constructed) context of eighteenth-century European power politics.[51] From the rationalist side,

[48] Katzenstein, Keohane, and Krasner 1998.
[49] See Fearon and Wendt 2002.
[50] March and Olsen 1998.
[51] Bukovansky 2002.

Dennis Chong attempts a "unifying theory" of individual choice in social contexts which, while not quite meeting with Bukovansky in the middle, takes seriously the function of normative concerns in strategic settings.[52] At a meta-theoretical level, Fearon and Wendt stake out a principled defense of the "complementarity" position, though with important provisos.[53]

A consideration of all these theories is important to the debate in IR about the relationship between IOs and states. The degree of influence of IOs on state decisions, and the sources of that influence, are generally thought to provide one way to distinguish between the main paradigms of IR. For realists, the practical power of international organizations comes from whatever power strong states are willing to invest in making the organization influential. Only when states apply their own resources do IOs have the capacity to exert power over other states. This conclusion seems inescapable given the realist presumption that material power, in military forms, moves world politics, and given that IOs lack military capacity of their own and are only likely to get such power when it is loaned by strong states under strict conditions. Without independent control of military capacity, IOs can only be conduits for the expression of underlying distributions of state power. For this reason Michael Glennon, upon finding that the Security Council is made up of states that disagree with one another, concludes that American unipolarity ultimately makes the Council immaterial.[54] Where IOs do exist, realists suggest that they so closely reflect the distribution of material resources among the states they are comprised of that they add little that is significant to the outcomes of interstate conflicts. Strong states generally win out in the construction of international institutions, and so the interests of these states should be privileged in the IOs. Lloyd Gruber, for example, argues that medium-sized states can be pressured into participating in multilateral schemes when strong states show their willingness to "go it alone." This, according to Gruber, is how Mexico ended up in the North American Free Trade Agreement (NAFTA), when its preference was to return to the status quo that existed before the Canada-U.S. trade agreement. It also explains why the European Monetary System (EMS) was accepted by some states (such as Britain and Italy) that strongly preferred other kinds

---

[52] Chong 2000. The remaining gap between Chong and Bukovansky is approximately this: for Chong, norms can be treated as "investments" made by actors in the past and which they value, thus allowing them to be calculated into cost-benefit equations; for Bukovansky, norms (or the legitimated "political culture") are internalized and so alter actors' preferences (and thus their estimation of various payoffs).

[53] Fearon and Wendt 2002. See also the empirical studies of Schimmelfennig 2005 and Lynch 1999.

[54] Glennon 2003.

of system.[55] Realists emphasize the power strong states have to influence the range of options open to weak states, and therefore to influence the kind of international organizations that come into being. Once in place, these organizations tend, by definition, to reflect the interests and desires of the powerful.

All approaches to international relations agree that state power is important and that the strong generally succeed in shaping the system to their interests. If there is a distinctive feature of the realist and neorealist traditions it is the assumption that *military* resources dominate states' thinking about power and threat. Non-realists are equally concerned about power, but they conceive of power in different ways.[56] For instance, neoliberal institutionalists similarly acknowledge that international organizations have little enforcement capacity, but they conclude that IOs can nevertheless have important effects on interstate outcomes. For neoliberals, international organizations begin life as solutions to coordination problems among states. Because states can be made better off by binding themselves to multilateral international commitments, both strong and weak states might find it beneficial to make such commitments.[57] In this neoliberal view, a pareto-superior end point is available if states can find a credible way to commit themselves to collective solutions. The "formalness" of the organization and the "publicness" of the commitment are tools by which this credibility is created and demonstrated.[58] The neoliberal institutionalist school of IR measures the power of international organizations in terms of their ability to reduce the costs of transactions among individual state actors.[59] This tradition derives its heritage from Ronald Coase's work in "positive" political economy on the reasons for the existence of firms and contracts.[60] Where individuals are seen in this way, it is logically required that institutions be seen "as nothing more than the set of processes, the machine, that allows . . . collective action" by individuals to take place.[61] International organizations exist, therefore, and states choose to respect them, because IOs allow states to reach utility levels that they could not reach without them. Once in place, path dependence may take hold and reduce the costs of continuing to comply as com-

---

[55] See Gruber 2000, chap. 7 on Mexico, and chap. 8 on the EMS. See also Cameron and Tomlin's (2000) version of NAFTA.

[56] For conceptualizations of power in IR theory, see Barnett and Duvall 2005.

[57] Ikenberry 2001.

[58] Abbott and Snidal 1998.

[59] See Baldwin 1993; Vaubel and Willett 1991; and Keohane 1984. An alternate branch of the model looks at the ability of international organizations to affect domestic politics by giving the government (or others) leverage in domestic competitions. See Cortell and Davis 1996; and Milner 1997.

[60] Coase 1937.

[61] Buchanan and Tullock 1962, 13.

pared to the costs of defecting, but the logic of instrumental cost-benefit analysis remains at the center of state-IO relations. In sum, it is sometimes in the *self-interest* of states to choose to follow an organization.[62]

A third approach to examining the influence of international organizations begins with the two central insights of constructivism: "that the fundamental structures of international politics are social rather than strictly material . . . and that these structures shape actors' identities and interests, rather than just their behavior."[63] From this starting point a research program has developed that charts how international institutions can constitute states and their interests; how they can define the terms by which states pursue those interests; and how they can be sites for the contest between states over status, legitimacy, and power. The constructivist program has both critical and positivist strands. Its empirical research includes, for example, how the fact that arguments at the Security Council are cast in legal language affects the politics that happen there,[64] how the terms used in domestic debates about state identity affect its international commitments and status,[65] and how negotiations in international crises can both break and remake bonds of community among states.[66]

By locating the concept of legitimacy at the center of the discussion, I adopt elements from all three approaches to international organization. In relation to the realist explanation, the legitimacy of an organization helps to explain *when* powerful states find it a useful tool in their arsenal, even if they do not believe in that legitimacy. It also gives a causal explanation for how legitimation changes the relative costs and benefits of complying or defecting, and this contributes an important element to the liberal argument. For constructivism, emphasis on legitimation shifts the focus from material power to the social construction of meanings around material resources, social institutions, and symbols.

## PLAN OF THE WORK

The structure of this book reflects the path of legitimation itself, from creation to reproduction to delegitimation or, to borrow language from

---

[62] This is a long-term view; there may be short-term reasons to defect from a cooperative system, and the neoliberal model allows that states may indeed defect in practice. What is important is that, in defecting in the short-term, states have considered the consequences of that defection for the long-term stability of the institutions they presumably value. "Self-interest" is understood here in the way described more fully in chapter 2.

[63] Wendt 1995, 71–72.

[64] Johnstone 2003.

[65] Lynch 1999.

[66] Mattern 2004.

economic markets, from investment to exchange to loss. Chapter 2 provides a theory of the legitimation process for international institutions. Centered on the power an institution gains by being seen as legitimate, this model introduces the concept of legitimacy to the study of international institutions and organizations. It addresses, first, how legitimated institutions affect individuals and their behavior, and, second, how institutions come to be legitimized in the first place. Legitimacy changes individuals' perceptions of their interests through the process of internalizing external norms. This change in individuals then creates a change in the structure of the system as the new behavior becomes more common. Even actors unaffected by the internalization process will find it rational to alter their behavior to account for the change in their strategic environment. The steps in legitimation are spelled out in chapter 2 in generic and abstract terms; their more interesting aspects are revealed only in later chapters when we can see these forces at work in concrete instances.

Chapter 3 presents a series of debates about how legitimation takes place in empirical settings and sets out a number of competing explanations. These address three broad questions that arise repeatedly in social science studies of legitimacy: (1) What makes an institution appear to be legitimate? (2) How does legitimacy affect strategic behavior? and (3) What difference does legitimation make in the relations between strong and weak actors? Each question has been answered in a number of ways, and this book provides some of the most common modes of thought on the subject. These controversies on how to interpret legitimation are then considered again in chapter 7 in light of the empirical material in the intervening case studies.

Chapter 4 begins the examination of the UN Security Council, starting with its early history. When the American proposals were first made in 1943 and 1944 for a prospective world organization, there was obvious tension between the desires of the major powers to retain ultimate control over the organization's biggest decisions and the need to gain widespread support among the small and medium states that were to be its rank and file. The unequal structure of the Security Council, which was necessary for the former goal, was an obstacle in achieving the latter. This tension could only be managed by a program of legitimization. Chapter 4 charts this program in the debates and conflicts over the shape of the Security Council between the Dumbarton Oaks Conference and the early years of the Council's operation after 1946, and centers on the UN Conference on International Organization (UNCIO) in San Francisco. Most striking was the degree to which the small and medium states that had opposed the veto allowed the procedures of the conference to structure, and ultimately limit, their chance to express that opposition. They took advantage of the opportunity the conference afforded to voice their dissent from the draft plan, but once their amendments failed to win the necessary super-majority and the Great Powers refused to concede to their demands, they gave up their fight and went on to support the Charter with enthusiasm. The substantive interests of the veto opponents were never satisfied, but they switched nonetheless from opposition to support of the draft. The key element of the Great Powers' strategy for the conference was to take advantage of the small states' commitment to the well-established procedures of international conferences and thus allow some careful circumscribed dissent. The opportunity for small states to voice their interests, even as they lost the substantive effort, was important in legitimizing the inequalities that remained in the Charter. Throughout we see the importance of proceduralism (conferences, deliberation, and the rules that organize contention) in creating legitimacy.

Once in operation, the strength of the Security Council lay in its ability to confer and withhold symbolic status to states and their actions. Chapter 5 examines how a legitimated institution comes to be seen as embodying a corporate identity, and how that identity causes the objects and practices associated with it to become symbolically powerful. The life of institutions is a constant effort by actors to appropriate, reinforce, and undermine the institutions' legitimacy, and much of the Council's role in international affairs since its founding, and especially since the late 1980s, demonstrates this. Chapter 5 considers the history of the Council as a problem in the long-run governance of a social system. It looks at several ways actors have sought to associate themselves with the symbols of the Council as a means of appropriating some of the legitimacy, and thus some of the power, that it represents. Notable here are the efforts of states to win collective legitimation for the use of force, the desire by states to occupy non-permanent seats in the Security Council, and the interest in adding items to the Council's agenda and keeping them there. These forces were evident in the the U.S.-Iraq crisis of 2002–3 insofar as international political support for the American operation was partly dependent on the symbolic authorization of the Council. In each of the instances in this chapter, states spend a great deal of energy to associate their cause with a symbol of the Council, with no expectation that this association will change the material facts of a dispute, but a strong expectation that a change in symbolism alters the way others understand the situation. This itself is equivalent to a change in material conditions and shows the power legitimation creates in an institution.

After chapters 4 and 5 examine the creation and deployment of legitimacy in an institution, chapter 6 takes the next step and looks at the process of delegitimation. If legitimacy gives an institution power over actors, how might one go about challenging that power? One should never assume that an institution that is widely seen as legitimate is actually morally good and always (or ever) acts for the benefit of all. Legitimacy is worth studying precisely because it is a powerful force and can transform a relation of overt coercion into something that appears more benign. That does not mean that it *is* benign. Examining the efforts of dissenting states and groups to *oppose* the Council and its decisions shows both the strengths and vulnerabilities of social orders buttressed by legitimated power. The material for chapter 6 is drawn from Libya's efforts to overturn the sanctions regime imposed on by the United Nations from 1992 to 2003. Libya made a clear and determined drive to manipulate legitimated values associated with the Council's sanctions as a means to undermine the authority of the sanctions regime. This strategy was based on associating the Libyan position with international institutions and practices that enjoyed wide support in the international community. It appropriated the justifications used by the sponsors of the sanctions and used them to separate the sponsors from their audience of third-party states. Noncompliance with the sanctions was a growing threat to the legitimacy of the Council by about 1997. The response by the United States and Britain reveals the lengths to which they would go to defend the legitimacy of the Council as a whole, even if it meant abandoning their short-run policy preferences. The history and theory of that effort is instructive for understanding the contestation over legitimacy and symbols around the Security Council in particular and international politics more generally.

Together chapters 4, 5, and 6 illustrate that the legitimacy of international organizations is a consideration for states at all ends of the power spectrum: it influences the behavior of small states, such as those that were considering whether to accept the Charter in 1945; of strong states, such as Russia and others, that fight over the legitimating power of peacekeeping symbols; and even of states ostracized from the mainstream of international society, such as Libya after Lockerbie.

Finally, chapter 7 gathers and develops several implications that may be drawn from the book. These are divided between those of interest to IR theory and those directed to the practical matters of designing new international organizations. Regarding the former, I concentrate on the relationship between rationalism and constructivism, on the implications the contents of this book may have for the study of other international organizations, and on the issue of sovereignty in the international system. I find that the existence of legitimated international organizations implies that sovereignty is distributed among very different kinds of international actors and is not monopolized by states. For the practical arts of institutional design and diplomacy, my findings offer constructive thoughts for legitimizing new institutions such as international courts, and for making sense of the Council's role in the 2003 U.S.-Iraq crisis. Chapter 7 also returns to the central controversies about legitimation that were outlined in chapter 3 and uses the empirical findings from the Council to help address them.

Chapters 4 through 6 are organized around the empirical study of aspects of the UN Security Council, but each depends on the development of a conceptual framework that is not usually associated with the study of international organizations. The larger goal, therefore, is to develop and defend such a conceptual framework. Chapter 2 sets out a trichotomy of "modes of social control" and shows that none can be ignored in international relations. Chapter 4 takes this concept of legitimacy and makes it dynamic, demonstrating how it is created through the processes of debate and deliberation. Chapter 5 then expands on the elements of symbolism and authority that were latent in the earlier chapters and uses them to investigate further the politics that occur in and around the Council. Chapter 6 completes the cycle by opening up space for the contestation and reinterpretation of legitimacy, adding a dynamic of change to what began in chapter 2 as a relatively static concept.

## METHODS AND SOURCES

The main source for the empirical materials in this book are primary documents of the Security Council, the UNCIO, and other UN bodies, as well as documents from national delegations. These provide direct evidence, from the life of the Council, of the politics of legitimation. In the chapters on international negotiations, they give a clear sense of what the states sought from the negotiations in substantive terms, as well as the procedural and discursive means by which they put forward their positions. There are times when reading the negotiating history between states might be misleading, and so I also make use of media sources and scholarly accounts to contextualize the primary documents.

The theoretical framework of the book derives from the sociological work of Max Weber and Pierre Bourdieu, and combines these with the work of Alexander Wendt in international relations. This produces a conceptual approach that in some ways is quite traditional in IR and in others quite atypical. It assumes, for instance, that states are unitary actors that generally act rationally, by which I mean that they calculate the relative costs of alternative strategies in the pursuit of their perceived interests. Following a typical state-centric model, I treat states as the main actors and examine the influence of international organizations in terms of their effects on states. This influence on behavior may either be direct or mediated through a process in which an international organization contributes to the construction of states' interests. International organizations are important, as they influence how states think and act. I do not inquire into how states came into being, how the position of states relative to other actors might be changing, or how individuals within governments or the public at large compete to control policy.

I also assume that, although states are the central actors, the environment in which they operate is populated by institutions and social forces that shape and influence them in significant ways. My interest is in the international organizations that exist among these forces, but other institutions are also clearly important, including market forces, ideologies, populist mobilizations, and a range of nonstate actors. All these outside influences on the state contribute to constituting the environment in which states make decisions. These factors contribute to constructing the payoff matrix for states. States take decisions in the context of an already existing set of institutions in the system, and the presence of these institutions changes the costs and benefits attached to actions. Even strong states take their decisions in this context; although they have more power than weak players to change the nature of their environment, in short-term situations like international crises this power is limited even for the strong.[67]

The power of international organizations is both "institutional" and "structural" in the terms provided by Barnett and Duvall.[68] Institutional power arises when "the rules and procedures" of an international organization are used to "guide, steer, and constrain the actions (or nonactions) and conditions of existence of others."[69] Each of the empirical chapters that follow shows that the Council is a location of institutional power and examines the implications this has for relations between states and for the Council itself. Structural power is evident in the relation of mutual constitution between Council power and state interests.[70] The process of legitimating the Security Council is inseparable from the constitution of states' interests. It contributes to making "the social powers, values, and interpretations of reality that deeply structure internal control" characteristic of state sovereignty.[71] Productive power, as defined by Barnett and Duvall, is not pursued in this book but could be the focus of research on international legitimacy. In such a work, the emphasis would be on the processes through which powerful discourses become authoritative and therefore legitimate.[72]

---

[67] Johnston (2001) develops a similar framework to study the process of socialization of states.

[68] Barnett and Duvall 2005.

[69] Ibid., 51.

[70] On "mutual constitution," see Wendt 1987.

[71] Barnett and Duvall 2005, 54.

[72] See, for instance, Williams 1999.

The combination of rational states in a social environment means that my approach straddles two of the conventional divides in IR theory. By assuming that states are rational but in a socially constructed environment, it overturns a false dichotomy that separates some versions of rational choice and constructivism, and by studying both the material and social content of the environment it links the materialist emphasis of realism with the ideational concerns of constructivism. I think it is more productive to combine these approaches than to treat them as mutually exclusive. This is true for both theoretical and empirical reasons. These are documented and defended in the chapters that follow and revisited in chapter 7.

# LEGITIMACY IN THEORY

# A Theory of Legitimacy

IN DEFENDING AS "legitimate" his government's exploitation of the Congo's natural resources, a spokesman for the government of the Congo said, "The Congolese government is the legitimate government of this country. Whatever we do is legitimate."[1] This claim is typical in that it reveals the value rulers place in being seen as legitimate, for legitimacy is one instrument to increasing power. Yet at the same time it begs for some empirical defense or support. In this, it nicely frames the two most important questions regarding legitimacy and political institutions: How are we to assess claims of legitimacy in order to distinguish the real from the preposterous? And what is to be gained by being seen as legitimate? Put differently, what is legitimacy, and what power does it have in society?

The goal of this chapter is to answer these questions and to outline for IR theory the related concepts of legitimacy, symbols, and authority, which are often overlooked in IR though they play crucial roles in many phenomena of great interest to the field. Legitimacy is the governing concept, above the other two. Having operational definitions of all three allows us to identify how and where they operate, and compare their contribution to outcomes to that of other forces. This gives new insight into the central debates in academic International Relations. Although relatively little attention is paid to these concepts in the literature on International Relations, a great deal of information on legitimacy is in the political science literature more generally and in allied fields, and I draw my resources from these studies. Part of my conclusion is that there is no principled reason why legitimacy should be a phenomenon of importance only to domestic society and not to international relations. This means, for instance, that neither international anarchy nor the nature of states creates decisive obstacles to the working of legitimacy in the international system. The empirical support for this claim comes in subsequent chapters, and the theoretical payoff for IR comes at the end of the book.

Each of the three sections of this chapter deals with a different aspect of the conceptual apparatus of legitimacy. The first asks, "What is legitimacy?" and defines the basic concept. In doing so, it defends a subjective approach to the psychology of legitimacy as against other approaches, and

---

[1] Interview with Kikaya Bin Karubi by BBC News, reprinted in *UN Wire*, United Nations Foundation, October 24, 2002.

shows how the macro-order created by legitimacy differs from that created by coercion or self-interest. The second section applies this model to international relations and asks, "What does legitimacy do in IR?" The answer comes in three parts, depending on whether one focuses on the unit level, the structural level, or the interaction between the two. At the unit level, legitimacy changes actors' interests through the process of internalization. At the structural level, widespread belief in the legitimacy of an institution changes the "objective" structure of payoffs faced by both believers and nonbelievers. The interaction between the two levels takes the form of symbolic resources that gain their power by their association with the legitimated institution. The three effects of legitimacy thus cover individual states, the international system, and the process of interaction between them. The final section of the chapter suggests that these effects of legitimacy indicate the existence of sovereign authority beyond the state. This is significant, because the conventional image of the international system as an anarchy is premised on the *absence* of authority at the international level. As concepts, anarchy and authority are incompatible with each other, but legitimacy and authority are natural complements. The chapter thus provides the conceptual resources to support the empirical evaluation of the legitimacy and authority of the Security Council that follows in chapters 4 through 6.

## WHAT IS LEGITIMACY?

Legitimacy refers to the belief by an actor that a rule or institution ought to be obeyed. Such a belief is necessarily normative and subjective, and not necessarily shared with any other actor. It has implications for behavior, as its presence changes the strategic calculation made by actors about how to respond to the rule or institution. When an actor believes a rule is legitimate, the decision whether to comply is no longer motivated by the simple fear of retribution or by a calculation of self-interest but, instead, by an internal sense of rightness and obligation. Mark Suchman defines legitimacy in similar terms as "a generalized perception or assumption that the actions of an entity are desirable, proper, or appropriate within some socially constructed system of norms, values, beliefs, and definitions."[2] This definition nicely encompasses both the sense within the individual of the appropriateness of a body or rule and the contextual, cultural origins of the standards of appropriateness themselves. Legitimacy therefore might be approached either as an explanation for individual behavior or as an element in the domination strategy used by leaders.

[2] Suchman 1995, 574; Habermas 1979, chapter 5.

The operative process in legitimation is the internalization by the actor of an external standard. Internalization takes place when the actor's sense of its own interests is partly constituted by a force outside itself—in this case, by the standards, laws, rules, and norms that exist in the community. A rule will become legitimate to an individual (and therefore become behaviorally significant) when the individual internalizes its content and reconfigures his or her interests according to the rule. When this happens, compliance becomes habitual (in the sense of being the default position), and it is *non*compliance that requires of the individual special consideration and psychic costs.[3] This is the kind of compliance that parents often try to instill in their children and that governments socialize in their citizens: "It is right to do as I say, because I say so." As Dahl and Lindblom contend, "Control is legitimate to the extent that it is approved or regarded as 'right.' "[4]

This is in line with Weber's usage where he takes "legitimate" and "considered to be legitimate" as having the exact same meaning.[5] This definition approaches legitimacy in terms that are internal to the psychology of the individual in question. Such a "subjective" approach requires that we accept the possibility of irreconcilable differences among individuals in their interpretations of legitimacy. Perceptions of legitimacy may be quite different for different individuals, even if the individuals are subject to the same forces of socialization, such as occurs among siblings.[6] Individuals experience legitimacy in their perception of the rule or institution, and, as with all perceptions, it is not directly accessible to outsiders. Outside observers cannot make determinations about legitimacy on behalf of those on the "inside," and legitimacy cannot be measured except through an assessment of whether the audience in question acknowledges it. In such an assessment, the opinions and perceptions of the audience give the final answer on the subject. For positivist methodology, this creates a great deal of difficulty. Internal conditions are hard to access and measure, and are subject to distortion by both the observer and the observed.

---

[3] "Habit" is often discussed as an explanation for patterned behavior that is quite distinct from legitimacy, for instance, as H. L. A. Hart does in his seminal treatment of the difference between "habit" and "rule" (1961, 54–57). Hart treats habit similarly to the way Weber treats "custom": Weber takes "*custom* to mean a typically uniform activity which is kept on the beaten track simply because men are 'accustomed' to it and persist in it by unreflective imitation" (Hart 1961, 319). My use of the term "habitual" here is not meant to evoke the debate over habits and rules; rather, it is simply to use the term's contemporary dictionary meaning of "usual" or "normal."

[4] Dahl and Lindblom 1992, 114.

[5] See, for instance, Weber 1978, 78. Voeten's (2005) definition of legitimacy is similar. His hypothesis for how legitimacy is created is from expected utility rather than socialization, which is discussed in chapter 3.

[6] For a review of the sibling-difference literature, see Plomin et al. 2001.

If legitimacy is based on internalization, how does one know if internalization has occurred? I employ two empirical tests in the forthcoming chapters to judge when legitimation has taken place in international politics. First, we can look for evidence that states are acting instrumentally toward their goals but within the context of taking existing rules or institutions for granted. In some cases this may be evidence that the states have internalized the content of the rule or the authority of the institution into their schedule of private interests. This is examined in chapter 4 in relation to the value many states placed on the deliberation at San Francisco in 1945 over the UN Charter, where the substantive outcome of the conference was prearranged by the Great Powers and not subject to change. It is also seen in chapter 5, in cases where small states pursue symbolic affiliation with the Council even though there are no immediate material gains to be had. The second kind of evidence comes where we see states attempt to manipulate others by deploying resources derived from legitimated institutions. In chapters 5 and 6 we see cases of states making apparently cynical references to the Council or to broader international norms in the expectation that other players will be forced to respond as if these were genuine. The "audience" in these instances is vulnerable to manipulation, as they have internalized the norms and believe that adhering to them is valuable in itself. Both kinds of evidence demonstrate how legitimated international rules and institutions affect the behavior of states. Indeed, the latter cases show that even states that have not internalized the Council's authority will find their behavior influenced simply because others believe in its legitimacy.

Allen Buchanan argues for joining legitimacy to justice, and I suggest separating them. He proposes a normative account of legitimacy in which a legitimated institution is one that "satisfies minimal standards for protecting individuals' rights by processes and policies that are themselves at least minimally just."[7] I see this as conflating two very different questions: "When do individuals perceive an institution to be legitimate?" and "When can we say that an institution is just?" This book is about legitimacy, not justice—at least not justice conceived in universalistic terms. Although insiders may perceive an indissoluble connection between the two, an outsider's assessment of the justness of a system is irrelevant to the insider's perception of its legitimacy.[8] Moreover, the concept of legitimacy loses its explanatory purchase if it is equated to the concept of "justness." In setting justice aside we give up the ability to answer certain im-

---

[7] Buchanan 2002, 718–719.

[8] Coicaud (2002, 7) defines legitimacy as the "just exercise of political command," which makes legitimacy and justice mutually implicating. To avoid confusion (over questions like "whose sense of justice is involved?") I prefer to maintain a bright line between the two.

portant questions, but we gain the capacity to understand legitimacy as a mechanism that produces one kind of social order and that affects the motivations of individuals in a social system. A legitimized institution operates, relative to its community, very differently than one without legitimacy, and these differences, significant in international relations as in other systems, are made invisible if we insist on reserving the label "legitimate" for systems which satisfy the outsider's values of universal justice.

The inability to make "objective" assessments of legitimacy puts my approach to legitimacy at odds with the approaches taken by a long line of writers, from Machiavelli to Marx to Gramsci, for whom legitimacy operates as a cloaking device between individuals' "true" interests and their "perceived" or "constructed" interests. For these writers, whom Zelditch describes as the "conflict school" of legitimacy, there is a constant and inherent conflict of interest between the rulers and the ruled, and legitimacy is used to sustain social order by masking this conflict. Legitimizing myths or ideologies are needed by the rulers in order to generate (artificial) consent on the part of the ruled and thus preserve the stability of the system.[9] Machiavelli, Marx, and Gramsci all use variants of this approach to explain the importance of legitimacy to social power. Such a view requires that one have faith in the ability of outside observers to identify the objective interests of the dominated in order to contrast them with the constructed interests defined by the dominant ideology. A subjective view of legitimacy is necessarily agnostic on this point of faith and so cannot be relied on to identify a gap between real and artificial interests.[10] It does not carry ethical content that would allow outsiders to declare whether an institution *ought* to be seen as legitimate by its audience or to judge whether an act or an institution is legitimate in the abstract. These judgments can only be made from the inside. To use the term "legitimate" in my approach says nothing about actual rightness or goodness; rather, it refers only to actors' internal perceptions of rightness and goodness. Richard Sennett, in his book *Authority*, explores the psychological complexity of legitimacy. He separates the psychological process of "perceiving an institution as legitimate" from the authoritarian process of "feeling internally compelled to obey."[11] In my approach these two processes are

[9] Zelditch 2001, 42–43.

[10] The subjective view also avoids the problem, inherent in these false-consciousness theories, of having to see through public strategies of compliance by subordinates that mask private thoughts of resistance. On disentangling this complex, see Spears, Jetten, and Doosje 2001, esp. 354–357.

[11] Working from a Freudian rather than Weberian starting point, Sennett (1980) suggests that individuals may feel normatively compelled to obey an institution or ruler that they perceive as *illegitimate* if they see in the institution or ruler a strong personality that mimics the needed paternal figure.

the same. This is a significant difference, as, in my approach, it is quite possible that an institution which outsiders view as morally reprehensible can still be seen and treated as legitimate by its intended audience. In fact, we *must* call it legitimate if its audience has internalized its authority and accepts it as right, regardless of whether the institution's values conform to those of the outside observer. Legitimacy does not rely on serving the "real" interests of the actor, and false consciousness is certainly a possibility.

This distinction is crucial for understanding the well-known power of motivated actors to legitimize to their constituents violent and destructive collective social projects such as genocides.[12] The long record of socially destructive acts by leaders gives ample evidence not only that it is possible to legitimize projects which outsiders find objectionable, but even perhaps that a logical connection exists between legitimacy and massive social projects.[13] The Rwandan genocide and the Nazi holocaust (for instance) were made possible by governments that encouraged the perception among their constituents that these were legitimate social projects set in motion by legitimate institutions of authority.[14] The genocides could never have reached their height of destructiveness had insiders felt the same revulsion as did many outsiders. Without legitimacy, each citizen mobilized to perform an act of violence would presumably have had to be forced at the end of a bayonet, making the project much less "efficient" on its own terms and perhaps even impossible. Such examples show that legitimacy is crucial to the operation of large-scale social mobilization, whether for good purposes or bad. Believing that the purposes are bad does not mean that an outside observer can deny the existence of legitimacy in the eyes of insiders. The behavioral and structural consequences of legitimacy, discussed below, will continue to exist regardless of whether the outsider objects to the values of the society.

## WHAT LEGITIMACY IS NOT: COERCION AND SELF-INTEREST

As a source of following rules in a society, legitimacy stands in contrast to two other equally grand concepts from sociology: coercion and self-interest.

---

[12] See Jackman 2001. The classic experiments of Stanley Milgram (1974) illustrated the capacity for legitimated authority to induce people to do harm to others. Scott (1998) gives further examples of the destructive potential of very large-scale social projects legitimized to populations and then executed without consideration for their interests.

[13] That norms might support activity which is destructive or morally bad is often acknowledged in IR (for example, Finnemore 1996; and Wendt 1999) but rarely explored at length; for an exception, see Barnett and Finnemore 1999.

[14] Berkeley 2001; Baumann 1989.

Legitimacy, coercion, and self-interest constitute ideal-types for modes of social control, and each generates compliance with society's rules by a different mechanism. Although each one can be analytically separated from the others, in practice they are rarely found in pure isolation. In this section I identify the conceptual features that make each concept distinctive and use these differences to highlight the distinguishing peculiarities of legitimacy.

### Coercion

Coercion refers to a relation of asymmetrical physical power among agents, where this asymmetry is applied to changing the behavior of the weaker agent. The operative mechanism is fear or simple compulsion; fear produces acquiescence. An actor who obeys a rule because of coercion is motivated by the fear of punishment from a stronger power. The rule itself is irrelevant except as a signal for the kinds of behavior that will or will not incur the penalty. If a social system relies primarily on coercion to motivate compliance with its rules, we would expect to see enormous resources devoted to enforcement and surveillance and low levels of compliance when the enforcing agent is not looking.

Thomas Hobbes presents a classic argument for why society must be based on the centralization of coercive power.[15] As Michael Doyle says, "Having assumed certain features of individuals (that they are rational but sometimes envious egoists), [Hobbes] showed how their interaction in anarchic conditions would lead them to want to form a truly sovereign state."[16] A group of individuals can be moved from the state of nature to a human society only if the group willfully concedes to a central agent almost all powers of self-defense and retribution. What matters in this process for Hobbes is the transfer of material capabilities in the shape of the physical resources needed for coercion. Centralized coercion is the solution to threats from one's neighbors. It does two things: it disarms the citizens relative to one another, pacifying their interactions, and it arms the Leviathan with overwhelming coercive capacity to enforce its rules. Although Hobbes's citizens join society by consent and retain a residual right to self-defense, the system is best seen as an example of a society based on coercion rather than consent, or even religious conviction, for three reasons: the motivation for joining is the fear of certain depredation in the state of nature; the motivation for obeying the sovereign is the threatened sanction; and the obligation to obey exists only while the sov-

[15] Hobbes, 1968 [1651].
[16] Doyle 1997, 113.

ereign maintains almost absolute power. The argument is sometimes made that Hobbes also relied on legitimacy or religion to help explain the maintenance of social order;[17] however, the Leviathan is necessary precisely because these other mechanisms cannot be counted on to do the job. Similarly individuals may hold powerful moral beliefs that influence their decisions, but because others cannot be relied on to act according to these moral precepts and the costs of being exploited might include death, internal motivations toward moral action cannot be the basis of society.[18] For Hobbes, it is the sword that ultimately maintains social order; neither self-interest nor legitimacy is reliably compelling.

In this same tradition we can also place John Austin and the classical legal positivists who find the essence of law in the act of enforcement. On this view, an attitude among the population of normative commitment to the rules or to their legitimacy is unimportant. Philip Soper, a legal theorist, writes:

> That many people may have such an attitude is simply a contingent fact about their personalities or about the coincidental convergence of their interests with the demands of a particular legal system; the attitude is not a necessary feature of law. After all, some people might respond positively toward gunmen too, sympathizing with a particular mugger's plight or with the justice of a terrorist's cause. Yet that possibility would not lead one to revise the judgment that in general the confrontation with gunmen is coercive.[19]

This model clearly establishes one pole in the triad of the mechanisms of social control. Its emphasis on threats and force in generating compliance comes at the expense of attention to either the normative content of rules or more complicated calculations of self-interest by actors. Coercion is a relatively "primitive" form of social control, because it is inefficient from the point of view of the central power. It does not generally provoke voluntary compliance. A common lesson of studies of complex organizations is that coercion and repression tend to generate resentment and resistance, even as they produce compliance, because they operate against the normative impulses of the subordinate individual or group.[20] As a result, each application of coercion involves an expenditure of limited social capital and reduces the likelihood that the subject will comply without coercion in the future. For this reason, few complex social orders are primarily based on coercion, although all likely resort to force at some point.

---

[17] See Eisenach 1981 and Williams 1996.

[18] See LeBuffe 2003. LeBuffe is responding to the alternative reading put forward in Warrander 1957.

[19] Soper 1984, 22.

[20] On these backlash and control costs, see Hechter 1987, chap. 8. See also Scott 1990.

Coercion and sanction are costly mechanisms of control, quite unsuited for regulating activities that require any measure of creativity or enthusiasm in subordinates. To anticipate, social orders based on coercion tend over time either to collapse from their own instability or reduce their coercive component by legitimating certain practices and creating stable expectations among actors.[21] Government based primarily on the centralization of coercive capacity looks like totalitarianism, like Leviathan, where each act of compliance comes from being at the wrong end of the gun.

## Self-Interest

A second possible motivation for compliance with rules is the belief that compliance, in fact, promotes one's self-interest. It is not uncommon in the social sciences to presume that such calculations of self-interest are the foundation of most social action.[22] This view suggests that, when individuals follow rules, it is the result of an instrumental and calculated assessment of the net benefits of compliance versus noncompliance, with an instrumental attitude toward social structures and other people. The governing agent's task is to structure incentives so that community members find compliance the most rationally attractive option.[23] If the system is constituted to manage incentives correctly, self-interest should, as Kant predicts, allow a peaceful society "even for a people comprised of devils."[24] In this perspective, social interaction is modeled as an exchange, and social obligations are the equivalent of contracts: individual decisions are calculated to maximize returns, and organizations are pillars of accumulated principal-agent contract relationships.[25] The fundamental political act is consent to a contract.

Self-interest needs to be carefully defined if it is to be a useful (and potentially falsifiable) concept for social science. The bounds of a self-interest explanation need to be clearly drawn so as not to subsume all other categories. The distinctions between self-interest and both coercion

[21] Kratochwil 1984.

[22] For instance, Chong 1995; and Ferejohn and Satz 1995; cf. Lohmann 1995. See also the discussion in Green and Shapiro 1994.

[23] Voeten (2005) suggests that legitimacy is itself a product of these incentives, so that, for instance, the Council is seen as legitimate by states to the extent that it promises a future stream of utility benefits. His concept of legitimacy has no sociological content.

[24] Kant 1984 [1795], 124. Kant did not imagine that this was an accurate description of society or of individuals. Rather, he used it show the resilience of a social order based on a correct arrangement of individual incentives.

[25] The literature in organization theory is large. A good overview is Williamson 1985. For critique, see Perrow 1986.

and legitimacy are important.[26] Self-interest is related to coercion in that both are forms of utilitarianism.[27] When an actor is presented with a situation of choice that involves threats of reprisals or where the available choices have been manipulated by others, the self-interest and coercion models will follow the same logic and predict the same outcome: a risk-neutral agent should compare the benefit to be had by going forward as against the costs of the punishment multiplied by the probability of the sanction being applied. Desmond Ellis contends that "clearly these two types of solutions embrace the view that the basis of the obligation to obey norms is prudence."[28] Turned around, this is the logic of deterrence. The key difference is that an application of coercion leaves the coerced worse off than before (even if the individual accedes to the coercion out of a sense of self-interest), whereas a self-interest perspective sees the individual as better off than had he or she taken any other available path (even if the menu of available paths has been coercively restricted by others.) Put differently, self-interest involves *self-restraint* on the part of an actor (as does legitimacy), whereas coercion operates by *external* restraint. This implies a difference in the complexity of the incentive structure and the consequent complexity required in the respondent in the self-interest approach. In other words, a coercive model is exclusively interested in the threat and use of physical violence, whereas the self-interested model is generalizable to a host of psychic, social, and physical incentives and disincentives.

The distinction between self-interest and legitimacy, on the other hand, can be specified through the distinction between interest and self-interest. All three models (coercion, self-interest, and legitimacy) assume that actors are "interested" in the sense of pursing their interests, and so self-interest must add something more. Actors who are interested act rationally to pursue goals, but we know nothing a priori about what those goals are. In order to assume *self*-interest, we need to add a presumption about the egoistic attitude of the self toward others or to the rules.[29] This instrumental attitude toward others remains true whether one uses a hypothetical model of absolute rationality, ignoring decision costs, or a more realistic model of bounded rationality, which accepts the cognitive and resource limits of actors. What matters is what gets included in the calculus of interest, and the actor's definition of the situation it finds itself in. Does the actor take for granted the existing structure of relations and institutions and seek to improve its position within it, or does the actor conceive

[26] Wendt 1999, 239–240, 287–288.
[27] Ellis 1971, 693.
[28] Ibid., 695.
[29] Jencks 1990; Wendt 1999.

of its situation *de novo* at each decision point and seek to create its maximally beneficial arrangement? The former is a status quo orientation, where at least some rules or relations are accepted and not generally challenged, and the pursuit of interests takes place within a set of structures that the actor takes for granted. Here we can say an actor is "interested." The latter is a "self-interested" orientation in the strict sense, which implies a continuous reassessment of every rule and relationship from an instrumental point of view.[30] Nothing is taken for granted or valued for its own sake, only for the payoff it brings the self. This stance is fixed, not variable. Self-interest is necessarily amoral with respect to one's obligations toward others; others are mere objects to be used instrumentally, although, of course, this does not preclude cooperative behavior if done for instrumental reasons.[31]

A society where compliance with rules is based principally on the self-interest of the members will exhibit several characteristic features. First, any loyalty by actors toward the system or its rules is contingent upon the system providing a positive stream of benefits. Actors are constantly recalculating the expected payoff to remaining in the system and stand ready to abandon it immediately should some alternative promise greater utility. Such a system can be stable while the payoff structure is in equilibrium, but the actors are constantly assessing the costs and benefits of revisionism. In this way, self-interested actors are ontologically inclined to revisionism rather than to the status quo. Second, and following from the first feature, long-term relationships between self-interested agents are difficult to maintain because actors do not value the relation itself, only the benefits accruing from it. Such long-term relations may exist, and indeed persist, but only while the instrumental payoff remains positive. David Beetham says of this attitude: "To explain all action conforming to rules as the product of a self-interested calculation of the consequences of breaching them, is to elevate the attributes of the criminal into the standard for the whole of humankind."[32] As a result, a social system that relies primarily on self-interest will necessarily be thin and held together tenuously, and be apt to change drastically in response to shifts in the structure of payoffs.

Therefore, we should avoid confusing the generic statement that individuals pursue "interests" in the sense of choosing means to achieve goals with the particular assumption of "self-interestedness," referring to an instrumental attitude toward other actors and toward rules.[33] Many diverse

[30] Wendt 1999, 240.
[31] Axelrod 1984; Axelrod and Keohane 1985; see also Jencks 1990. On self-interest in economic and political realms, see the review in Citrin and Green 1990.
[32] Beetham 1991, 27.
[33] Wendt 1999, 239.

models of human behavior accept that actors pursue "interests," but they disagree on whether they are "self-interested" in this strong sense. The distinction is essential, because the difference between self-interest and legitimacy comes from the divergent accounts of how each thinks of its goals; both take the position that states do pursue goals. Models that take interests to be equivalent to "self-interest" end up being circular, for there is no behavior that could contradict the self-interest hypothesis.[34]

The relationship between coercion, self-interest, and legitimacy is complex, and each is rarely found in anything like its pure, isolated form. Further, they are probably sometimes related in a patterned, systematic fashion, in that many social structures that are eventually legitimized emerged first from relations of coercion or from individual self-interest. Once established, it is logical for the powerful to spend energy legitimizing structures from which they benefit. As a result, it is sometimes argued that legitimacy is derivative of coercion because the social consensus upon which legitimacy is premised can be created by coercion. Many social relations that are accepted today as legitimate began as relations of coercion, including perhaps all modern liberal democratic states.[35] Although I agree that the creation of legitimacy by the use of power is one of the more interesting aspects of legitimacy, this cannot mean that legitimacy and coercion are the same or that the former is reducible to the latter. Even if begun through coercion, legitimacy, as a product of internalized norms, operates differently than does the power relation in which it originated. It is precisely because something changes when a relation of coercion becomes legitimized that it is worth studying legitimacy in the first place.

## WHAT DOES LEGITIMACY DO IN IR?

A structure of legitimate power relations operates in notably different ways than do structures of coercion or self-interest. The former has different costs and consequences, different means of achieving compliance, and different modes of reproduction and contestation. These distinctions are worth knowing about. Legitimate institutions in society are behaviorally significant in three ways: through their effects on the internal makeup of actors, through their effects on the structure of payoffs, and through the construction of resources available to all actors in the system. In the following sections I examine these effects and explore their operation in the international system. At the unit level I emphasize that legitimacy is a process of

[34] Ibid., chap. 6
[35] Tilly 1992.

internalization which shapes states' sense of their interests. The result is a kind of socialization of states that produces congruence between (perceived) interests and the legitimated rules and institutions. At the structural level I explore Max Weber's sophisticated account of the embeddedness of the individual in an environment of legitimated power, what he called the "validity" of the system. Validity encompasses both the power of intersubjective norms over individuals and an account of the change such norms create in the decision-making context for all actors. For international relations, this provides an explanation for the structure of payoffs and constraints faced by states as they operate in the international system, where even states that reject the legitimacy of an institution are faced with a changed environment because of others' belief in it. Legitimate institutions also affect the distribution of resources in the system, because such institutions create new kinds of resources that are available to actors and are useful in their varied pursuits of power and interest. These resources, in the form of symbols of the institution, are brought into being by the legitimation of the institution and themselves become powerful tools that any rational actor might have an interest in using. The connection between legitimacy and symbols is important, and it is revisited in chapter 5 in the context of the Security Council.

### Legitimacy at the Unit Level: States

The process of legitimation alters the character of the units in a social system. A legitimate rule or institution is one that has been internalized by the units so that its procedures or proscriptions have been incorporated into the unit's own sense of its interests and identity. Internalization is the process by which an individual apprehends an "objective" reality and endows it with meaning shared by others. The individual is thereby altered, or, as Habermas put it, one's " 'inner nature' is adapted to society with the help of normative structures in which needs are interpreted and actions are prohibited, licensed or enjoined."[36] Legitimation begins, according to Berger and Luckmann, with "the immediate . . . interpretation of an objective event as expressing meaning, that is, as a manifestation of another's subjective processes which thereby becomes subjectively meaningful to myself."[37] The result is a "bringing in" to the individual intersubjective material provided by the social context, what Berger and Luckmann call the individual "taking over" the world. This provides the

---

[36] Thomas McCarthy summarizing Habermas in the translator's introduction to Habermas 1975, xxii.

[37] Berger and Luckmann 1966, 129.

individual with both a map of the external environment, populated by other actors and institutions and useful for navigating that environment, and—more important for my purposes—a comprehension of its interests relative to that environment.

For states, internalization is part of the process by which the state acquires its interests and preferences—part, in other words, of the state learning what it *wants*. State interests come from two sources: the intrinsic qualities and needs of the state itself (the state qua state), and the role, identity, and culture which the state inhabits.[38] Into the first category fall interests such as those for survival, power, and autonomy whose failure to satisfy would result in the elimination of the unit from the system. Providing for these interests ensures the fundamental continuity of the state and so is the precondition for the existence of the state in the first place; it is the precondition for *all* states. Into the second category fall interests that depend on the context or social setting of the state and so cannot be generalized across all states. These might include the interest of a Great Power aspirant to be recognized as a "pole" in the system, of a status quo state to be seen as a rule follower, of a capitalist state in a low inflation rate and steady growth of GDP. How these two classes of interests might be satisfied is not at all clear, and turning interests into strategies for choice and behavior is a messy process. There will never be universal agreement among policy makers on the appropriate strategy to satisfy interests, and the conflicts of domestic politics are generally over these strategies—for instance, what constitutes the most efficient path to "autonomy" for a state or how to balance the trade-off between imperial dominance and overstretch. Fighting over strategies to achieve goals, and over goals themselves, constitutes the normal stuff of domestic interest-group politics.

Internalization can affect states both at the level of defining basic interests and at the point of deciding on strategies with which to pursue those interests. Both pathways of internalization require that an external rule, institution, norm, or idea exist before the process begins, and that this outside feature affects the internal constitution of the state. At the level of basic interests, this might take the shape of actors "discovering" a new need, or perceiving a new interest, based on the prescription, example, or ethics of the external feature. Once internalized, the external features "enter directly into the constitution of the actors' ends themselves."[39] Such norms, therefore, "are constitutive rather than merely regulative."[40] As Martha Finnemore says of national science bureaucracies, "states

---

[38] Wendt 1999, chap. 5. Wendt describes these, respectively, as "objective" and "subjective" interests.

[39] See the discussion by Wrong 1961, 186.

[40] Wrong 1961, 186. See also Wendt 1999.

adopted these bureaucracies because of a new understanding of necessary and appropriate state behavior" originating at the international level.[41]

At the strategic level two processes can be seen. The first is the normative shaping of strategies by the "logic of appropriateness" set out by international rules or institutions.[42] This is evident in the normative commitments made in war strategies, for example, where there is a clear demarcation between the goals of the war and the (appropriate and inappropriate) modes of fighting it. The chemical weapons taboo is an example of one such normative commitment on war strategy derived partly from international sources.[43] Strategies are seen as either legitimate or illegitimate means of problem solving by states. The second is the strategic use of legitimized resources or institutions in the political competition between groups. This second process includes those identified by Keck and Sikkink, among others, where domestic actors make an appeal to an international rule as part of their domestic politicking.[44] This process relies on internalization only indirectly, since internalization by some members in the community creates resources that are powerful for all. I therefore treat it below under the heading "Symbolic Politics."

Internalization requires more than simple "learning" by states. Learning refers to improving the decision-making calculus between means and ends. It does not entail any change in the interests or goals of a state, just in the thinking that governs how best to achieve them.[45] Ikenberry and Kupchan distinguish between "socialization" and "learning," where the former entails internalization and the latter does not.[46] Confusion between learning and internalization makes it impossible to distinguish between habitual, instrumental, and legitimized patterns in society.[47]

Both learning and internalization might or might not be "fitness enhancing." There is nothing necessary in the logic of either to suggest that all changes should be "improvements" in any objective sense over the prior situation. Clearly, in an evolutionary model, changes that improve the fitness of the unit will be more likely to survive in the long run, but since this pattern relies on the "death" of unfit units rather than a reason why units should be able to recognize "good" changes over "bad" ones,

[41] Finnemore 1996, 65.

[42] March and Olsen 1998.

[43] Price 1995. See also Tannenwald 1999, on the nuclear taboo; Eyre and Suchman 1996, on weapons procurement; Krause 2002, on light arms; and Cameron Lawson, and Tomlin 1999, on land mines.

[44] Keck and Sikkink 1998. Also, Cortell and Davis 1996; Müller 1993.

[45] One can "learn" to have new goals but only through internalizing new values, as when one learns to occupy a role in society. I separate these two functions, which are joined in Wendt's (1999, 327) discussion of "complex learning."

[46] Ikenberry and Kupchan 1990.

[47] Wrong 1961, 187.

it is still entirely possible for units to internalize or learn new goals and strategies that turn out to be harmful in the long run. Those units may then die, but this step in the life cycle of norms is separate from internalization. Moreover, under the right circumstances, several formal models find that altruistic or other non-optimal norms might survive in an evolutionary setting.[48] One model in this vein, by Herbert Gintis, is especially interesting in that it identifies as the crucial feature the existence of institutions that reinforce the norm. This creates a path for the "oblique" transmission of norms by socializing authorities recognized by the individual (as opposed to more direct transmission by parents or peers) and may explain the persistence of fitness-reducing norms.[49]

Recognizing the role of internalization in legitimacy means that we should separate our discussion of legitimacy from that of compliance. Several recent treatments of international treaties equate an increase in legitimacy with an increase in compliance,[50] but the measure of legitimacy does not lie in its ability to generate compliance with the rule or institution. Legitimacy might sometimes lead to an increase in compliance, but the connection between the two is not inherent in the concept of legitimacy. Instead, legitimacy changes the relationship between rule and actor in a manner that *might* increase the compliance pull of the rule but might not.[51] The behavior of the actor relative to the rule or institution is dependent on many factors in addition to legitimacy, including the relative payoffs of different options and the actor's customs and habits. What matters for legitimation is the internalization of the external norm, not the behavioral result of compliance or noncompliance. Even in cases where the rate of compliance is not affected by legitimacy, the process of internalizing the rule must still have taken place for legitimation to happen.[52] Legitimacy changes the relation between the actor and the institution—*that* is the heart of the concept; any change in the rate of compliance as a result is a subsequent consequence of this change. Compliance may indeed be affected, but this is secondary to the internalization that is the crucial feature of legitimation.

[48] Gintis 2001; Axelrod 1984.

[49] Gintis 2002. This model is a formalization of Herbert Simon's more casual description of altruism.

[50] Chayes and Chayes 1995; Albin 2001.

[51] Wrong (1961), following Freud, sees the relationship as much more complex. For him, internalization *increases* the psychic tension in the individual, rather than decreasing it, by producing guilt and anxiety among those with the strictest superegos. This might create compliance in the short run but at the expense of feelings of repression and frustration. More basic drives and instincts are being repressed and must eventually express themselves. Although I do not pursue this line of thought, it is consistent with the approach used here of keeping compliance questions separate from legitimation issues.

[52] Weber 1978, pt. 2, chap. 10.

One incidental consequence of internalization is that it makes problematic all statements structured in the following form: "the power of legitimacy is shown when an actor complies with a legitimate rule that goes against its interests." Wendt has observed that such a starting point for research is internally inconsistent because the process of legitimation has affected the actor's own definition of its interests, not just the value of the payoffs of the different options.[53] Legitimacy changes interests, and it changes them systematically in the direction of being supportive of norms. Thus, in the presence of a legitimated institution, the actor may have lost any sense that previously existed that its interests are in conflict with the institution. Attempting to separate interests and legitimacy at this point is fruitless. For models of legitimacy that base themselves on consent (in other words, that assume legitimacy is produced by individuals' giving their consent) this creates a problem: the process of rational consent involves assessing the difference, if any, between one's interests and the available options. But if we accept my definition of legitimacy, then legitimacy contributes to structuring the decision situation. Legitimacy changes the actor's perception of both its interests and the payoffs of the available options. As Weber says, "Every genuine form of domination [legitimated power] implies a minimum of voluntary compliance, that is, an *interest* (based on ulterior motives or genuine acceptance) in obedience."[54] All talk of "interests" becomes more complicated in the presence of legitimacy, since legitimacy works by affecting one's definition of interests.

### Legitimacy at the Structural Level: The International System

In Max Weber's discussion of legitimacy, the effects of legitimacy go beyond change in the individual to include structural effects on society that arise when the belief in legitimacy is widely shared. Weber called this structural condition the "validity" of the system, where validity refers to the probability that an action in society will be guided by the dictates of a given legitimated rule or institution.[55] He used the concept to explain the stabilizing effects of legitimized legal orders, but it is also useful in thinking about the international system because it identifies a structural consequence of the individual-level process of internalization. When that process is widely shared at the individual level, it affects the structure of the system overall by shaping the expectations for all actors about what constitutes a normal pattern of behavior.

[53] Wendt 1994b.
[54] Weber 1978, 212; emphasis in original.
[55] Ibid., 311–315.

Where legitimacy, as a psychological phenomenon based on internalization, is a quality that exists in the minds of individuals, validity is a quality of the system that exists when the general expectation is that one might encounter a believer of norms in one's international interactions. In the valid social system, nonbelievers cannot simply ignore the rules and institutions that they do not view as legitimate. That enough others do believe in their legitimacy means that nonbelievers must consider them when estimating the likely effects of different courses of action. Thus, even though validity is ultimately derived from the individual psychology of the units in the society, it is seen by all actors as an "objective" element of system structure. The effects of validity on individual behavior reflect both shared beliefs in society and also how these beliefs change the strategic decision setting for *all* actors, not just those who share the beliefs. In the "valid" social system that Weber defines, perpetuation of the system has more to do with the system-reinforcing behavior of the members of the system than it has with their belief in the normative foundations of the system. In his words:

> It is by no means necessary that all, or even a majority, of those who engage in such [compliant] conduct do so from this [normative] motivation. As a matter of fact, such a situation has never occurred. The broad mass of the participants act in a way corresponding to legal norms, not out of obedience regarded as a legal obligation, but either because the environment approves of the conduct and disapproves of its opposite, or merely as a result of unreflective habituation to a regularity of life that has engraved itself as a custom.[56]

From the structural perspective, according to Weber, "it is the 'orientation' of an action toward a norm, rather than the 'success' of that norm [in getting internalized] that is decisive for its validity."[57] The "validity of a norm" is measured by "the very likelihood that a coercive apparatus will go into action for its enforcement."[58]

A "valid" international system exhibits a structure of constraints and incentives that appeared to all actors in the system as an objective reality.[59] On a local rather than systemwide scale, this is very much like how James and Lake describe the second face of hegemony: the structure of opportunities faced by states is changed by the actions of the hegemon, which in turn changes "the likelihood of a given individual acting on any particular opportunity in the new distribution."[60] The hegemon's impact on

[56] Ibid., 312.
[57] Ibid., 312–313.
[58] Ibid., 319–320. We should understand "coercion" here to mean any kind of pressure on an individual to ensure compliance, not just as physical aggression.
[59] This includes both material and normative incentives and constraints.
[60] James and Lake 1989, 6.

the "broader material environment" of the international system appears to states as the given context for analyzing policy choices. For James and Lake, who are looking to explain the effects of hegemony on the trading system, what is interesting about hegemons is their choice of trade policy and of other domestic policies with implications for trade patterns. This is not my focus here, but the structural role played by legitimated power in creating the objective structure of incentives faced by others is the same.[61]

A single legitimated international institution will not result in the comprehensive "valid" social system that Weber imagines in the well-ordered domestic society. However, that single institution will still create this structural effect in its area of competence. It will be recognized as an authority in its sphere. This implies a local form of validity within the realm in which the institution is perceived as legitimate. Separating society into such spheres, under locally dominant institutions, is the insight behind the concept of social "fields" as used by Pierre Bourdieu and others; these scholars recognize the distinct but interlinked realm of authority for institutions in society.[62] The Security Council, if seen as legitimate, might have social power in crises relating to international peace and security, but it has no special power over issues outside that sphere of official competence.[63]

The structural component of legitimacy affects how states calculate their decisions by changing the structure of incentives that they face. Legitimacy in an international institution changes the strategic environment for states and so affects their behavior, even beyond those states that have been socialized to see the institution as legitimate. This means that two kinds of actors who might resist the force of internalization—namely, the strong and the "nonbeliever"—will nonetheless be affected by the presence of a legitimated institution. First, both strong states and weak states are affected by a valid social order. Although the effects are felt differently by the two groups, in that the higher (absolute) costs of breaking rules are easier for the strong to bear, the cost-benefit calculus is changed for both. The strong can find themselves constrained by a legitimated social system and restricted from following their preferred course of action, even if they themselves had a hand in creating the system. Legitimate social structures reduce the scope of freedom for the strong, as well as for the weak. As Bukovansky says: "The hegemonic state does not stand outside the hegemonic order, but is subject to it. . . . Leadership and great

[61] We cannot treat this structure of incentives as objective for the *long-run*, of course.

[62] Bourdieu 1991. Hayward (2000) applies a similar concept, and it is also the foundation of Walzer's (1983) argument about "spheres of justice," each under the domain of its own social institutions and normative principles.

[63] Arguing about the limits of the Council's competence takes a prominent role in debates over the legitimacy of its actions. See the references above in chapter 1.

power status are roles contingent on the broader social order."[64] We return to this theme in chapter 4 with regard to the origins of the Security Council.

Second, actors who "believe" in the legitimacy of the order as well as those who do not are both affected by its existence. Actors who are socialized to accept the legitimacy of the system might still behave in ways that conform to its dictates because they see instrumental advantage in doing so. Thus the validity of the system opens up the possibility of a purely strategic use of legitimacy. As Weber says, "sheer expediency" may cause actors to alter their behavior in light of norms that are legitimated at a structural level in the society. "A thief orients his action to the validity of the criminal law in that he acts surreptitiously. The fact that the order is recognized as valid in his society is made evident by the fact that he cannot violate it openly without punishment." Further, "a person who fights a duel follows the code of honor [a "valid" legitimated structure]; but at the same time, insofar as he either keeps it secret or conversely gives himself up to the police, he takes account of the criminal law [an instrumental incentive structure]."[65] This does not mean that legitimacy is being "abused" by those who do not believe in it or that the beliefs of those who do perceive legitimacy are "wrong" in any meaningful sense. Rather, it illustrates that legitimacy, when widely shared and acted upon, has effects on even nonbelievers that cannot be ignored. It demonstrates the unavoidable structural implications of legitimacy, so that legitimacy cannot be treated entirely at the individual level.[66]

The structural effects of legitimation are evident in Mlada Bukovansky's study of "international political culture" and its effects on domestic politics.[67] In the context of the American and French revolutions, she sees "international culture" as providing resources to domestic actors struggling against challengers. Domestic players are strengthened to the extent that they can draw on strong currents in international culture, and although these currents are themselves constituted by the beliefs of many individuals, their systemic power comes from the perception by any one individual that they are part of the international structure and not changeable. Over the long term, of course, the international structure is changed by the addition of new intellectual currents that alter the domi-

[64] Bukovansky 2002, 46.

[65] Weber, 1978, 32. For the same argument in international law, see Kratochwil 1989 and Johnstone 2003. On the limits of stretching to justify, see Franck 1990 on "determinacy."

[66] There might also be domestic implications, which I do not examine here. For instance, legitimized international norms might also be used instrumentally by domestic actors in their battles with other domestic players. See, for instance, Cortell and Davis 1996; and Leheny 2006.

[67] Bukovansky 2002.

nant ideology; in Bukovansky's case, the ideology of absolutism was replaced by the revolutions with versions of republicanism, meaning that
future generations of republicans would have an easier time in their domestic contests because of the compatibility of their demands with the
prevailing international culture. In the short term, however, the international political culture is part of the structural background that defines
the incentives and resources that domestic actors face.

### Legitimacy and Resources: Symbols

Between the unit level and the structural level lies a set of processes that
channel power and information from one to the other. These processes
take a material form in the shape of symbols. It is symbols, and their
power when used instrumentally by actors, that are the consequence of
the successful legitimation of institutions. Legitimate institutions beget
symbols which actors recognize and use as forms of power. The practical
implications of this for studying international relations are explored in
chapter 5, but a conceptual introduction to the issue is given here.

The study of symbolic politics has at times been marginalized in social
science and remains so in International Relations. Prior to Barry O'Neill's
recent book,[68] symbols that entered IR discussions were largely in the
form of the occasional example in works not otherwise interested in the
phenomenon.[69] To some early-twentieth-century sociologists and anthropologists, the use of symbols and rituals in political order was the hall-
mark of primitive, non-modern, or foreign societies.[70] Weber's typology
of political legitimation, which separated charisma, tradition, and rational-
bureaucratic law, contributed to the exclusion of symbolic power from
modern social study.[71] Weber's ideal types left room for symbolic power
only in traditional and charismatic systems, and thus performed a "double
move" with respect to the substantive concerns of sociology: first, it rele-
gated symbolic power to those social structures that were defined as "non-
rational" or "pre-rational;" and, second, it suggested a teleological progres-
sion from non-rational ordering principles toward the "rational society."
Together these created the assumption, which governed subsequent research and still affects the study of international relations, that complex

---

[68] O'Neill 1999.

[69] For example, in his discussion of globalization and backlash, Benjamin Barber (1995)
takes seriously the symbolic power of "McWorld" but does not explain how or why its symbols are important. One welcome exception to this is Kaufman 2001.

[70] This view, expressed in the study of French political symbolism, is treated in Agulhon
1985.

[71] Weber 1978.

societies and advanced systems should be examined as rational-bureaucratic structures in which symbolic power, when it is manifested, is a sign of residual pockets of primitive polities in need of modern socialization.

This view is undermined by a careful look at any political system, domestic or international. People fight passionately over what flag is to fly over the statehouse, over whose face is to be on stamps and currency, over prayers in public spaces—over the "labour of representation."[72] These fights go beyond the issues that affect an individual directly—even people without children hold strong opinions about prayer in school; people in Connecticut care whether people in Nevada have access to abortion.[73] The importance of symbolism to politics is as old as politics itself; that is, it is inseparable from human social existence. As Kertzer says, "At its root, politics is symbolic, because both the formation of human groupings and the hierarchies that spring from them depend on symbolic activity. [No] political identities are based on objects I can touch or see or perceive in any way except through symbolic representation."[74]

The symbolic struggles at the heart of politics exist also in the international community, perhaps even more so than in domestic politics. The status of the PLO delegation to the UN, the presence of blue-helmet troops in a war zone, and the outcome of an ICJ hearing are the kinds of issues, primarily symbolic, that animate foreign offices and constitute the stuff of international relations, even for states not directly involved in the dispute.[75] Like all political systems, the United Nations makes heavy use of symbols. Symbols are used, inter alia, to legitimate the institution, to define social classes among members, to conceal or bolster power relations, to communicate and to act, to delegate power, and to establish authority roles. Even if scholars have paid little attention to the power of symbols in international relations, practitioners and states appear to take them seriously.[76] To say that a matter is of symbolic importance is not to

---

[72] Bourdieu 1991, 234.

[73] This is a key weakness of the "deontological" project in political theory, represented by John Rawls. Rather than being independent, the interests of an individual are partly shaped by the symbolic question of what the society permits others to do and whether this fits with or goes against the values of the individual. For instance, one might not want to live in a society where children are taught creationism as fact in schools, even though one may have no personal or familial stake in the curriculum of schools.

[74] Kertzer 1996, 4.

[75] This concern with how others live is not limited to within one's national borders. Thus, to the extent that foreign policy is concerned with how those in other countries live or are allowed to live (as in crusades for anticommunism, human rights, or pro-democracy), the theory of sovereignty is inherently flawed when it coexists with any universal theory of the good life. The universalizing tendency of liberalism is at odds with the dividing tendency of sovereignty.

[76] This is one way in which it is true, as Abbott and Snidal (1998, 29) note, that "for several decades, states have taken IOs more seriously than have scholars."

contrast it to matters of "real" importance, as in "such-and-such a debate doesn't really matter because it is only symbolic, not material or substantive." In politics, as in language, it is the symbols that can constitute substance. Symbolic stakes, in as much as institutions and relations of authority are socially constructed, are the real thing.

Barry O'Neill provides a conceptual foundation for thinking about symbols in international relations but not a definition of the term. He surveys many competing definitions and decides that such a complex phenomenon will not likely yield to a universal definition. So rather than offering a general definition, O'Neill provides definitions of three subtypes and then identifies the "family resemblances" among them in order to learn something about the whole set.[77] The subtypes he defines include message symbols (those that carry a message between actors), focal symbols (those that induce players to "commonly expect a certain outcome" in an interaction), and value symbols (those that express and reinforce an identity). O'Neill claims that it is impossible to specify precisely a common thread among the three: "there is no set [of features] that is necessary and sufficient" to define the group to which all three belong.[78] Instead, he illustrates by example the characteristics and operation of each subtype in international politics, and allows the reader to infer from the examples the commonalities they share. Kertzer's seminal book on symbols and rituals follows suit, giving no definition but rather a series of examples of the central place symbols and rituals occupy in politics.[79]

Among attempts at a universal definition, a few stand out as notably unique. Alfred North Whitehead, for instance, gives a catholic definition of "symbol," focusing on the simple act of connecting in the mind two physically unconnected sensations: he says that symbolism takes place "when some components of [an agent's] experience elicit consciousness, beliefs, emotions, and usages, respecting other components of its experience. The former set of components are the 'symbols' and the latter set constitute the 'meaning' of the symbols."[80] This approach is sufficiently broad enough that he can include as "symbolic" the connection between noticing a colored shape before us and the observation that this is a chair we can sit down on—an encompassing definition which gathers under a single heading all acts of representation.[81]

Whitehead's approach is too expansive for my purposes. There is an im-

---

[77] O'Neill 1999. He borrows "family resemblance" from Wittgenstein 1968.

[78] O'Neill 1999, 4.

[79] Kertzer 1988.

[80] Whitehead 1928, 9.

[81] He says "colored shapes seem to be symbols for some other elements in our experience, and when we see the colored shapes we adjust our actions toward those other elements" (ibid., 5).

portant difference between the mental act of recognizing patterns in one's physical environment and the political act of mobilizing others by manipulating these secondhand meanings. I wish to reserve the term "symbolism" for those representations that carry political significance but at the same time provide a concrete working definition so that we can distinguish the boundary conditions of symbolism and thus recognize the difference between things that are symbols and things that are not.[82] This means finding a definition that extracts the essence from the examples given by O'Neill and Kertzer but also identifies the connection between a "symbol" and social and political power.

Alison Brysk provides a definition that moves in this direction. She suggests that a "symbol involves the maintenance or transformation of a power relationship through the communication of normative and affective representations."[83] This emphasizes the purposes to which a symbol can be put (maintaining power relationships) rather than the nature of the symbol itself, but it has the advantage of putting power at the center of the concept. We can use Brysk's insight to extract what O'Neill's three symbol types have in common, namely, a sense that social power is being exercised by an object or action which in strictly materialist terms has no capacity to cause these effects. A symbol, therefore, can be defined as an object vested with social power beyond its physical, material powers. The power of a symbol is power exercised at a distance from its material source. For instance, the destruction of Saddam Hussein's statue in Baghdad by Americans on April 9, 2003, symbolized a changing of the Iraqi regime, even though the statue itself made no material contribution to the old power structure.[84] Similarly, also in the context of the U.S.-Iraq war, a French flag flown in a window in the United States could evoke a violent response from neighbors, even though the flag itself has no material capacity to undermine American foreign policy.[85] The physical separation between the power of the symbol and its material origin helps to account for the flexibility that is available to the users of symbols: each step removed from the material source adds a degree of freedom in how the symbol can legitimately be used or interpreted while still maintaining its integrity and social power.

A symbol, once constituted, is a form of power: it allows a person or object to do things that could not be done before. Objects (such as a flag, a uniform, or a scepter), phrases (a judge saying "I sentence you to . . ."), procedures (the General Assembly making a decision by majority vote),

[82] Or, more accurately, between things that are *treated as symbols by actors* and things that are not.

[83] Brysk 1995, 561.

[84] Associated Press 2003.

[85] *New York Times*, "Frisson of Unease Among the City's French," March 23, 2003.

or manners of speaking (the dialect speaker meeting with disrespect in the capital) all become imbued with power, because they are associated in the minds of the audience with the authority the audience perceives in a particular institution. Symbols, as Wolin says, "serve to evoke the presence of authority despite the physical reality being far removed."[86]

The object in which symbolism is lodged need not bear a resemblance nor carry any connection to its symbolic meaning. The object itself is quite irrelevant: in Whitehead's words, it is "indifferent;" in Bourdieu's, it is "arbitrary."[87] To "make" a symbol means to couple a physical object to a recognizable and meaningful social institution. This results in a change in the object's political function, perhaps a change from having no political function to having one, from being, for instance, a piece of cloth to being a nationalist flag.[88] The "message symbol" of a handshake could easily be imagined being transmitted by any other physical ritual and still carry the same meaning, and the "value symbol" of a national flag could easily be replaced by arrangements of sticks. What matters is the intersubjective understanding of the meaning of the symbol, and this is independent of its physical shape or manifestation.[89] Symbols are therefore a subset of the two categories of "ideas" and "material power." They straddle the typical distinction in IR between what Goldstein and Keohane call the ideational domain of "human beliefs" and the materialist "realities" of "interests in the context of power."[90] Examining the power of symbols in IR requires setting aside the classification scheme that separates ideational and material resources.

Where does this social power come from? As hinted at by the intersubjective basis of symbolism, the social power of a symbol comes from the shared belief among those in the society that it represents an institution with an independent source of (non-symbolic) power. For the symbolic meaning of an object to function, its referent must be understood by both the user of the symbol and the audience.[91] "The goal of [symbolic] communication is coordinated thinking, so the receiver must decipher the sender's meaning and the sender must choose a symbol that promotes a correct understanding."[92] Both sender and receiver must be members of a community of meaning in which the symbolic contents of actions are relatively settled and readily deciphered. Only people with a common un-

---

[86] Wolin 1960, 76.
[87] Whitehead 1928, 2; Bourdieu 1991.
[88] Harrison 1995, 263.
[89] Cf. Saussure, as discussed by O'Neill 1999, 5. See also Harrison 1992, 235.
[90] Goldstein and Keohane 1993, 13, 26–27.
[91] This leaves aside interesting cases of misunderstandings, as well as O'Neill's (1999) "focal symbols."
[92] Ibid., 241.

derstanding of the flag and nationalism will read the colored cloth as a symbol of the nation. Thus symbols are collective goods, part of the inter-subjective baggage of individuals situated in a community.[93] They are a currency of power because enough individuals believe that others believe in them.

The symbol is a representation of something else, and this other thing must be a powerful institution in the society, whether a formal organization, a powerfully held value, or a popular historical memory. Symbolism is a medium for "lending" the power of an institution through the society, and so for extending the scope and reach of the institution itself. It lies between the state and the international system. As a representation, a symbol "is the product of subjective acts of recognition and, in so far as it is credit and credibility, exists only in and through . . . trust, belief, and obedience. . . . It is a power which exists because the person who submits to it believes that it exists."[94]

The power of symbols is a logical corollary of the legitimacy of an institution. In a socially constructed world populated by social actors, political acts and statements acquire meaning through associations of one object to another. Symbols are created out of "a socially specific set of stories about justice, rights, and identity," and an institution is a readily available stock of meanings from which symbols can be hewn.[95] John Searle describes symbols as "institutional facts," making explicit the connection to the legitimating institution. He says an institution "permits the creation of institutional facts out of social facts and brute facts."[96] The legitimacy of the institution of sovereignty, for instance, creates a set of symbols with which states can be associated and which bring them some strength: a flag outside the UN headquarters, an ambassador inside it, and anthems, slogans, and emblems for schoolchildren to memorize. The legitimacy of an institution can be transferred to any other actor authorized to deploy its symbols.

Since in international relations the power of institutions comes from the belief in their legitimacy (or in the faith in others' belief in their legitimacy), we must therefore look for the origins of international symbols in the legitimacy of their originating institutions. The symbols that are unique to the international system (as opposed to those that are borrowed from domestic society) all come from legitimized international institutions.[97] If IOs had some other basis for their power—for instance, the

---

[93] Bourdieu 1991; Searle 1995.

[94] Bourdieu 1991, 192. Also Kertzer 1996.

[95] Brysk 1995, 563. There is a connection here to how Saussure describes language, where words acquire meaning only through associations with other meaningful objects. See the discussion by Edkins and Pin-Fat 1999, 3.

[96] Searle 1995, 113–114.

[97] "Institution" is used here to refer broadly to organizations, norms, practices, and so on.

coercive power of a "world state"—then symbols could be created by them without reference to legitimacy. But this is currently not the case. Even the UN Security Council, with its broad mandate to intervene forcefully in member states, must rely on perceptions of its legitimacy to accomplish its goals. Therefore, its symbols are also derivative of this legitimacy. The power of the institution in the background creates the social power vested in the symbol in the foreground.

This recalls the discussion above regarding the absence of a normative presumption in the concept of legitimacy. Since we are not understanding "legitimate" to mean the same as "good" or "moral," it is possible to see that symbols can be generated by reprehensible as well as "good" institutions. The symbols of a dictatorship are socially powerful, because the regime they represent has coercive power over the society.[98] This would be conceptually impossible if we erroneously took "legitimate" to mean "moral." This is less of an issue in international relations, since, as mentioned, the power of IOs comes from their legitimacy rather than their coercive power. The legitimated power in IOs provides the foundation for many international symbols.

Symbols are tools of power in two ways: first, in their instrumental use by actors; and, second, in giving power to the international organization that acts as their gatekeeper. While neither has received much attention in International Relations, the second is more seriously underexplored. I look at both forms of power in the following sections, tracing the ways that the symbols of the Council are resources of international power both for states and for the Council itself.

### Symbols and Individual Power

When symbols are used by actors in the pursuit of their goals, the symbol itself can be modeled as an intervening variable. This approach is already a commonplace in International Relations, although generally it is done at the level of domestic and nonstate actors.[99] For instance, much of the recent literature on the domestic effects of international norms relies on an

---

[98] Some might go further and say that the symbols of coercive institutions can entrance even individuals who object morally to the nature of the institution. The history of film, for instance, contains movies such as *Triumph of the Will* and *Birth of a Nation* which many liberals consider "dangerous" for their effective use of cinema technique in the service of fascist political agendas. They are dangerous to the extent that one believes that their symbolic power is capable of tempting the audience to absorb the intellectual program behind them.

[99] O'Neill is an exception in treating the symbolic content of inter-*state* bargaining.

implicit theory about how the symbols of international organizations can be used in a strategic and instrumental manner by domestic actors. Domestic nonstate actors often seek to use the symbols of international organizations in their struggles against the local state. The Chiapas protesters in Mexico, for example, chose the first day of NAFTA, January 1, 1994, to launch their rebellion.[100] Keck and Sikkink document how the international women's movement used the symbols of international conferences to bring attention to their work and to "legitimize the issues."[101] Alison Brysk, in her study of rights movements among indigenous peoples in Latin America, brings the power of symbols to the forefront: despite a long history of oppression and violence brought by Europeans, she finds today that the empowerment of these groups depends in large part on their strategic use of the symbols of international power. These might include reference to UN declarations, participation in international conferences, strategic access to the world media, and appeal to first-world rhetoric. By such strategies in the 1990s, she says, "Indian rights movements have gained voice in the village, presence in the state, niches in the market, influence in international institutions, global alliances, and standing in civil society."[102]

Stuart Kaufman similarly makes a very strong case for seeing the phenomenon of contemporary ethnic war in terms of symbolic motivations. He charts the mobilization of ethnic groups to war, particularly in post-Soviet regions, and finds that a theory of "symbolic choice" rather than "rational choice" provides the best explanation for the conditions which bring societies to ethnic war. Kaufman's view of symbols include myths of ethnic or historical oppression, and are generally of domestic origin and applied in domestic politics. His examples include few cases of symbols arising from the international system itself. At a conceptual level, Kaufman limits himself unnecessarily by defining symbolic politics as "any sort of political activity focused on arousing emotions rather than interests."[103] This definition fits well with the approach he takes—showing how chauvinist leaders appealed to the fears and emotions of populations to incite them to ethnic hatred—but his analysis relies on an untenable separation between interests and emotions. Indeed, in Kaufman's own accounting, the leaders' appeals to ethnic myths worked by changing citizens' perceptions of their own interests. In the disintegrating Yugoslavia, for instance, "the scapegoating rhetoric and discriminatory policies of the leaders led ethnic groups to mobilize against each other, causing residents of ethnically mixed areas to begin seeing their neighbors as threats. As ethnic ten-

[100] Cameron and Tomlin 2000. Also Brysk 2000; Bob 2005.
[101] Keck and Sikkink 1998.
[102] Brysk 2000.
[103] Kaufman 2001.

sions rose, those mixed communities, aided by extremist leaders, engaged in a kind of arms race that quickly led to the outbreak of violence."[104] Interests, then, are precisely the prize being fought over by competing narratives of chauvinism and harmony; divisive narratives and aggressive myths are often effective strategies in convincing a population to see its interests in ethnic terms. These legitimating myths must be recognized as appealing to interests as much as to emotions, since it is by altering perceptions of interests that emotions have their impact. This distraction aside, Kaufman illustrates nicely the importance of symbolic politics to the conflicts in riven societies.

Kaufman, Brysk, and Keck and Sikkink all demonstrate how domestic actors can use symbols, often borrowing them from international organizations, to achieve their goals. This borrowing might be for either constructive or destructive uses, but either way it shows how domestic political actors can use symbols in an instrumental manner. From these examples we can see that some in IR have taken seriously the way in which international politics is changed as a result of actors making use of symbols provided to them by international society.

These authors are not primarily concerned with the *limits* to the use of symbols, yet any conceptual scheme that sees the symbol as an intersubjective act of "representation" clearly must include a boundary beyond which the representation no longer makes sense. There are limits to the ways actors can deploy symbols and still have them accepted by the community as meaningful in their original terms. Investigating these limits helps to introduce the second form of social power created by symbolic politics in international relations. An audience's belief in the credibility of a symbol depends on its being used within the boundaries of meaning as understood in the society. The act of representation entailed by the symbol can be destroyed if the symbol is used outside these bounds. At some point of misuse, the connection between the symbol and its base of institutional power is broken, and the symbol loses its credibility. In international relations, these limits are set by the intersubjective understanding among states regarding the proper meaning of the symbol, and this in turn depends greatly on how the symbol is managed by the international institution that created it.

Because of the political power of symbols to give meaning to objects and events, we find, not surprisingly, that control over the symbolic field is itself a location for the highest political contestation. There is real power to be had in being the one to choose which symbols shall apply to a situation. Bourdieu makes this point strongly: "Knowledge of the social world and, more precisely, the categories which make it possible, are the

[104] Ibid., 166.

stakes *par excellence* of the political struggle." He goes on to say that "this is a struggle which is inseparably theoretical and practical, over the power of preserving or transforming the social world by preserving or trans-forming the categories of perception of that world."[105] Edelman uses sim-ilar language: "The critical element in political maneuver for advantage is the creation of meaning: the construction of beliefs about events, policies, leaders, problems, and crises that rationalize or challenge existing inequal-ities."[106] If meaning defines the situation, then to control meaning is to control the situation. Politics is partly about the struggle over symbols and over the right to use them.

When an actor exercises power over another using symbols, the result-ing relationship of dominance is different than dominance by coercion or physical force. In addition to resting ultimately upon legitimacy, rather than coercion or self-interest, the power intrinsic to symbolic dominance is inherently unstable. The instability manifests itself in two ways. First, the user of the symbol is relying in part on the institution that generated it. A state that appropriates a symbol receives a form of power that is del-egated from the institution and over which it does not have complete control.[107] This inevitably means that power in a system of legitimated hi-erarchy is partly decentralized, because it is dispersed between strong ac-tors and the institutions of authority through which they rule. The strong cannot completely dominate the institution without threatening the legit-imacy which is the basis of its influence.[108] Second, even the weak must perceive the institution and its symbols as legitimate, or else, the symbol carries no "social magic." This also contributes to the decentralization of power, this time between the strong and the weak (or the "sender" of the message and the audience). Domination via symbols requires the com-plicity of the dominated, which may create an opening for them to appro-priate, manipulate, and perhaps subvert the meaning of the symbols.[109] The legitimacy of the Security Council, and the reliance by the permanent members on its symbolic power to achieve their objectives, may some-times be a source of power to the rest of the UN membership. The exer-cise of power through symbols involves "complicating" the relations of coercion and dominance that would otherwise prevail. This is explored in chapter 6 in the case of Libya versus the United States and Great Britain over UN sanctions in the 1990s.

[105] Bourdieu 1991, 236.
[106] Edelman 1988, 103–104.
[107] On delegation and authority, see Barnett and Finnemore 2004.
[108] Slater (1969) shows that American dominance of the Organization of American States in the Dominican crisis of 1965–66 contributed to delegitimating the OAS.
[109] Bourdieu 1991; Scott 1990.

## Symbols and the Power of the Institution: Gatekeepers

International organizations act as gatekeepers to their symbols, regulating states' access to them and setting terms and conditions on their use. The organization has what amounts to a property right over the symbol and controls how and by whom this property can be used. Developing this metaphor, Simon Harrison suggests that one can apply an "intellectual property" model to thinking about ritual and symbolism. He investigates a number of social settings in which the right to control a ritual is treated by the society as intellectual property, capable of being owned, bought and sold, and taken by force. Bourdieu follows a similar path in describing "symbolic capital" as a disguised form of "economic capital" where the former can be cashed in for economic and material wealth at terms of trade established by the prevailing rates in a general moral economy.[110]

Not all international symbols have an associated formal organization as their gatekeeper. Some symbols, such as those associated with informal institutions and practices, can be claimed and used by states at almost no cost. The boundaries of informal institutions are sufficiently unclear that the regulatory function of the institution is almost nonexistent. When formal organizations are involved, however, the matter is quite different. The symbols associated with formal organizations can only be used in co-ordination with those organizations, and this creates the possibility of gatekeeper control by the organizations.[111]

The intensity of interest by other actors in gaining access to the symbol reveals the underlying value of the good. States value what the symbols can do for them, and they are willing to make concessions to gain the authority to use them. In international politics, the ability to extract these concessions gives international organizations a measure of power over states, even over powerful states. For instance, in the lead-up to the 2003 U.S.-Iraq war, the United States approached the Security Council seeking approval for the military operation to remove Saddam Hussein and was prepared to make concessions over the terms of the mission in exchange for that approval. Regardless of the actual beliefs in the Bush administration regarding the Council's legitimacy, the U.S. recognized that winning the Council's approval would make a difference in how third parties responded to the mission, and so it pursued that symbolic prize and offered material concessions to win it. The Council was thereby placed in a position of power relative to the United States, since it controlled something

---

[110] Bourdieu 1990.

[111] This repeats the common distinction between international organizations and international institutions, which is found in Young 1994, among other sources, and may provide a concrete and observable difference between the two.

that the latter wanted. In the end, the Council could not agree on terms and so no exchange was possible, and of course the operation went forward without the Council's legitimizing imprimateur. Although some consider this as indicating the Council's lack of power, it is actually quite the opposite: the U.S. failure to win Council support increased the military and diplomatic costs to the U.S. of the mission and its aftermath.[112] We may yet see retribution against the United Nations by the U.S. for the UN's use of its power in this way, but that retaliation is not evidence that the Council was powerless in this case. Similar examples can be found in every instance of negotiation over the terms of Council approval for state action.[113]

Two important features of this institutional power are worth highlighting: first, even actors with only instrumental attitudes toward the symbol will be willing to pay some costs to be allowed to use it; and, second, the power that is thereby gained by the organization may not be evident in its official charter. Together, these two factors mean that even the most powerful states in the system, as well as those with nonconformist attitudes toward international norms of legitimacy, might find it in their interest to pay lip service to the legitimacy of the organization as a strategy for winning access to its symbols. In theory, therefore, we might observe strong states acting as if they recognized the superior authority of international organizations, even perhaps beyond the formal powers of the organization. With the support of the evidence in the coming chapters, I conclude that this inversion of the traditional hierarchy of authority in world politics has already taken place.

## AUTHORITY, SOVEREIGNTY, AND ANARCHY

When an institution is seen as legitimate, it occupies a position of authority in society, and in international relations authority signals the existence of sovereignty. These connections mean that finding evidence of a legitimated international organization such as the Security Council has broad implications for the concepts of authority, sovereignty, and anarchy.

Authority is a central concept in social science, and the mysteries of its use and misuse, its creation and loss, are perennial themes in political study. Max Weber traces the many forms of authority in his *Economy and Society*.[114] Weber understood authority, or *Herrschaft*, as the condition in which power is married to legitimacy. Authority describes the relation that exists between an actor and an institution when the actor perceives

---

[112] For the contrary view, see Glennon 2003. For a response, see Hurd 2003.
[113] For instance, see Malone 1998 on Haiti.
[114] Weber 1978.

the institution to be legitimate. Where an actor sees a rule as legitimate, the rule has been internalized into interests and takes on the quality of being authoritative over the actor. It is hierarchically superior to the actor and partly determines the actor's behavior.[115] Two effects of this for compliance with rules are that the rule becomes naturalized and only occasional deviance needs to be policed.[116] A relation of authority remains a relation of power or of social control, but it allows control and compliance to be maintained with minimal direct coercion. Indeed, coercion is a symptom of the lack of authority or its decline. Peter Blau says, reflecting a generally Weberian approach:

> Resort to either positive incentives or coercive measures by a person in order to influence others is *prima facie* evidence that he does not have authority over them. . . . We speak of authority, therefore, if the willing unconditional compliance of a group of people rests upon their shared beliefs that it is legitimate for the superior . . . to impose his will upon them and that it is illegitimate for them to refuse obedience.[117]

The character of power changes when it is exercised within a structure of legitimate relations. As Ruggie says, "Political authority represents a fusion of power with legitimate social purpose."[118]

It is increasingly common in IR to see references to 'international authority' when discussing institutions of global governance, but the connection between legitimacy, authority, and sovereignty is not often made clear.[119] A wide range of institutions, actors, and social forces have been described as authoritative in international relations, ranging from states to international organizations to religious movements to firms to the market itself. States are said to have "authority" over their polities and territories,[120] and changes in the rules and practice of sovereignty may be transferring some of this authority to other kinds of actors.[121] Sovereignty is itself sometimes said to be a form of authority, but so, too, is the international administration of failed sovereign states.[122] A recent volume by

[115] Ruggie (1998, 61) prefers to say that the actor and the rule are in a "transordinate" rather than super/subordinate relationship, because "the institutionalization of authority [in IR] takes place at the level of the state" and therefore should be seen as coming from below rather than above.

[116] Thus the phrase "legitimate authority" is redundant. See Onuf and Klink 1989. Ernst Haas (1990) disagrees.

[117] Blau 1963, 307.

[118] Ruggie 1998, 64; Wendt 1994.

[119] Barnett and Finnemore (2004), however, elaborate the link between authority and legitimacy.

[120] Krasner 1999.

[121] Strange 1996.

[122] Compare Philpott 1999 & Caplan 2004.

Hall and Biersteker focusing on "private" international institutions finds that "markets, market actors, transnational movements, mafias, and mercenaries are each recognized socially as possessing authority within certain issue domains."[123] Authority may lie in the self-regulatory schemes organized by firms in an industry or in an exchange rate regime.[124] Coordination among states of their laws on bankruptcy, intellectual property, and electronic commerce have all been described as pieces of international authority,[125] as has the set of legal competencies of international tribunals.[126] Yet, for all the talk about international authority, there is little discussion of what the concept means or how it relates to the larger issues of legitimacy and power.

Barnett and Finnemore have done much to clarify what is meant by the authority of international organizations relative to states. They define authority as "the ability of one actor to use institutions and discursive resources to induce deference from others."[127] Discursive resources, such as symbols and norms, are powerful to the extent that their audience understands them as legitimate. Barnett and Finnemore show how the effects of IO authority create distance between the organization and its state members, and allows its staff a measure of autonomy in setting goals and designing programs. The authority of IOs, they say, is based on the legitimacy states see in both the bureaucratic procedures they follow and the substantive goals they address. Bureaucratization and liberal, humanitarian goals are considered legitimate in international society, and IOs that are seen to embody these values gain legitimacy of their own by association.

The UN Security Council cannot be a rational-legal bureaucracy. Its purposes and structures are inherently political in a way that conflicts with the essence of modern bureaucracy, and so Barnett and Finnemore do not consider it among their cases.[128] The substantive goals it aims for (maintaining international peace and stability) could indeed be a source of its legitimacy, and so it might follow their model in this respect. In chapter 4 I examine the early history of the Council and trace the legitimating effects of the negotiating procedures over the UN Charter at the 1945 San Francisco Conference. The substantive goals of the Council were not part of the debate, probably because they were uncontroversial to the states assembled there, and any legitimating effect they may have had is hard to

[123] Hall and Biersteker 2002, 205.
[124] Compare Lipschutz and Fogel 2002 to Pauly 2002.
[125] See generally the work of the UN Commission on International Trade Law (UNCITRAL) on model laws: http://www.uncitral.org/en-index.htm. For instance, Halliday and Carruthers 2004.
[126] Helfer and Slaughter 1997.
[127] Barnett and Finnemore 2004, 5.
[128] See also Voeten 2005, 552.

discern. More prominent was the effect generated by the deliberative process itself: the conference structure with known procedures that organized the process of arguing, amending, and voting on the draft Charter. Demonstrated at the conference was the creation of legitimacy in a setting different than the bureaucracies of interest to Barnett and Finnemore; more generally, however, it reinforces their point about the power that comes to IOs when they succeed in fitting themselves into prevailing international norms.

The existence of international authority in these terms suggests that the sovereign state is not the ultimate unit of the international system. Sovereign states are embedded in a social system of authority relations where sometimes states are subordinate to other kinds of institutions. Both Daniel Philpott and Christian Reus-Smit describe this broad context as the foundational "constitution" of the international system.[129] It defines the conditions of possibility of states and also regulates their behavior. The Security Council is a specific institutional location where this constitutional structure meets and interacts with individual states. The legitimated power of the Council has important effects on state behavior and state interests, and state behavior also redefines the power of the Council.

Sovereignty is not monopolized by states. The implications for traditional IR theory are significant, because the absence of authority at the international level is an important axiom of all IR models that assume that the international system is anarchic. Anarchy is traditionally defined in IR as the absence of authority.[130] All the "structural" schools of thought in IR, including neorealism, neoliberalism, and constructivism, agree that the defining feature of the international structure is its anarchy. The paradigm debates of the 1980s and 1990s were conducted around the shared premise of international anarchy, with the result that the possibility of sovereignty beyond the state was assumed away from the start. Waltz made the case most clearly in his strict distinction between domestic and international spheres: "National politics is the realm of authority," he contends, whereas "international politics is the realm of power, of struggle."[131] The constructivist position on anarchy has been more complex in that where Waltz presented a dichotomous choice between hierarchy and anarchy, his constructivist critics have argued that there can be different *kinds* of anarchy, each with distinct characteristics. For instance, Wendt suggests that the quality of international anarchy depends in part on the distribution of ideas and interests in the system so that one can speak of different "cultures" of anarchy.[132] Similarly Rodney Bruce Hall examines the different

---

[129] Philpott 2001, chap. 2; Reus-Smit 1997.
[130] Milner 1991.
[131] Waltz 1986, 111.
[132] Wendt 1999, chap. 6.

types of anarchic international relations that arise from differences in the dominant "national collective identity" in a given period.[133] Bruce Cronin's *Community under Anarchy* charts variation in anarchy owing to variation in the strength of the inter-actor "community."[134] Research on "pluralistic security communities," starting with Deutsch and elaborated by Adler and Barnett, gives empirical evidence of what might be called "the difference that community makes to anarchy."[135] The idea of a continuum of "cultures of anarchy," from self-help enmity to pro-social "weness," has proved very powerful and has been adopted in different forms to account for a variety of complex phenomena in international life. However, while these works might disagree with Waltz's interpretation of how anarchy affects state behavior, they accept that the system can still be described as anarchic. They see that the quality of the anarchy can vary, but they remain committed to the position that international authority, and thus sovereignty, does not exist outside the state.

If authority is found to exist in international organizations, then the defining feature of international anarchy would be missing and the system would deserve a new description. The presence of authority undermines the concept of anarchy but not the concept of state sovereignty. The meaning of sovereignty changes when the system contains elements of authority rather than anarchy, because the institution of state sovereignty is embedded within a structure of legitimated power, of which the UN Security Council is one piece.[136] Chapter 7 brings together the strands of evidence from the rest of the book on this theme and suggests strategies for reconsidering international anarchy in light of the connection between legitimacy and authority.

## CONCLUSION

This chapter has set out the conceptual foundations for the empirical investigation of legitimacy in international relations. The concept of legitimacy, long in casual use in international relations but rarely given formal specification, can be made tractable for IR scholars when treated in the following way: as the subjective condition in which actors internalize rules given by institutions. This internalization changes the relationship between the rule and the actor, redefining the actor's sense of its own inter-

---

[133] Hall 1999.
[134] Cronin 1999.
[135] Deutsch et al. 1957; Adler and Barnett 1998.
[136] Connolly (2005, 148) says "For sovereignty now implicates suprastate institutions and capitalist processes that confine and channel state and interstate activities." See chapter 7 below.

ests, and gives the actor an internal orientation that is biased toward following rules. It also produces a form of stability in the international system that is markedly different from that produced by either the deployment of coercion or the arrangement of self-interests. By internalization, shared beliefs in the legitimacy of an international norm or institution affects the behavior of states that share the belief, and the patterns of behavior that result then affect the calculations of all states. The resulting systemwide structure is its "validity."

The chapter also examined the link between legitimacy and symbolism, and found that legitimized institutions generate symbols. These symbols are then useful tools in the hands of states and other actors as they pursue their strategic interests in political struggles with other actors. The power of symbols is inextricably linked to the power of the underlying institution that created them. In the international setting, that power comes from perceptions of the institution's legitimacy.

Finally, the chapter looked at the connection between authority, legitimacy, and sovereignty. To the general observation that "international authority" is increasing, we can add a theory of what constitutes authority: authority is the relationship that exists between a legitimized rule or institution and its audience. Thus the proliferation of claims by IR scholars that some phenomenon or other is evidence of new international authority can be assessed critically by examining whether there is evidence of legitimation underpinning the phenomenon. Where we find authority in these terms in the international system, the traditional notion of the international realm as anarchical cannot be supported. International organizations may exercise sovereignty over and alongside states.

The next chapter examines three contemporary controversies about legitimacy, specifically about its creation, use, and effects. Competing accounts of legitimation and its impact are considered and then form the foundation for the empirical chapters that follow. The cases from the Security Council that are discussed in the empirical chapters allow conclusions to be drawn regarding these controversies.

# CHAPTER 3

# Legitimacy, Rationality, and Power

THE PREVIOUS CHAPTER defined several of the key concepts that appear throughout this book, including legitimacy, symbolic politics, and authority, and explained the relationships between them. This chapter introduces three controversies about legitimacy that follow from those definitions. These are substantive disagreements about the nature of legitimacy that divide IR scholars into diverse schools of thought.

The controversies may be framed as three questions:

- How does an institution come to be seen as legitimate?
- How does legitimacy affect an actor's ability to think and act strategically?
- How does legitimacy affect relations of power between weak and strong actors?

Each question can be answered differently and the answers defended by competing evidence and methodologies. My contribution to these debates over legitimacy, rationality, and power shows that legitimacy is not reducible to favorable outcomes, to instrumental behavior, or to hegemony. Since interests are constituted by socialization, as shown in chapter 2, the process of legitimation leaves room for resistance and strategic behavior, but how states conceive of these is conditioned by the presence of the legitimated institution.

## WHERE DOES LEGITIMACY COME FROM?

There are many theories of how legitimation occurs. The long history of debate on the subject in sociology suggests that the issue is unlikely to be resolved soon, and that there likely are multiple causal paths to legitimation. Even if it is not possible to settle the matter definitively, it is useful to understand the competing claims as it helps to clarify the different ways that legitimacy is treated by scholars.

Scharpf, among others, divides models of legitimacy into two categories based on whether legitimation is thought to take place as a result of procedural factors ("input-legitimacy") or substantive outcomes ("output-legitimacy").[1] This is useful but glosses over important differences within the categories and so I prefer a three-way typology. Theories of

---

[1] Scharpf 1999. Thomas Franck (1995, 26) discourages the effort to disaggregate the two.

legitimation differ, in my framework, according to whether the active legitimizing force is (1) favorable outcomes, (2) fairness, or (3) correct procedure. Scharpf's distinction becomes important in subdividing the "fairness" school into input- and output-oriented variants.

### The "Favorable-Outcomes" Approach

To the extent that IR has an implicit model of legitimacy, it is probably this: states accept as legitimate those international laws or institutions that generate outcomes from which they stand to benefit. This is what Morris Zelditch calls the "favorable outcomes school of legitimacy."[2] This hypothesis deals exclusively in Scharpf's "output-legitimacy" model, since it is the ultimate distribution of payoffs from the institution that is important for its legitimation, and the process by which outcomes are determined is irrelevant.

Two possible mechanisms have been suggested for how this model works. The first holds that actors perceive legitimacy in institutions that provide them with material benefits.[3] The second contends that people are more inclined to give their *consent* to institutions that provide them with material benefits and that this consent then generates perceptions of legitimacy.[4] The first is more direct, the second mediated through the individual act of consent. These different causal paths lead to the same result: legitimacy is ultimately derived from the production of material payoffs and the satisfaction of perceived self-interests. It is this basic causal logic that underlies the very popular account of late-modern capitalism in Habermas's *Legitimation Crisis*, where a threat to the legitimacy of the state is found in its inability to provide citizens the protections and benefits promised by the welfare state.[5] Gilpin makes a similar case to account for the rise of economic nationalism and regional trading blocs, namely, that the nation state finds it increasingly difficult to satisfy citizens' interests in a globalizing economy.[6] Taken together, consent and self-interest

---

[2] Zelditch 2001.

[3] Kelman 2001. In IR, see Voeten 2005. Caldeira and Gibson (1995) discuss, but discount, this approach.

[4] See, for instance, John Locke (1980 [1690], §134): "for without this [the approval of the legislature] the law could not have that, which is absolutely necessary to its being a law, the consent of the society." Consent, for Locke, is "the final legitimating mark of all political action and institutions" (Shapiro 1986, 116). See also Raz 1990, 12, on the bounds outside of which it is impossible for consent to create legitimate authority, and Simmons 2001 and Zelditch 2001. Bodansky (1999) gives some reason to suspect that consent is less unproblematic as a source of legitimacy than many claim.

[5] Habermas 1975.

[6] Gilpin 1987, 227.

as the basis for legitimation are central to the social contract theorists and to the political mythology of most modern democracies.

This instrumental hypothesis on legitimacy has a strong appeal for many reasons. It provides an a priori explanation for why the "winners" in a social system might perceive it as legitimate, and also might account for why those who lose *this time* but perhaps will win in future rounds might perceive legitimacy in the system as a whole. In studies of quiescence and inequality at the level of individuals, it has been found that rebellion among the disadvantaged is significantly reduced when upward mobility is possible.[7] Further, at the group level, it is often argued (following Schumpeter) that one of the virtues of democratic elections is that they give even losing parties a reason to remain loyal to the system as a whole, thus stabilizing the system.[8] The chance of being a winner tomorrow helps keep today's losers from overturning the social order.[9]

This instrumental approach to legitimation can take either a subjective or objective form, depending on whether we are concerned with people's *beliefs* about the satisfaction of their interests or an *objective* measurement of their needs and interests. The latter provides the basis for Kelman's claim that a national system is legitimate to the extent that it meets the needs and interests of its citizens,[10] and also in the many versions of "false consciousness" theory in which we must measure objectively the match between system payoffs and actors' actual (not perceived) interests.[11] The subjective instrumentalist variant leaves it up to the individual in question to assess the relationship between the institution's outputs and his or her needs.[12]

In a very different vein, but still focused on how outcomes match interests, Crandall and Beasley emphasize the individual's sense of justice as the crucial element in legitimation; they argue that individuals have an interest in seeing justice done. This leads to their empirical hypothesis that people perceive legitimacy in an institution when its outputs accord with their sense of justice.[13] Pursuing this theme, one could imagine a number

---

[7] Wright, Taylor, and Moghaddam 1990. Others, however, for instance, Gaventa 1982 and Bourdieu 1987, imply the reverse: those at the bottom of a system with no possibility for upward mobility may be *more* likely to accept the system as legitimate because of its apparent inevitability. This may make them even less likely to rebel than if they could conceive of paths to social mobility.

[8] Schumpeter 1942. See also Huntington 1991; Shapiro 2001.

[9] For an IR version, see Ikenberry 1999, 27.

[10] Kelman 2001. Buchanan (2003) uses an objective measure of legitimacy based on safeguarding the human rights of citizens.

[11] See, for instance, Jost and Banaji 1994.

[12] The deontological branch of Anglo-American social-contract theory suggests that while consent generates legitimacy, it is *perceptions* of procedural justice that generate consent. This makes it possible to maintain differences of opinion on matters of substantive justice and still create agreement on constitutional questions. See, for instance, Rawls 1971.

[13] Crandall and Beasley 2001.

of distinct sub-hypotheses, varying on how people define "justice." For Crandall and Beasley, who wish to promote a "naïve analysis" attitude toward legitimacy and justice, this is operationalized as the hypothesis that people measure justice based on their perceptions of others' moral worth: in their words, "that *bad people deserve bad treatment* [and] this belief is applied to issues of punishment, social control, disqualification from positions of authority, jail terms, shame, and humiliation."[14] The legitimacy of a social system is therefore measured by each individual on the basis of how well it is perceived to give "bad treatment to bad people" and "good treatment to good people." Legitimacy comes to an institution that is perceived to generate outcomes that match the individual's sense of the moral worth of others.[15] This is still part of the favorable-outcomes school, but it extends the notion of individual interests to include the psychological as well as material factors.

It is possible to take the self-interest approach so far in the direction of rationalist individualism that it denies any important role for legitimacy in society at all. If one's perception of the legitimacy of an institution is a function of the degree to which the institution serves one's interests, then outcomes are determined by the distribution of interests in the society and not by any independent force flowing from legitimation.

The favorable-outcomes model provides a hypothesis about why those who benefit from a system might see it as legitimate, but since what is interesting to many about legitimacy is its contribution to social order even where inequalities are well entrenched, we still need an explanation that can account for why those who do relatively badly in a system might nonetheless perceive it to be legitimate. Getting at this issue requires considering the two main competitors to the favorable-outcomes school: the fairness hypothesis and the procedural approach.


### Fairness


It is common to claim that people perceive as legitimate rules or institutions that they believe are "fair." There are many variants of this approach, each one interpreting distinctively how to judge what is "fair." All are committed to a model of individual psychology which suggests that the belief in the legitimacy of a social institution is derived from a sense that it treats people fairly.

Thomas Franck, and Abram Chayes and Antonia Chayes, among others, apply this approach to international relations. These writers are inter-

---

[14] Ibid., 2001, 78; emphasis in original.
[15] Compare this account of justice to Rawls 1971, for whom variation in perceived status of individuals is precisely the thing that justice is designed to ignore.

ested in supplanting the favorable-outcomes approach with something they believe to be a more empirically satisfying account of legitimacy as applied to international law. Chayes and Chayes make two distinct claims: first, that fairness is a key component of legitimation; and, second, that compliance with international norms is closely related to whether they are seen by states as fair.[16] Their causal theory of legitimation is therefore subordinate to a story about how people think about fairness, which they separate into the categories of fair procedures, fair application, and substantive fairness.[17] Franck's work in *Fairness in International Law and Institutions* works in the other direction, with a causal story that sees a person's belief in the legitimacy of the institution producing the sense that it is operating fairly. For Franck, legitimacy in the institution creates a belief in the fairness of its outputs; for Chayes and Chayes, fairness creates the perception of legitimacy.

The fairness hypothesis has both a substantive and a procedural version, depending on whether one believes that fairness of the decision-making process or fairness of the substantive outcomes is the motor behind legitimation. Erik Voeten describes, but does not endorse, the procedural version of the fairness hypothesis. It is a "common argument," Voeten states, "that the main threat to SC [Security Council] legitimacy is that the institution is dominated by a few countries and that its procedures are opaque and unfair."[18] Although conceptually distinguishable, in most scholarship the substantive and procedural versions of the fairness argument are intermingled without a clear line between them. Chayes and Chayes, for instance, explicitly combine the two in an effort to reflect more accurately how they believe people's minds work with respect to legitimacy. They say that "the question of the legitimacy of a rule or system cannot be kept wholly distinct from the fairness of its substantive content."[19] Their observations of how people think lead them to conclude that individuals mix the two in practice, and so scholars should follow suit.

### The Procedural Approach

In IR, debates over the legitimation of IOs and international law tend to take place between advocates of the favorable-outcomes school and the fairness doctrine. But in sociology and psychology, controversy over legit-

---

[16] Chayes and Chayes 1995.

[17] Ibid., chap. 5.

[18] Voeten 2005, 538. In his study of the Security Council, he finds this thesis to be less useful and instead prefers a favorable-outcomes model.

[19] Chayes and Chayes 1995, 127, 134.

imation is generally an argument between favorable outcomes and a procedural view. Although the proceduralist approach has not been widely adopted in IR, it merits attention as an alternative to both fairness and favorable outcomes.

The procedural model in sociology was originally inductive, based on the observation that as an empirical matter people sometimes accept as legitimate decisions that seem to go against their interests. As long as rules are passed according to accepted procedures and by established authorities, people appear to accept them as legitimate, all else equal. This school of thought has been advanced in domestic legal settings by Tom Tyler. Tyler has shown, among other things, that, in American society, satisfying certain procedural criteria is more important in explaining people's perceptions of legitimacy about the law than are favorable outcomes. He finds that "judgments about the favorability or fairness of the outcomes themselves have little impact upon people's evaluations of the legitimacy of those authorities or of the institutions that they represent."[20] Notice that what matters to the procedural school is not the *fairness* or *justice* of the procedures per se but rather what we might call the *correctness* of the procedure, that is, the following of accepted rules of procedure for the decision in question. An outsider might find these rules to be biased in favor of one group in society or to be otherwise unfair, but the proceduralists suggest that even in such situations legitimation will accrue from adhering to the rules. Thus, in this approach, structural power over decision situations, including agenda setting, is not in itself a barrier to legitimation. It is for this reason that proceduralists tend to speak of the importance of following "correct procedure" and not of achieving "procedural justice."

In international politics Jens Steffek follows Weber and Habermas to conclude that "the characteristic feature of legitimate governance is the rational exchange of arguments, which eventually arrives at a conclusion in the form of agreement."[21] This suggests that legitimation is made possible by having procedures in place which facilitate that rational exchange of arguments, and the process of legitimation begins when the procedures are followed by actors as they argue over the issues. Fragments of this hypothesis also appear in the work of Joseph Weiler, insofar as he distinguishes between the "formal" legitimacy that comes from following the right procedures and the "social" legitimacy that derives from having the active support of the society. His conceptualization provides a clear statement of the procedural approach, even if in his empirical work he prefers the explanatory power of the latter over the former. By way of illustration,

---

[20] Tyler 2001, 416; 1990.
[21] Steffek 2003, 263. The deliberative element in Steffek's argument is not inherent in the procedural model of legitimation.

he points out that "most popular revolutions since the French Revolution occurred in polities whose governments retained formal legitimacy but lost social legitimacy."[22]

Franck is more sympathetic than is Weiler to the procedural explanation of the causes of legitimation. The model Franck provides incorporates a wide range of variables, giving it a complexity that makes it both appealing but also more difficult to apply in practice. In *The Power of Legitimacy among Nations* he concludes that legitimacy accrues to a rule or institution when it "has come into being and operates in accordance with generally accepted principles of right process. . . . Legitimacy is that attribute of a rule which conduces to the belief that it is fair because it was made and is applied in accordance with 'right process.' "[23] This is a clear statement of what I am calling the procedural approach. But Franck also wants to include consideration of the substance of the rule. His "four indicators of legitimacy are: *determinacy, symbolic validation, coherence,* and *adherence.* . . . The extent to which any rule exhibits these qualities will determine its legitimacy."[24] In practice, it may be very difficult to separate the legitimating effects of "correct" procedures from those of the substantive outputs of the institution or process, but conceptually the two are clearly distinct causal mechanisms.

The procedural approach helps explain how highly unequal social systems can sometimes be seen by their members as legitimate.[25] This is the fundamental insight of the "third-face of power." Gaventa observed that "power serves to maintain prevailing order of inequality . . . through the shaping of beliefs about the order's legitimacy."[26] A procedural model of legitimation provides at least a partial explanation for how this can come about. Where legitimation comes from following correct procedures in institutions, then it is possible that inequality, poverty, powerlessness, and hierarchy should not necessarily lead to delegitimation.

One difficulty with the procedural approach is that it depends on a prior understanding of what constitutes an appropriate procedure for the subject in question. In some cases this may be clear, but in many it is not. Arguments over the content of "correct procedure" undermine its legitimating power. In the context of the UN Security Council, as we shall see in the coming chapters, this is less of a problem than it might be in other

[22] Joseph Weiler, "The Transformation of Europe," in idem, *The Constitution of Europe* (Cambridge: Cambridge University Press, 1999), 80–81; cited in Howse 2001, 361. Weiler also identifies a third quality, "substantive legitimacy," defined as the degree of congruence between the rule and society's main values more broadly understood.

[23] Franck 1990, 24, 26

[24] Franck 1995, 30; emphasis in original. See also Franck 1990.

[25] In IR this phenomenon is noted by, among others, Wendt 2003.

[26] Gaventa 1982, 42.

settings, because the procedures by which the Council operates are relatively clear and well codified, as were those by which it was established. Acceptance of the procedures is strong from the outset, giving rise to relatively few procedural arguments that might undermine its legitimacy. That said, the Libya case in chapter 6 is partly centered on a contest over which elements of international procedure should dominate others.

## LEGITIMACY AND STRATEGIC BEHAVIOR

How does legitimacy affect states' instrumental calculations about the strategies they might pursue to achieve their goals? Attention to the relationship between strategic behavior and legitimacy is important for at least two larger issues in IR: first, it determines how models that incorporate legitimation relate to models premised on rational-choice assumptions, and so it affects the shape of the paradigm debate between rationalism and constructivism. Second, it begins to unpack the relationship between legitimacy and compliance, and so gets at the more general question of how legitimacy affects state behavior. It is common in IR to assume that the main behavioral implication of legitimacy in IOs is higher rates of compliance by states with international rules, but precisely how and why this works is usually left unexplained.[27] Thinking about the connection between strategic thought and legitimacy is a first step in building such an explanation.

March and Olsen suggest that there are two basic models for interpreting human behavior: the logic of expected consequences and the logic of appropriateness. These lead to two distinct debates: one concerning which is a more useful starting assumption for those seeking to understand human behavior, and the other over the conditions under which "one logic is more likely than the other to be observed as the basis for actual behavior."[28] In other words, the two logics are intended to be at once analytic and descriptive categories. The logic of consequences prioritizes strategic behavior over legitimated norms, and the logic of appropriateness does the opposite. They form the poles of a debate in IR theory, against which Wendt provides an alternative that subsumes the two.

### Legitimacy over Strategy: The Logic of Appropriateness

The "logic of appropriateness" rests on a view that legitimated norms supplant strategic or instrumental calculations of benefit. March and

---

[27] Chayes and Chayes 1995.
[28] March and Olsen 1998, 949.

Olsen describe the intuition behind this approach as the belief that "action involves evoking an identity or role and matching the obligations of that identity or role to a specific situation."[29] States, on this view, assess possible behaviors according to criteria defined by the "identities, roles, and institutions" to which they have been socialized, rather than according to their instrumental payoffs.[30] Thinking about interests is replaced by thinking about a structurally derived notion of what is appropriate given the situation and the actor's role or identity. An example is provided by Eiko Thielemann in his examination of "burden sharing" of the costs of refugees in the European Union (EU). He uses the logic of appropriateness to hypothesize that a state will accept a rule that gives it a higher share of the costs if it has "a greater commitment to a particular norm" that underpins the rule.[31] In this hypothesis, the social attachment to the norm takes the place of the consideration of interests. The conceptual heart of the logic of appropriateness model is a commitment to the view that some international behavior by states is governed by beliefs about what is appropriate rather than by the anticipated consequences for the actor's utility.[32] To sustain this model, it is necessary to conceive of interests as separate from the rules to which actors may be socialized. Only by doing so is it possible to see the demands of rule following as leading down a distinct path from that suggested by the demands of interest following.

### Strategy over Legitimacy: The Logic of Expected Consequences

The opposite view outlined by March and Olsen is a model of behavior that sees "history . . . as the consequence of the interaction of willful actors" in which the "action of individuals, organizations, or states is driven by calculation of its consequences."[33] In this view of the social world, actors use instrumental and individual criteria for judging the possible actions. These criteria are posited in this "logic of consequences" to be distinct from, and more relevant than, normative and communal criteria. This consequentialist frame is often equated to rational choice and is also often seen as connected to materialism—the former because it rejects the socialized view of actors and the latter because it often measures consequences in materialist terms.[34]

[29] Ibid., 951.

[30] Ibid., 951.

[31] Thielemann 2003, 258.

[32] March and Olsen 1998. Because actors' identities might be made of several competing elements, and these might lead to different behaviors, it may be impossible to predict perfectly how actors will respond in all situations

[33] March and Olsen 1998, 950.

[34] See the critique in Fearon and Wendt 2002, 58–59.

Stephen Krasner's history of sovereignty attempts to show the explanatory superiority of models that start with a logic of consequences rather than a logic of appropriateness.[35] He draws a connection between consequentialism as an analytic assumption and the assumptions of rationalism and materialism.[36] His history of sovereignty documents a long tradition of hypocrisy around the norms of sovereign statehood which to him shows that "statehood" has meant more or less whatever the strong players wanted it to mean, and they have not been shy about violating or changing the apparent norms when it suited them.[37] Krasner's evidence makes clear that states retain a strong sense of their particularist interests despite the proliferation of claims about legitimized norms of sovereignty, and this is powerful evidence against the claim that norms somehow "disable" states' pursuit of their interests. Even while the general rules of sovereignty are usually respected, its content is a function of the material needs of strong players.[38]

The consequentialist and appropriateness schools define themselves in opposition to each other. Each lays claim to a distinctive approach to social science defined by referring back to what the other approach leaves out. This is made explicit when March and Olsen present them as alternative frames for action and for scholarship. Therefore they wish to keep them analytically separate, even while they acknowledge that actual behavior is usually a product of both kinds of logic, and concede that neither is likely to be found to dominate the other in all situations. The relationship they see between the two is precisely that: a relationship *between the two*. They say that "the two devices are sufficiently distinct to be viewed as separate explanatory devices."[39] This is maintained by scholars, including Jeffrey Lewis, who seek to operationalize the distinction from March and Olsen by testing *which* of the two models best explains foreign policy outcomes. Lewis, like Thielemann cited above, aims "to test competing claims side by side and assess which image . . . more accurately accounts for the behavior of national officials" in negotiations in the European Union.[40] He sees the two logics as amenable to "competitive testing" against each other.[41] However, since the two logics are simply mirror images of each

---

[35] Krasner 1999.

[36] See also Krasner 1993.

[37] Krasner 1999.

[38] He says that material and technological needs "created a need for legitimating rationales" and these rationales were "easily found" among the many competing norms of European intellectual traditions. Krasner 1993, 261.

[39] March and Olsen 1998, 953.

[40] Lewis 2003, 99.

[41] Ibid., 122.

other, they share a common problem of reifying the poles in a dichotomy. As a result, the "legitimacy over strategy" view leads to an image of states as "cultural dupes" that are so thoroughly socialized by the norms that they lose the corporate autonomy that would allow them to be independent actors, whereas the "strategy over legitimacy" view risks the overstated claim that actors are completely unswayed by the processes of legitimation and socialization, and that their social context is irrelevant to their strategic calculations. Both Lewis and Thielemann, in their efforts to test empirically which of these is more "true," end up concluding, not surprisingly, that both matter.[42] But the prior commitment to seeing the two as mutually exclusive leaves few resources for understanding how or why both matter.

### Legitimacy and Strategy

A third possibility for the relationship between legitimacy and strategic behavior lies outside the continuum anchored by March and Olsen's two poles. This approach, which I follow, suggests that interests and socialization are both important in understanding state behavior, and neither is reducible to the other. This is founded on Wendt's model of the co-constitution of states and international structure, which implies that it is not necessary to accept the two logics as exclusive or exhaustive.[43] It is possible to conceive of states as goal-driven actors that are conditioned by their social context without trying to reduce either agents (goals) to structures (norms), or vice versa. This approach suggests that states, by virtue of being corporate entities, have strong beliefs about their interests, and they pursue strategies to maximize them. But they are also corporate entities only by virtue of the social recognition of that identity by the community, and so their understandings of their interests are shaped by the expectations of the community.

Martha Finnemore's account of the changing understandings of the use of force is an example of the empirical application of this perspective. She finds that states' "perceptions of utility are tightly bound up with [their] perceptions of legitimacy. Separating the two or treating them as competing explanations is not only difficult but probably misguided, since it misses the potentially more interesting question of how the two are intertwined and interdependent."[44] This approach avoids problems

[42] Ibid., passim, Thielemann 2003.

[43] Wendt 1987. In this article Wendt does not use the language of the two logics. I am suggesting that the two logics map onto the two poles that Wendt identifies in the agent-structure debate.

[44] Finnemore 2004, 16.

associated with reifying either state interests or social norms, and so moves beyond the dichotomous logics proposed by March and Olsen.

The usefulness of this approach can also be seen by reconsidering Krasner's history of the instrumental use of sovereignty norms. Taking agent and structure together helps reveal aspects of this history which Krasner identifies but discounts. Even while he shows that the hypocritical use of sovereignty norms is pervasive, he reveals at the same time that powerful actors find it useful, perhaps even necessary, to refer to norms of sovereignty in defense of their positions. He shows that there is a material payoff that comes from having an ideological justification for one's behavior and, conversely, that the absence of suitable justifications may make certain policies inconceivable. He explicitly argues that the range of options for leaders is constrained by the availability of normative justifications.[45] This creates a gap between Krasner's empirical evidence and his theoretical pre-commitments. The evidence does indeed lead to the conclusion that strong states manipulate norms in their own interests, but it also undermines the assumptions of rationalism and materialism that underpin his analysis. Out of this irony emerges a compelling set of research questions, about *how* and *why* norms are useful to strong states in the pursuit of those interests. Addressing them requires moving beyond the dichotomy that treats materialism as an alternative to ideas.

## LEGITIMACY AND HEGEMONY

There is controversy also on how legitimation affects the relationship between the strong and the weak. Legitimation is usually conceived as a conservative force that contributes to the stability of the status quo.[46] It is inherently bound up with subjugation and power because it affects individuals' obligations, either absolute or perceived, toward rules or rulers. Habermas noted the intimate connection between legitimacy and power hierarchies in a class context: "Because the reproduction of class societies is based on the privileged appropriation of socially produced wealth, all such societies must resolve the problem of distributing the surplus social product inequitably and yet legitimately."[47] Thus the progress of legitima-

---

[45] Krasner (1993, 263–264) suggests, for instance, that the Aztec response to the Spanish was constrained by the ideational categories available to the Aztecs, and that the poor fit between the available categories and the reality of the Europeans left the Aztec even more vulnerable than they were in purely material terms.

[46] Keeping in mind, of course, that existing political institutions might be undermined to the extent that they do not conform with legitimized basic values in the society, but the "legitimacy question" is whether the basic values are made stronger by beliefs in their legitimacy.

[47] Habermas 1975, 96.

tion results in changes in the relation between strong and weak—but what kind of change? The main debate on this question concerns whether legitimacy makes the strong stronger or whether it makes the rules of the system stronger.[48]

On the first view, legitimation grants almost absolute power to strong actors by changing the perception the weak have of their own interests; it makes for hegemony. This approach sees legitimacy as making the strong players in the system even more powerful and their position even more entrenched.[49] The Gramscian model of hegemony, for instance, is in this category. It provides a theory of legitimation to account for the change that takes place in subjects' beliefs about the inequalities they experience. There can be no resistance to legitimated institutions, at least not directly. If legitimation causes the weak to fail to see that the current system works against their interests, then an institution that is seen as legitimate is immune from attack from the subordinated classes precisely because its legitimacy masks any interest the weak may have in resisting it. Evidence of this position is on display in Habermas's suggestion that the loss of legitimacy makes an institution more vulnerable to disruption. He says, "As soon, however, as the belief in the legitimacy of an existing order vanishes, the latent force embedded in the system of institutions is released—either as manifest force from above . . . or in the form of expansion of scope for participation [from below]."[50] Thus only when legitimacy *fails* can resistance be conceived by subordinates, and only once it is conceived can it be expressed. This is the foundation of the Marxist view of legitimacy and hegemony presented by Gill and Law:

> With time, the coercive use of power may become less necessary and also less obvious as consensus builds up on the basis of shared values, ideas, and material interests on the part of both ruling and subordinate classes. . . . In this way, a hegemonic structure of thought and action emerges, one which militates against the raising, or even conception of alternative types of political, economic, and social arrangements.[51]

The progress of legitimation leads to a decline in social conflict between classes and to a more peaceful and stable (though still exploitative) order. There remain, for the Marxists, conflicts of interests between the classes, but the effect of legitimation is to disable the subordinate classes from recognizing or acting on them. The relationship between the strong and the weak thus comes to look consensual and pacific, with fewer reasons

---

[48] It may often do both together, but interesting aspects of power and legitimacy are revealed when the rules go against the perceived interests of strong actors.

[49] Bukovansky 2002, 8.

[50] Habermas 1975, 96.

[51] Gill and Law 1988, 78.

for the weak to complain and less opportunity for them to behave strategically in defense of their "true" interests. Indeed, the distinction between the classes begins to disappear as they perceive their interests to be in harmony. The distribution of power under legitimacy is, in this view, entirely in the favor of the strong.

An alternative view sees legitimacy as strengthening the rules of the system rather than the most powerful actors directly. Because legitimacy is often invested in a rule or institution, rather than directly in an actor, the stabilizing force of legitimacy in this view accrues to the basic rules of the system and its offices, not to particular individuals personally. Strong actors may well seek to legitimize certain principles as a tactic in cementing their rule, but thereafter it is those principles and not the strong actors themselves that are respected by the audience. As a means of increasing one's power, this is indirect, although potentially very useful. Maintaining the hegemony thereafter requires that the strong subscribe to a minimum standard of compliance with the legitimized rule or institution lest the connection be lost. This allows subordinates the capacity to pressure the strong into conforming with the rules. The behavioral implications of this difference between the two views are significant, for in the second lies the possibility that the strong (and not just the weak) may be induced to alter their behavior by the effects of legitimated rules. The change in the distribution of power is therefore not unambiguously to the benefit of the strong.

## CONCLUSION

This chapter examined a series of controversies about the making, and effects, of legitimacy. Resolving these debates requires careful attention to the details of the practical empirical case in question, and universal answers to any of these questions are unlikely. However, the empirical study of the forces described in this chapter and the previous one entails overcoming obstacles in the observation and measurement of legitimacy and internalization. As a rough guide, we have reason to suspect that legitimation and internalization of a rule or institution have taken place in states when we observe: (1) that states treat the rule in question as a necessary part of the strategic landscape for decision making; (2) that they cease making cost-benefit calculations about the effects of breaking the rule as they consider future behaviors; and (3) that they use as resources the symbols that derive from the rule or institution.

Having set out the conceptual framework for studying legitimacy in the international system, I next explore the empirical complexities of these concepts. Using the UN Security Council as the focus, this is done in three stages: first, in chapter 4 I examine the construction of legitimacy in the process of founding the Council at San Francisco in 1945; second, in chapter 5 I look at the power of the legitimized Council, emphasizing how its legitimacy affected how states pursued their interests in a number of controversies in the 1980s and 1990s, including on the use of force; and, finally, in chapter 6 I document the diplomatic struggle between Libya and the United States and Britain in the 1990s over economic sanctions on Libya—in this confrontation, the legitimacy of the UN was front and center, and was used as a resource of power for both sides. In chapter 7 I return to the controversies on legitimation in light of the evidence about the Security Council gathered in the intervening chapters.

# LEGITIMACY IN PRACTICE

# CHAPTER 4.

# San Francisco, 1945

THE SAN FRANCISCO conference in 1945 brought together 282 delegates from 46 countries to deliberate over the draft Charter of the new United Nations Organization. From late April to late June the delegations, along with thousands of consultants, reporters, translators, and others at San Francisco, produced half a million pages of documentation per day before the Charter was unanimously approved on June 25.[1] The process was crucial in the legitimation of the UN and, as a result, marks an important constitutional moment in modern international history. The politics of legitimacy are central to the San Francisco conference.

The need for legitimacy is well known to those who propose new international organizations and is a preoccupation of those who design them. It is also well known to opponents of new institutions, leading to an opportunity for political and symbolic struggles between legitimation and delegitimation in the early stages of institutional development. Observing how the designers of new international institutions handle the issue of legitimation reveals a process of historical and political contestation.[2] As the most prominent and perhaps most powerful international organization, the UN has through its first sixty years been the subject of intense competition between the forces of legitimation and delegitimation. The UN's extensive powers, conferred by the Charter and mostly lodged in the Security Council, and its representation of a broad, almost global, constituency, make it a prime location for observing the dynamics of legitimation in practice.

Legitimation is central to the UN Security Council, and can be traced in the drafting of the Charter, in the process of negotiations at San Francisco in 1945, and in its operation since then. This chapter examines the legitimating strategy of the Great Powers at the creation of the Council. Later chapters examine legitimation in the politics of the Council since then. At San Francisco the framers of the UN Charter were centrally concerned

---

[1] Russell 1958, 625 n. 1.

[2] See, for instance, Ikenberry's (1992) examination of the Bretton Woods negotiations. In the domestic setting, Anthony Marx's (2003, 9) discussion of nationalism focuses on "moments when the idea or imperative for nationalism began to emerge but was not yet consolidated. And western Europeans at midmillennium were confronted by precisely such a moment, with monarchs seeking to hold and build state power before their subjects had vested that power with popular loyalty and obedience."

about the Council's legitimacy in the eyes of the small and medium states, and this concern structured both the design of the UN organization and the process by which it was debated at San Francisco. The legitimating motive behind the conference carried even into the visual representations of the UN system. Oliver Lundquist, the official in charge of "visual presentation" for the State Department at San Francisco, reported that his office was instructed to devise "a circular organization chart so it didn't have the hierarchy of one organization [the SC] being at the top and the rest filtering down from it."[3] The Great Powers recognized the importance of legitimacy to the new UN organization but faced a great deal of hostility to the design they proposed. The inequality inherent in the veto, and that it was drafted without the input of the small states and was nonnegotiable at San Francisco, meant a difficult challenge. This challenge was met by a strategy of legitimation by the sponsoring states that relied above all else on the legitimating power of procedural correctness. The legitimating power of the procedures of the international negotiation shaped and constrained how the Great Powers could use their influence to maneuver the small states into accepting the veto. The small states valued the deliberation afforded by the procedures of the conference and accepted the veto only once all avenues to oppose it were exhausted. The debate between the Great Powers and the small states at San Francisco over the veto right of permanent members *is* legitimation in action.

The chapter expands on three issues related to the larger themes set out in the previous chapters. First, it shows how the early history (and prehistory) of the Security Council was designed by the Great Powers to increase the legitimacy of the institution; from early on, legitimation was identified as an important element in the power and usefulness of the Council for the Great Powers. Second, it provides evidence regarding the two competing claims about the process of legitimation described in chapter 3: a procedural view versus a "favorable-outcomes" view. The former argues that legitimation occurs when a decision is reached by following procedures that are generally accepted as appropriate to the situation. The latter suggests that actors see outcomes as legitimate when they produce tangible benefits for themselves. The evidence in the chapter comes from a case in which some potential intervening variables are not present, such as logrolling and substantive concessions, and so we can isolate more clearly the relative effects of deliberation and of "favorable outcomes" in this case. The historical evidence presented here supports a procedural view of legitimation relative to other theories. Finally, the chapter demonstrates some overlooked aspects of the power of "talk" in international politics. How and why states argue, deliberate, and posture among each

---

[3] Lundquist interview, UN Oral History, April 19, 1990, p. 13.

other are questions that are increasingly getting attention among IR scholars,[4] and the evidence in this chapter extends this literature to consider cases where deliberation is valued by states even when there is no expectation that it will affect the substantive outcome of the case.

This chapter presents three sections of historical evidence from the early debates over the UN Security Council. The first section shows how the design of the Council was completed among the Great Powers prior to the San Francisco conference. The second examines the deliberative process that took place between the Great Powers and the others at San Francisco. The third considers the impacts of this deliberation on the final product of the conference. A fourth, concluding section uses this historical material to help develop further the controversies over legitimation identified in chapter 3.

## BACKGROUND TO SAN FRANCISCO

The Charter negotiations took place in two broad stages, starting with an agreement over the main questions among the Great Powers and ending with a universal conference of likely members. This follows what Odell calls a "most influential first" strategy of negotiation.[5] The UN organization, as we now know it, was first imagined in memos within the U.S. government which were then circulated to the governments of Britain and the Soviet Union. These three governments (the "Big Three") met at Dumbarton Oaks in Washington, D.C., in 1944 and at Yalta in the Crimea in 1945 to specify the plans further. China participated at Dumbarton Oaks as well. The deliberations were held in two sessions as China and the Soviet Union refused to sit together at international meetings. The first conference at Dumbarton Oaks was between the Big Three, and a second meeting had China replacing the Soviet Union. The Chinese session added nothing of substance to the plan, although it did recognize China as a formal equal to the other Great Powers (and so after Dumbarton Oaks it is common to refer to these states collectively as the "Big Four").[6]

In the main discussions, both at Dumbarton Oaks and Yalta, the Security Council clauses generated most of the controversy, and the debate centered largely on crafting the terms of the veto for the Great Powers. The following year the veto also became the centerpiece of controversy between the Great Powers and the rank and file at San Francisco. Indeed,

[4] For instance, Risse 2000; Sartori 2002.

[5] Odell 2000, 191–194. This is consistent with insights from the veto-players approach of Tsebelis (2002) and, as applied to IR, of Spruyt (2005).

[6] Notter 1949, 328–334. By the first days of the San Francisco Conference, France is informally included in the group, making it the "Big Five."

today it remains the icon of inequality in the UN system and continues to fuel controversy over the unequal distribution of responsibilities and privileges in the UN.[7] Given this history of controversy, the debate over the veto is the most important location at San Francisco for observing the politics of legitimacy and illegitimacy in the Charter negotiations.

The general shape of the veto for the Great Powers in the Security Council was agreed upon at the Dumbarton Oaks meetings. Prior to that, the concept was contained in an internal study by the U.S. State Department in 1943, which itself originated in earlier informal papers.[8] From their earliest discussions, the Big Three were in agreement that it was unacceptable that they should commit themselves to an organization that could embark on any type of enforcement action which they themselves had voted against. The Council had to be structured so that the Great Powers had an escape route out of the decisions of the majority in the Council. An outlet was needed either by making Council decisions nonbinding (in which case majority rule could be maintained) or by giving the Big Three special voting powers (which would require giving way on majority rule). Since the former was reminiscent of the League of Nations in an unappealing way, the Big Three decided that the Council should have the power to bind the UN members but that they themselves should have some form of veto over Council decisions. This was agreed to prior to Dumbarton Oaks, and so the only question to be worked out at Dumbarton Oaks was the scope of the veto, such as whether it should apply to procedural or only substantive decisions, whether it should apply to "peaceful" dispute settlements or just military enforcement measures, and whether it should be available to a Great Power when it was itself a party to the dispute before the Council.

Agreement on these three questions among the Great Powers did not come easily at Dumbarton Oaks. The limits and use of the veto in the Council was probably the most contentious issue in the entire worldorganization plan, and disagreement over it seriously threatened to alienate the three from one another and ruin the whole project. "The issue of the veto would seem so vital to all three nations that they would prove willing to break up the conference—and jeopardize all their hopes for a postwar organization—rather than accept what they regarded as an unsatisfactory formula for its use."[9]

---

[7] Many statements are collected at www.globalpolicy.org/security/reform/index.htm. It is noteworthy that while activists agitate to abolish the veto, the proposals coming from think-tanks and expert panels generally take for granted that it is unrealistic, and so not useful, to make proposals that include changing the veto. See, for instance, the UN's High-Level Panel Report of 2004 and the essays in Zedillo 2005. See also Hurd 2008.

[8] Notter 1949, 526–634; Hilderbrand 1990, 25; and Luard 1982, 17–18.

[9] Hilderbrand 1990, 183.

The real sticking point was whether a Great Power should be able to veto Council action with respect to a dispute to which it was a party. The British view at Dumbarton Oaks was that it would be impossible to win the support of the small and medium states if the veto were unrestricted, and so it proposed that the veto should not be available to a permanent member when it was a party to the dispute in question. This would apparently include both peaceful settlements and enforcement measures.[10] The Soviet Union countered that the principle of Great Power unanimity could not be compromised, particularly should it come to a case where the organization was considering acting against a permanent member, without opening the organization to the threat of serious rupture. The U.S. delegation contained elements sympathetic to both positions, but eventually it settled on the British stance, adding the concern that the U.S. Senate would have problems with an unlimited veto.[11] President Franklin D. Roosevelt told Stalin, "I know public opinion in the United States would never understand or support a plan . . . which violated that principle [of parties to a dispute losing their vote]."[12] The U.S. view was that the British proposal preserved the principle of equality while also protecting, "in its essential aspects," the Great Power veto, thus satisfying simultaneously the needs of the relevant domestic publics, the small states, and the Great Powers.[13]

The rift between the Soviet and Anglo-American positions hardened over the course of several days at Dumbarton Oaks, to the point where Stettinius, Gromyko, and Cadogan, the heads of the three delegations, reluctantly conceded that the problem might be unsolvable. For a while they discussed possible avoidance maneuvers, including postponing the final document, sidestepping the issue with vague language, or omitting mention of the issue altogether and leaving it for the full conference at San Francisco to decide.[14] Disliking all three choices, the parties pressed on in discussions for the remaining fortnight of the U.S.-U.K.-Soviet phase of the conference, but they made little substantive progress and focused increasingly on the management of the disagreement rather than its

[10] The historical record on what was to be included is unclear, probably the result of confusion in communicating the British proposals to others as well as the fact that the British delegation had not themselves thoroughly thought out all angles of the idea. See Russell 1958; and Hilderbrand 1990.

[11] Russell 1958, 447; Hilderbrand 1990, 204. Possible objection by the Senate was used by both sides in this argument. It was also suggested that the Senate would not abide a structure that allowed action to be taken without U.S. concurrence. See Hilderbrand 1990, 186–187, 194.

[12] Cable from FDR to Stalin, September, 1944; cited in Hoopes and Brinkley 1997, 150.

[13] Informal minutes of the Joint Steering Committee, August 28, 1944; cited in Hilderbrand 1990, 195.

[14] Hoopes and Brinkley (1997) recount these discussions.

solution. A final twist before the end of the conference was the switching of sides by the British, apparently owing to the belated personal attention that Churchill gave to the question, as well as his concern that the more limited veto arrangement might prove insufficient to protect the empire from the Council's interference. Nevertheless, this left the imbalance at 1 to 2, as opposed to 2 to 1, and the final report was released on time on October 9, 1945, with a blank section VI-C and a note reading: "The question of voting procedure in the Security Council is still under consideration."

A solution was found in the run-up to the Yalta conference in January 1945, once the three heads of state became directly involved. The compromise that eventually found its way into the San Francisco draft involved excluding from the veto cases where "pacific settlements" were recommended in a situation to which a permanent member was a party but that, for all enforcement actions, parties to a dispute could continue to vote (and veto) as usual. This was a formulation which the negotiating committees had previously rejected at Dumbarton Oaks, but it was revived in the pre-Yalta planning. With military enforcement against one's self subject to the veto but a peaceful settlement not so, the permanent members were assured of being able to avoid hostile action against themselves while at the same time maintaining at least an appearance for the small and medium states that the permanent members could not foreclose all critical discussions against them in the Council.

After Dumbarton Oaks, the draft Charter was circulated by the Big Four to the capitals of all potential UN members several months in advance of San Francisco. At this point the substance of the proposals were largely in place, and the attention of the Great Powers turned to the task of winning support for them among the smaller states. Having invested so much in reaching an agreement among themselves, the Big Four were in no mood to reopen the question of the veto with other states at the general meetings in San Francisco.

While most histories of the conference document the debates that took place among the Great Powers themselves,[15] the San Francisco conference was designed principally to facilitate discussion *between* the Great Powers as a bloc and the small and medium states. It was to be the one global, public opportunity for this latter group, which was to make up the rank and file of the new United Nations organization, to express opinions on and influence the draft inherited from Dumbarton Oaks. It is in this context that the forty-six states gathered at San Francisco.[16] They were in-

[15] For instance, Schlesinger 2003; Russell 1958; and Hoopes and Brinkley 1997.
[16] The conference began with forty-six states and added four more (Belarus, Ukraine, Denmark, and Argentina) in the course of the conference. Poland was not at the conference but was allowed to sign the Charter shortly after the close of the San Francisco meetings. Together these states make up the fifty-one "original" members.

vited to come to San Francisco to discuss the text drafted by the Big Three. In the intervening months governments had studied the proposals and developed both individual and coalitional positions on them. By the time of the meetings at San Francisco, all were well versed in the texts of the sponsors' proposals. The unanimity of the Big Four was well publicized before San Francisco and surprised no one who was there.

In this sense San Francisco was not a postwar peace conference on the model of the Versailles Peace Treaty after World War I. Ikenberry has argued that Great Powers use postwar moments to entrench their powers with new institutional and military orders.[17] After the Second World War, Ikenberry says, there were two distinct institutional "settlements;" these are linked to each other but each has its own logic: one was within the Western bloc and the other between that bloc and the Soviet alliance. In neither settlement does he find the founding of the UN to be a major event. In Ikenberry's history, the early UN is seen as being *conditioned by* (and perhaps a victim of) the tentative military settlement reached elsewhere between the U.S. and Soviet blocs rather than as itself contributing to the settlement.

Ikenberry is right that San Francisco was not central to either of the two settlements he documents. However, the conference was crucial to the institutional architecture of the post–World War II world because of the universality of its membership and its areas of competence. That San Francisco was not a peace conference is evident from two factors: the big issues, like territorial settlement and armistice terms, were not on the table; and it both explicitly excluded enemy states and was begun before the end of hostilities. The importance of the conference lies in its attempt to legitimize a universal legal system among all countries that would entrench a system of Great Power dominance through the Security Council.[18]

Prior to the San Francisco conference, many states made strong public statements of opposition to the place of the veto in the draft text. They were critical of both the substance of its broad terms and its nonnegotiable status in the conference. According to Hoopes and Brinkley, states across a broad spectrum "deeply resented the enormous authority conferred on the Great Powers by the veto [and] were determined to exploit any differences between them in an effort to win liberalizing changes in the formula."[19] This coalition of states included influential members of all the main groupings at the time, including the Arab states, Latin Americans, Western medium powers, India, and Africans. It was a broad and diverse group. The Great Powers in turn were forced to campaign in defense of

[17] Ikenberry 2001.
[18] Simpson 2004.
[19] Hoopes and Brinkley 1997, 198.

their draft of the veto, and the San Francisco conference was the main venue for their legitimation strategy. Ultimately they succeeded in convincing all the participating states at the conference to sign and ratify the Charter, and by all accounts most were genuinely enthusiastic about it.

Two explanations are commonly given for why the small states agreed to the UN Charter in 1945 despite their initial objections to the veto. The principal axis of disagreement between the two lies in their interpretations of the interests of the small states before the conference. Some historians contend that the small states were genuinely opposed to the veto but were convinced to accept it in the end as a result of "side payments" made in the form of Great Power concessions on issues other than the veto. In this view, the contribution of the conference was that it allowed for the trading of concessions across unrelated provisions in the draft Charter, with the small states giving in to Great Power demands for the veto and the Great Powers in exchange conceding to a larger role for the rank and file in other parts of the organization, and for a larger Economic and Social Council (ECOSOC), for instance.[20] The competing view is that the small states were eager from the start to accept the draft Charter even with the veto, and so there was little need for the Great Powers to make concessions.[21] This position is strengthened by recent publication of evidence from American and British spying at San Francisco which shows that these two governments had good information about the preferences of the small states, and they did not believe any states were willing to wreck the conference over the issue of the veto.[22] In this view, the conference itself was irrelevant to the ultimate outcome of the bargain between the big and small states.

Both these views capture an important aspect about the relationship between the two blocs of states, but, rather than resolve the issue, together they help to clarify a more fundamental puzzle: although very few substantive concessions were made to the small states, all sides reported that the conference itself was extremely important to the process of setting up the United Nations. The lack of meaningful concessions undermines the central empirical claim of the first explanation of San Francisco, and the degree of seriousness with which the governments treated the negotiations undermines the second explanation's view that the conference was immaterial. Thus a paradox exists in prevailing interpretations of the San Francisco conference. On the one hand, it generated few substantive changes in the text of the Charter that might have mollified the small states; on the other, the deliberative opportunities it created allowed for

[20] Russell 1958; Lagoni 1994.
[21] Schlesinger 2003, 172.
[22] Schlesinger 2003; Daws 2004.

vigorous debate on the draft, to such an extent that it lasted many weeks longer than originally planned. The energy invested in argument, deliberation, and debate does not seem matched by a comparable payoff in the development of the text of the treaty. I argue that the process of deliberation was itself a powerful legitimating device and that the conference therefore had a "payoff" for both sets of states, even if it did not result in changes to the text.

## PROCEDURAL CORRECTNESS AT SAN FRANCISCO

The procedures adopted to manage the San Francisco conference combined well-established and novel components. For the most part, the organizers imported the accepted protocols for international conferences and diplomacy that had been developed over the preceding decades, but in some important areas they needed to develop original rules to cover the unique circumstances of the meetings. These rules were both enabling and constraining for the small states: they ensured that *some* participation and deliberation would be possible but also circumscribed the input of the small states in ways that aided the Great Powers. Reus-Smit has provided a useful model of the central importance to international relations of what he calls "systemic norms of pure procedural justice."[23] In his model rules of procedure have a constitutive function in society at two levels: they help shape the "institutional imaginations" of actors as they design new political institutions, and they also contribute to actors' beliefs about how they " 'ought' to resolve their conflicts, coordinate their relations, and facilitate coexistence."[24]

The specific procedures of the conference were written by the conference Secretariat in the opening days. For the most part, these followed the standard rules of procedure that existed at the time for running international conferences.[25] There would be a series of concurrent committees made up of all the attending states, each committee tasked with debating a separate section of the draft Charter. In these committees each state had one vote, and decisions were taken by two-thirds majority vote on substantive matters and by simple majority for procedural decisions. Any state could propose an amendment to the draft before the committee, although amendments that originated from among the conference sponsors would always be voted on first with other amendments coming to a vote only in the absence of sponsors' amendments. The topic of the vot-

[23] Reus-Smit 1997, 569.
[24] Ibid.
[25] The contemporary rules are presented in Kaufmann 1996 and Sabel 1997.

ing procedure in the Council was delegated to Committee III of Commission I.[26]

All committees took the Dumbarton Oaks proposals as the foundation for their discussions. Thus the language of those proposals was the default position of the conference. This was agreed in advance by the sponsors of the conference, and the invitations to states indicated that the Dumbarton Oaks proposals would "afford the basis for" the San Francisco deliberations.[27] This gave the sponsors tremendous agenda-setting power and slanted the debate at San Francisco in their favor, since adopting an amendment required two-thirds approval. The Great Powers needed only to muster a "blocking third" against any proposed change to guarantee its failure. Moreover, in cases where a provision generated many proposed amendments, the sponsors often collected them together and considered them in a subcommittee to reconcile them down to just one or two versions of the clause. These would then be brought back to the committee for a vote.[28] By managing this process, the Great Powers could winnow proposed amendments and filter out those they considered most dangerous to their interests. The procedures of the conference left the rank and file at a significant disadvantage in the amendments process. This experience led one of the Canadian delegates to comment more generally on agenda setting in international negotiations, saying, "The influence of a delegation at an international conference called to draw up an international instrument is greatly increased if, before the conference opens, [it] publishes a well worked out complete draft of the international instrument. Unless there are competing drafts, equally well worked out and complete, the chances are good that the state's draft will be taken as the basis of discussion at the conference."[29] Evan Luard made a similar point about San Francisco: "Because discussion began from the Dumbarton Oaks plan, the Charter emerged rather as a variation of this theme than as an independently conceived creation. . . . The result was that some features of the Charter were accepted which would never have come into being if the Conference had started from scratch."[30] Nonetheless, the procedures of the conference guaranteed to the small states the opportunity to deliberate on the proposals and to participate in votes on both the amendments and the original clauses in the draft. Nothing could be ac-

---

[26] There were twelve technical committees organized under four general commissions. The Third Commission was responsible for the Security Council provisions of the Dumbarton Oaks proposals and its First Committee was tasked with matters of Council structure and procedure, including voting and the veto.

[27] Cited in Russell 1958, 643.

[28] Schlesinger 2003; Russell 1958, 642.

[29] Reid 1989, 192.

[30] Luard 1982, 43–44.

cepted, either in the form of amendments or of the original draft, without approval by the committees. As a result, a great deal of active debate took place on almost all aspects of the draft Charter.

In this debate the clauses on the veto in the Council generated the most controversy of any element in the entire document.[31] Although it is true, as Ruth Russell reports, that there was "no serious objection to the veto on enforcement actions" in the Council and that "its main structure was adopted almost without debate,"[32] we should not understate the degree of controversy over the veto. The limits of the veto were vigorously debated, even while the basic concept was not. These limits were controversial, including the veto's application to peaceful settlements, its relationship to disputes in which a Great Power was a party, and its application to mere discussion of a dispute as opposed to concrete decisions on disputes. On these details, the Council proved to be the most contentious organ in the entire UN plan, and its articles were the subject of the most proposed amendments of any section in the draft Charter. According to Hoopes and Brinkley, "it was soon apparent that the sponsoring powers would have to address these questions seriously or risk wholesale dissension among the smaller nations."[33] The small states raised objections, for instance, about the application of the veto to selecting the Secretary General, to admitting new members to the UN, to votes on judges of the International Court of Justice, to Charter amendments, and to the pacific-settlement procedures. Attempts were also made to subordinate the council to regional security arrangements and to strengthen the more egalitarian General Assembly relative to the Council. None of these made it into the final Charter.

Opposition to the proposed structures of the Security Council was most effectively presented by the Australian delegation led by the Australian Foreign Minister H. V. Evatt. Evatt was not the most radical critic at the conference, but he was seen by the sponsoring governments as something like the respectable face of the opposition.[34] Escott Reid said, "Evatt gloried in being the flamboyant leader of the middle and small powers."[35] He championed many of the proposed amendments mentioned above, including requiring General Assembly ratification of Council decisions, making Council decisions subject to judicial review at the

[31] UNCIO 1945, 11:766–782. On these debates generally, see Russell 1958, chap. 26–28.
[32] Russell 1958, 723, 646.
[33] Hoopes and Brinkley 1997, 199.
[34] The Philippines delegation initially shared Evatt's position but quickly abandoned that stance when the U.S. government signaled to Manila that its position was unappreciated. See UN Oral History interview with General Carlos Romulo, 1982, on deposit with UN Library, New York.
[35] Reid 1989, 195.

World Court, and excluding the veto from decisions on Charter amendment or from all peaceful settlement measures (and not just peaceful settlements *against themselves*, as in the Yalta formula).[36] His proposals, although they sought to reduce the institutional power of the permanent
members, did not go as far as those of Cuba, Ecuador, or Iran.[37] Evatt's
influence was also a product of his energetic diplomatic style. He has been
described as "in effect a one-man delegation, as he rushed from committee
to committee urging the Australian viewpoints on all matters, clearly taking great pleasure in contending with the Great Powers and in trying to
reduce their representatives to size. He became in effect a public defender,
a belligerent champion of the smaller countries, anxious to prevent the
United Nations from becoming a private preserve of the Big Powers."[38]

For all his vigor, Evatt embodied the paradox found more generally
among the small states between vociferous opposition to the veto and a
willingness to accept it in the end. He recognized a special place for the
Big Powers in any postwar organization, just as he recognized the value in
ceding to them authority to direct the war itself. The Australian Parliament, led by Evatt's government, was, by 1944, already virtually unanimous in support of "an international security organization [built] around
the nucleus of the Big Three."[39] Evatt himself said in early 1945 that the
Great Powers must be free to act "unitedly to deal with aggression in its
incipient stages."[40] However, he felt that the lack of input from smaller
states, which characterized the war effort, should not be institutionalized
in the new body, and he suggested that the Dumbarton Oaks proposal
did just that. A favorite phrase was that "leadership is acceptable; domination is intolerable."[41] Changes were essential to the effectiveness of the
organization, since "the world organization to be successful must be capable not merely of giving the smaller Powers an opportunity and right of
participation, but also of evoking an enthusiastic contribution from them,
and particularly their peoples."[42] It is notable that Evatt, the most prominent of the Council's critics at San Francisco, found it possible to at once

---

[36] Evatt 1946, chap. 7.

[37] These three proposed amendments that would have eliminated the veto in enforcement decisions were as unpopular with the rank and file as they were with the Great Powers.
Cuba's proposal eliminated the veto for non-enforcement decisions but required that enforcement decisions be supported by two-thirds of permanent members as well as two-thirds
of non-permanent members. Iran and Ecuador both proposed versions of super-majority
rule in the Council. See UNCIO 1945, 11:766–782. See also Hoopes and Brinkley 1997,
chap. 16.

[38] Pearson 1972, 276.

[39] Harper and Sissons 1959, 41.

[40] Evatt speech at the University of California, March 1945; printed in Evatt 1946, 13.

[41] Evatt 1946, 129.

[42] Ibid., 13.

maintain this commitment to the principle of state equality and at the same time believe that a Security Council without the veto was neither realistic nor desirable.

## RESULTS OF DELIBERATION AT SAN FRANCISCO

Three independent lines of evidence stand out when assessing the impact of the San Francisco conference. First, in the text of the Charter, there was very little change as a result of San Francisco. The Dumbarton Oaks proposals were adopted by the conference with no significant changes to their most controversial elements. Second, the sponsors' reactions to the debate centered on a series of informal commitments regarding the use of the veto which the small states understood as important statements, even if not legally binding changes to the treaty. Finally, there was a shift from hostility to acceptance in the attitudes of the small states that took place abruptly as soon as the deliberative phase of the conference ended. The next section of the chapter traces these threads through the conference. The last section draws together their insight for a theory of legitimation.

### No Changes to the Text on the Veto

The small states won *no* significant changes to the Charter as a result of all the deliberation. In that sense, the debate at San Francisco was a futile exercise for the small states. A number of changes to the original text were made in the course of the deliberations, yet all but one of these were the result of amendments proposed by the sponsors themselves and all were in areas far from the central concerns about the Council and the veto. These so-called sponsors' amendments had priority ahead of other proposed amendments in the procedural rules of the conference. They were generally negotiated among the Great Powers behind closed doors and then presented to the relevant committee the next day for a vote. For instance, the sponsors suggested increasing the Council's role in issuing recommendations of peaceful settlement and adding "equitable geographic representation" to the criteria for non-permanent Council membership. Many of these sponsors' amendments developed from new disagreements among the Great Powers themselves that emerged in the course of the conference, the most famous concerning the application of the veto to "discussion" in the Council as opposed to action by the Council.[43] But several of these disputes had their origins in proposals coming

[43] Russell 1958, chap. 28.

from smaller states, and so, although legal authorship for these lies with the sponsors, their spirit comes from the complaints of the small states.[44]

A handful of textual changes did result from pressure by the small states, but these were very minor. For instance, the General Assembly was given slightly greater freedom of operation in Article 10.[45] On the role of ECOSOC, the small states won some minor increases in its authority, including, in Article 56, that the members should undertake "joint and separate action" to achieve the economic and social goals of the organization rather than just "action"; Article 64, on how ECOSOC can consult with other international organizations; and Articles 71 and 72, on the right to consult with nongovernmental organizations (NGOs) in the operation of ECOSOC. These were all formally proposed in sponsors' amendments but were motivated by continual pressure from one or more small states. The single instance in which a small-state amendment officially made it into the final Charter appears to be a Peruvian amendment regarding the Military Staff Committee in Article 47.[46]

The depths of the Great Power commitment to an unrestricted veto is evident in how these powers handled the controversy over "regional arrangements." The relationship between regional agreements for collective security and the global security regime of the Charter was discussed among the Big Three at Dumbarton Oaks, where they agreed that the former should be subordinate to the latter. Regional security arrangements "should be auxiliary to, consistent with, and under the supervision of the world body," reports Russell. Although supportive of regional organizations in principle, the Dumbarton Oaks draft stated that "no enforcement action should be taken under regional arrangements . . . without the authorization of the Security Council."[47] This was not controversial at Dumbarton Oaks, and the Big Three did not have significant differences of opinion on the subject.[48]

[44] For instance, the right of what are now called "troop-contributing countries" to participate in Council deliberations on their use (Arts. 31, 32) was the result of a British reworking of a Canadian proposal (Russell 1958).

[45] Where the Dumbarton Oaks draft gave the Assembly the right to "make recommendations for the purpose of promoting international cooperation" and to "consider the general principles of cooperation in the maintenance of peace and security" (V-B-6 and V-B-1), the small states managed to change this to "the right to discuss any questions or matters within the scope of the Charter" except where already being treated by the Council (Art. 10).

[46] The change was very slight and involved adding the right of the Military Staff Committee to "consult with appropriate regional agencies" ahead of establishing regional subcommittees (Russell 1958, 678). Given the fate of the MSC after 1945, the practical import of this change went from negligible to nil.

[47] Dumbarton Oaks paragraph VIII-C-2.

[48] China sought even greater control by the Council over regional arrangements and wanted to require that the Council give prior approval to all such arrangements (Russell 1958, 472–473).

At San Francisco, however, several Latin American states objected, including Chile, Colombia, Costa Rica, Ecuador, and Peru.[49] Their initiative drove the matter onto the agenda at San Francisco. These countries feared that the Dumbarton Oaks language would nullify the automatic authorization of collective reaction under the Act of Chapultepec to an attack on any of their members, or at least cause a delay in responding to an attack while the approval of the Council was obtained.[50] They organized their opposition to the Dumbarton Oaks draft both through formal amendments and informally by pressuring the American delegation to take up their position,[51] and their argument was strengthened when other countries with potential regional security plans pushed in the same direction.[52] The Great Powers resisted at first, in the interest of defending the primary position of the Council over matters of international security, and to maintain their veto over all determinations of threats to the peace and of appropriate enforcement actions. But they had reasons to be internally conflicted on the matter, since each also sought to protect a sphere of influence of its own and also wanted to defend the general principal that local dispute-settlement regimes should be encouraged where they could be complementary with the Council.[53] As with the broader veto debate, the concerns of some small states forced the Great Powers to reconsider the matter among themselves, and they eventually returned to the general conference with compromise language, acceptable to the Big Five, that they presented to the others.

This compromise, which entered into the final Charter in Chapter

---

[49] Ibid., chap. 27. Also interview with Alger Hiss, UN Oral History Project, February 13, 1990; and interview with Lawrence Finkelstein, UN Oral History Project, November 23, 1990.

[50] The Act of Chapultepec, which entered into force in March 1945, declared that aggression against any member would be considered an attack against all. It was signed by the U.S. and a number of Central and South American countries. Some members feared that the collective obligations of the UN Charter would nullify the implicit promise of U.S. assistance against aggression contained in the Act.

[51] In an underexplored instance of private influence over international affairs, Hiss reports that one member of the American delegation, Nelson Rockefeller, acted on his own initiative to influence conference outcomes in directions favored by the Latin American states. He suggests that Rockefeller's motives were to further his private business interests in the region. See Hiss UN Oral History interview. See also interview with Lawrence Finkelstein, UN Oral History Project, November 23, 1990.

[52] Russell (1958, 688) identifies "Australia and New Zealand and . . . the Arab states" as countries interested in preserving the possibility of creating new regional collective-security systems.

[53] Alger Hiss emphasizes the American interest in defending its Latin American influence by endorsing regional arrangements. Interview with Alger Hiss, UN Oral History Project, February 13, 1990. In the formal negotiations, however, the U.S. never accepted that regional organizations should trump the Council. See also Smith 1994.

VIII, involved changing the definition of self-defense rather than taking away anything from the Great Power veto. It made explicit that regional collective security was automatically acceptable as a subset of self-defense, and preserved without exception the broad power of the veto in the Council over all cases of enforcement.[54] It appears in Article 51 as "the inherent right to individual or collective self-defense."[55] This satisfied the concerns of the small states, both the Latin Americans who were defending Chapultepec and others who imagined future regional security systems, as well as maintaining the Great Powers' overriding interest in Security Council supremacy. The issue never threatened to disrupt the negotiations over interpreting the veto, and it supports the argument developed here in that it further demonstrates that the Great Powers were unwavering in their defense of the unrestricted veto over security measures and thus found ways to satisfy small states' concerns on other issues without conceding to changes in the Council. In resolving the regional-organizations puzzle, the Great Powers gave up none of the authority of the Council, or their position within it, but maintained small-state support for the whole package by recasting the problem as one that related to the separate concept of self-defense.

In sum, the small states accomplished virtually nothing toward the goal of making the draft Charter less unequal or in any other way reducing the privileges of the Great Powers. As Wilhelm Grewe concludes, the result of the conference was "the adoption and enactment of the draft negotiated [at Dumbarton Oaks] by the Great Powers without significant amendments or firm opposition."[56]

## A Discourse of Reassurance on the Veto

Although there were moments of tension behind the scenes in the coalition of the Big Four, the public face they presented to the critics of the veto at San Francisco was united and wholly consistent with the agreements reached at Dumbarton Oaks and Yalta. Some changes to the Charter texts were agreed to by the Great Powers, but, as seen above, these concessions came on points of contention other than with respect to the veto. On the matter of the veto, Great Power flexibility took the form of clarifications and promises rather than formal amendments. They offered a series of "interpretations" of the draft of the Charter, designed to satisfy critics that the veto would be used only within certain limits. The power

[54] Russell 1958, 703.
[55] Goodrich, Hambro, and Simons 1969, 348.
[56] Grewe 1994, 11.

of this extra-Charter commentary and justification to satisfy critics deserves a closer look.

When the work of the Committee became entirely wrapped up in the debate over the veto, rather than bring the matter to a vote (which the Big Four would likely win but which would leave many unhappy delegations), the sponsoring governments agreed to a system whereby a subcommittee composed of critics would submit written questions about the nature of the veto, and the sponsors would reply in writing. The Big Four approached the problem as one that could be resolved through incremental legitimation rather than as needing substantive concessions; they had no intention of altering the text, but they had faith that by continued discussion they could weaken and eventually win over opponents. They were prepared to continue to offer justifications but not compromises. Leland Goodrich, of the American delegation, remembers that the Big Four "felt that it was desirable . . . to have some appearance that the views of the smaller States were being taken into account" even though the Big Four felt that "on what they regarded as the essentials, their position was definitive."[57] The twenty-three questions that the subcommittee came up with for their query document reflected the general concerns of the committee with clarifying the kinds of situations where the veto would or would not be allowed.[58] They were particularly interested in the point, during the investigation of a dispute by the Security Council, at which the veto would be available to a permanent member: would the veto be possible at the time the Council recommended a settlement? When a decision was made as to whether a matter was a "threat to international peace and security"? or at the initial point when a party requested the Council's attention on an issue? Questions also dealt with whether the veto applied to electing a Secretary General and whether an abstention by a permanent member would constitute a negative vote, that is, a veto.

The reply by the sponsoring governments took the form of an essay rather than a point-by-point list of responses.[59] The essay dispensed quickly with the questions, essentially by restating in two paragraphs the language of the Charter (that the veto would not apply to procedural matters such as its operating rules, establishing subcommittees, adding items

[57] Goodrich, UN Oral History Project interview, September 16, 1985, p. 6

[58] The document of questions is *Questionnaire on Exercise of Veto in Security Council,* UNCIO v.11, 1945, 699–709.

[59] *Statement by the Delegations of the Four Sponsoring Governments on Voting Procedure in the Security Council,* UNCIO 1945, 11:711–714. It is widely reproduced as the "Statement by the Sponsoring Governments on Security Council Voting" or, simply, "The Four-Power Statement." See Hartmann 1951, 179–184. The government of France, which was not a sponsor of San Francisco but was included by the Charter among the permanent members, noted at the time that it "associates itself completely" with the Four-Power Statement.

to the agenda, or inviting non-Council members to appear, but would apply to all matters under the headings of peaceful settlements and enforcement measures),[60] and went on to elaborate a long, conceptual justification of the veto. It emphasized the inevitability and naturalness of an inequality between the Great Powers and the rest, and suggested that the proposed voting procedure was simply a way of responsibly dealing with that fact. Moreover, the proposed Security Council was not giving the permanent five anything new, according to the statement, since the five already had a veto power in the Council of the League of Nations under the League's rule of unanimity: "As regards the permanent members, there is no question under the Yalta formula of investing them with a new right, namely, the right of veto, a right which the permanent members of the League Council always had."[61] The question was restricting the right of non-permanent members to veto a decision, a power which they formerly had in the League but which would be restricted in the Security Council in the interest of making "the operation of the Council less subject to obstruction than was the case under the League of Nations rule of complete unanimity."[62] The statement cast the Council as a continuation of an existing system, improved by a small, reasonable change. This interpretation of the League of Nations was useful, because it let the Big Four frame the choice as one between everyone having the veto (as in the League) or just the permanent members.[63] Opponents could therefore be made to look like partisans of "obstruction."

While denying as many limits on the veto as possible, the Big Four kept up a discourse of reassurance that the veto would not be used often and would not create a problem between the permanent five and the rest. This is epitomized by the sponsors' reply to the key question of whether deciding that a matter is procedural or not was itself to be considered procedural—and thus not subject to the veto. To this the sponsors replied that they saw it as "unlikely that there will arise in the future any matters of great importance on which [such] a decision will have to be made", but nevertheless such an "unlikely" question would not be considered procedural.[64]

Throughout the committee's deliberations, the rhetoric of the Big Four exhibited this reassuring tone, even while denying substantive concessions. The sponsors made continual reference to the logic of collective

[60] Except as limited by the Yalta compromise against the veto on peaceful settlements against a permanent member.
[61] UNCIO 1945, 11:713.
[62] Ibid.
[63] On the later use of the "hidden veto" (i.e., when the non-permanent members act collectively to defeat a proposal), see Bailey and Daws 1998, 249–250.
[64] UNCIO 1945, 11:714.

security and to the greater responsibilities of the permanent members. The U.K. delegate, in defense of the veto, emphasized the "willingness of the great powers to accept the obligations laid down in the Charter" and contended, apparently seriously, that this "represented one of the most remarkable advances in all human history."[65] In the same meeting the U.S. delegate called on the small and medium states to fall in behind the sponsoring powers on the veto "in the same spirit of cooperation on the part of all the members as had been displayed by the sponsoring governments in reaching agreement."[66] He may have been carried away when he went on to emphasize the equality of UN members, saying: "There should be no distinction in the world organization between little powers, medium powers, and great powers," except that by their material resources the latter have responsibilities which the others don't, and which they had not sought.[67] Finally, the U.S. "pledged" that, for its part, it "had no ambition [in defending the veto] except the ambition to preserve peace; it sought no territories and no conquest but only cooperation with the other nations of the earth."[68] All the Big Four delegations emphasized the naturalness and inevitability of an unequal international system, and that the Great Powers did not choose their status but, given this situation, it was their "responsibility" to devise a world body which they dominated.

### Attitudes and Behavior of the Small States

These reassurances had a powerful effect on the critics in the committee, even when they had no basis in the text of the Charter. The behavior of the small states changed after this episode. In this light, the third place to examine the effects of the conference is in the positions and behaviors of the governments that opposed the inequalities of the veto. Many of the small states changed their behavior over the course of the deliberations, and how and why they did so provides important evidence regarding the impact of the Great Powers' legitimating strategy. For their part, the sponsoring governments retained essentially the same position regarding the veto and general powers of the Security Council throughout the deliberations. They admitted very few changes, and none of real substance. But changes in the behavior of the small states were significant and need explaining.

The opponents of the veto entered San Francisco with a declared public position against the veto as presented in the Dumbarton Oaks plan.

[65] Ibid., 11:435.
[66] Ibid., 11:432–433.
[67] Ibid., 11:433.
[68] Ibid.

They used all the available procedures in the conference to express that position and to rally support for amendments. The opponents of the Yalta voting formula, as expressed in the joint statement, included Belgium, Australia, the Netherlands, Honduras, Cuba, Chile, Mexico, Peru, Norway, New Zealand, Colombia, and Canada. Within this broad group, and among the many other small states that discretely sided with them, there were a number of positions regarding how to respond to the proposals. Colombia said it would vote against the original veto scheme, and, as noted above, others proposed amendments that would seriously curtail or entirely eliminate the veto. Several others proposed only to remove peaceful settlements from the domain of the veto, and the Australian version of this proposal became a centerpiece of the debate on the veto more generally.

The Australian amendment modified the veto rule such that in cases where the Council made an official recommendation on the peaceful settlement of a dispute between states, a majority of seven (of the original eleven members of the Council) would be sufficient to pass the recommendation. This effectively eliminated the veto for peaceful settlements. Because this was the most "moderate" of all the small-state amendments to the veto rule, it was treated as a bellwether and votes on all others were deferred until full deliberation and a vote could be taken on it; if the Australian amendment failed, all stronger changes would certainly fail as well. The Sponsors' Statement, described above, was part of the Great Powers' reaction to the Australian proposal.

The climax of the debate on the veto came once the committee had before it three formal documents: the original Dumbarton Oaks/Yalta text on the veto, the Sponsors' Statement offering an "interpretation" of those clauses, and the Australian amendment that would reduce the veto power to enforcement decisions only. Since the rules of procedure stated that amendments must be voted on before votes could be taken on the sponsors' original text, the amendment came up first. It was defeated by a vote of 10 in favor, 20 against, with 15 abstentions and 5 absences.[69] In its next meeting, the committee decided not to consider any other amendments (on the bellwether theory) and moved to vote on the original text of the veto clauses proposed by the sponsors. The crucial section was adopted with 30 in favor, 2 against, and 15 abstentions plus 3 absences. Finally, the committee voted on approving the entire text under its jurisdiction, including the veto clauses already adopted, and the result was success with 25 votes for and 2 against.[70]

The outcome of the voting is important for two reasons. First, we cannot account for the failure of the Australian amendment except by also

[69] Russell 1958, 738.
[70] Ibid.

considering the Great Powers' threats to abandon the UN entirely should it be adopted. This application of political leverage outside the negotiating framework was reported by many states as heavy-handed and improper, but it was also seen as sincere and so it was effective in reducing the support for the amendment.[71] The impact that this use of ad hoc political power has on legitimation is considered in the next section.

Second, after the vote, we observe an immediate shift in the behavior of the small states that had previously fought for restrictions on the veto. Having lost, the opponents of the veto ceased trying to alter the text of the Charter and switched to supporting the new organization, making much of the justificatory reasoning in the Great Powers' statements. Many states that had voted for the Australian amendment subsequently voted for the original Dumbarton Oaks text, even though the two were contradictory.[72] This should be interpreted in light of the information they had about the future: knowing the originals would certainly pass, they had no incentive to continue to oppose them.

Evatt told the committee that, although he could not justify the veto to his constituents, it was enough that he "could tell his people that the United States Delegate had said the 'veto' would not be used capriciously and that the Soviet Delegate had told the press that the five great powers would rarely exercise the veto."[73] Evatt relied heavily on these assurances when, after the conference, he undertook to win support for the Charter in a series of speeches on "Australia's achievements at San Francisco."[74] These statements were powerful in deflecting opposition at San Francisco. This might have been because they were convincing to the small and medium states' representatives, or, perhaps more likely, because they gave these leaders texts they could use to satisfy their domestic constituents that no great injustice was being done to their countries. Evatt's statements are ambiguous as to how he was interpreting the promises made by the U.S. Either way, however, the reasons given in defense of the veto played an important role in legitimizing the Security Council. Whether heard by cynical ears, or taken as honest commitments, they provided the governments of the rank-and-file states with justifications for the outcome of San Francisco.

Having reached the limits of their procedural options for change, these countries began to support the very thing they had just been working to change. Despite strong feelings on elements of the veto, none among the veto-weakening coalition was willing to violate the limits set by the delib-

[71] For instance, Russell 1958; Reid 1989; and New Zealand 1945.
[72] Russell 1958, 738–739.
[73] UNCIO 1945, 11:p 434.
[74] See speeches of July 25, 1945, Sydney; and August 30, 1945, in the Australian House of Representatives, both in Evatt 1946.

erative and voting procedures of the conference, even though these procedures were strongly biased in favor of the sponsors. Universally the small states allowed their opposition to be contained within, and limited by, the pre-set procedures of the conference; once their procedural channels were exhausted for making statements, proposing amendments, and rallying support against the veto plan, every state gave up on making any changes and shifted to acceptance of the whole UN package. The position of the veto opponents on the substance of the matter remained relatively stable through the conference: after the failed vote on the Australian amendment, the distribution of states and positions was essentially the same as at the opening of the conference. There is no evidence that any had really changed their view of the veto itself, and yet the behavior of all these states shifted after the vote, from opposition to acceptance, as they reached the end of the procedural opportunities for resistance.

The procedures of the conference opened a window of opportunity for the small states to voice their opposition to the veto plan. But they also defined the limits of that opportunity, and so closed the window after the Australian amendment failed. The opponent states then accepted their loss and shifted to support for the Charter as a whole. Restated in the terms used by Reus-Smit, the constitutive force of procedural norms regarding how conflicts ought to be resolved shaped how the small states expressed their opposition: the channels for deliberation, the voting rules on amendments, and the procedural limits on opposition were all accepted as the structure for the process.[75] The structure was in this sense *prior* to the pursuit of their particular substantive interests on the veto, and it limited their conception of their interests. The veto opponents appeared to value more highly respect for the accepted procedures of international diplomacy than they did defeating the Great Powers on the question of vetoes over peaceful settlements of disputes.

The deliberations around the veto are valuable for revisiting my general theory of legitimation. First, all parties to the deliberations at the San Francisco meetings probably expected the veto provisions of the draft to be accepted, though with some controversy. The deliberative process was nonetheless treated by both the Great Powers and the rest as an important contributor to legitimation. No party appears to have been willing to forego the deliberative stage and rush immediately to ratification. The procedure by which agreement was achieved contributed something important to legitimating the outcome. Second, many small states experienced a development in their position during the conference, going from strong and public opposition to acceptance of the veto. For most, this

[75] Reus-Smit 1997.

change occurred immediately after the failure of the Australian amendment and thus is closely linked to both the deliberation that took place and the procedural rules governing the limits for how and when amendments could be made. The moment when the rules of conference procedure shut off further discussion marked the turning point for the small states. Having fought and lost within the rules of international diplomacy, they expressed their interests in opposing the veto within the limiting framework provided by the legitimated procedures of the conference.

## IMPLICATIONS FOR THE THEORY OF LEGITIMATION

The San Francisco case is instructive for all three controversies outlined in chapter 3. These relate to the source of legitimation, and to the relations between legitimacy and strategic thought and between legitimacy and power. If we accept that the Great Powers saw the conference as a legitimation device, and that this was successful in inducing the small states to accept the veto's inequalities as legitimate, then we can ask these three questions: What element of the procedure was the source of that legitimation? Did legitimacy affect the strategic thinking of governments? Where and how did power manifest itself in the process?

### *The Sources of Legitimation*

Chapter 3 presented competing hypotheses for how legitimation takes place, and we can use these to organize the San Francisco history into alternative explanations for the outcome. The three main competing explanations for legitimation in the San Francisco case are (1) that the procedures of the conference encouraged deliberation, and this deliberation helped legitimize the inequalities of the Charter; (2) that the small states were bribed with incentives elsewhere in the Charter to accept the veto; or (3) that the small states simply so desired that the UN come into being that they were content to accept the inequalities as the price of getting Great Power support for the organization. The second and third of these are variations on the favorable-outcomes hypothesis.

What accounts for the small states' change in position? Clearly they did not receive concessions in the text of the Charter as compensation for accepting the veto. There were no changes to the substance of the veto, and so these cannot account for the decline in the opposition voiced by the small states. Neither did they receive compensating benefits in other areas of the draft. Their support was not "bought," and so the favorable-outcomes school cannot account for the turnaround in their positions. If we define the favorable outcome as securing changes to the veto, then we can conclude that it is not a powerful explanation in this case.

Disentangling the two remaining arguments is more difficult, because they predict the same outcome. Did the small states accept the veto because they believed in the appropriateness of the San Francisco process, or did they accept it because they wanted the UN to exist and would put up with the veto as a *sine qua non*? The difference between these two lies in the internal processes of interest assessment and strategic decision that led to the outcome, and for this reason it provides an opportunity to assess the legitimating power of deliberation.

That the small states were eager, before San Francisco, that the United Nations come into existence is well documented, both in the public record and in the secret intelligence gathered by the sponsors. They were therefore predisposed to accept the general structure proposed by the draft charter and would have been unhappy to see the conference end without an agreement on the new organization. In that sense, the outcome satisfied the basic interests of the small states even without any diminution in the power of the veto. However, their very public and vociferous opposition to the veto in the run-up to the conference suggests that at least some of these states were not prepared to accept the UN plan without the opportunity to deliberate on it at a general international conference. There is no evidence to suggest that national capitals thought the conference was an unnecessary exercise; quite the contrary, for most capitals appear to have armed their delegations with lists of unacceptable provisions and preferred changes for them to carry to the committees. A few delegations, such as that of the Philippines noted above, were ultimately instructed by their governments simply to accept what was offered and back down in the face of pressure from the Great Powers.[76] But many others continued to present alternatives right to the end. The behavior of these states suggests that they believed they were defending their interests in the deliberations, and saw their interests as different than the draft text of the Great Powers. They took seriously their opportunity to make and vote on amendments. By the end of the conference the small states had exhausted these opportunities for influence under the procedures of the conference. They were then faced with a choice between accepting what was offered or walking away. At this point their general preference for having a UN organization won out over their distaste for the inequalities of the veto.

Thus the most plausible explanation for the success of the conference is one that includes both components: in other words, the small states were content to accept the draft Charter essentially as presented, as long as

[76] See n. 34, above.

they had the opportunity to discuss, criticize, and vote on it. The deliberative opportunities were crucial to making the conference work, even without a significant chance that they would result in substantive changes to the draft in line with the opponents' proposals.


### Deliberation and Strategic Thought

The deliberative process at San Francisco also reveals patterns of interest to the debate between legitimacy and strategic thought. This is generally treated in IR theory as an either/or dichotomy, but in this case both must be present to explain the outcome. The deliberation at San Francisco was both strategic and normative: it was strategic in the sense that states were using the procedural devices available to them in a calculating way for instrumental purposes, but it was normative in that it depended on a shared belief in the appropriateness of those procedures in order to promote the legitimacy of the conference output. The two kinds of consideration are not on display sequentially, as the two-step model suggests.[77] Instead, states appeared to be motivated by both at the same time, such that neither makes sense without the other.

The relationship between deliberation and outcomes in international relations is the subject of a good deal of literature. Thomas Risse, for instance, suggests that the arguing that took place between the U.S. and the Soviets at the end of the Cold War led to a change in how Gorbachev framed the options under discussion, and this led to him changing national policy regarding the terms of German reunification.[78] Neta Crawford shows that arguing over norms of self-determination was important in shaping states' actions with respect to decolonization, among other matters.[79] But, in general, the new literature on deliberation looks at situations where principled arguments are used to attempt to influence which among several possible outcomes actually occurs, that is, situations where there is uncertainty over outcomes and a number of possible outcomes are in play, some of which are cooperative but many that are not. Deliberation, as treated by Jon Elster and his colleagues in *Deliberative Democracy*, can increase the chances that a cooperative outcome is reached.[80] Abbott and Snidal use a focal-points metaphor to explain cases where deep disagreement over substantive outcomes is avoided by first agreeing on procedural devices. Finding consensus on procedures may be easier

[77] Legro 1996.
[78] Risse 2000.
[79] Crawford 2002.
[80] For the framework, see Elster 1998.

than on substance, even if actors know that the procedural rules constrain the set of future possible outcomes.[81] Deliberation, either over procedures or substance, affects the probabilities attached to different outcomes. The emphasis on changing outcomes is driven partly by methodological needs, in that it is easier to assess how and when deliberation affects outcomes by examining cases where negotiations produce changes in the document, and partly by tactical needs, to meet the counterclaim that deliberation is inconsequential in light of prior state interests. But it also threatens to become a tacit substantive assumption that deliberation is important (only) to the extent that it moves immediate outcomes from where they would otherwise be.

The evidence from this chapter suggests that we need not limit ourselves in this way. The question, "Why argue?" is even more pertinent in cases where the outcome is not expected to change. The mismatch between the energy expended by the participants and their expectations of returns on that investment suggests that the anticipated payoffs are not measured by substantive concessions. Strategic behavior continues in these cases, but the resources by which it is conducted and the currency of payoffs take the form of symbols and legitimation. At San Francisco the negotiated outcome is overdetermined in the sense that it was seen as the most likely outcome for most parties. The debate over the Council is notable precisely because the prior situation is one where existing theories suggest that deliberation should not be particularly important. In this it is exemplary of a set of cases that are noteworthy from a theoretical point of view: where no change in our substantive outcome is expected, the mechanisms by which deliberation matters are more clearly visible as they are unencumbered by the complicating influence of side payments and logrolling.

### Power

Power politics played an important role in the negotiations, in that the most powerful states used their advantage to structure the draft and then ensure that it was adopted by the general membership. However, the need to legitimize the outcome conditioned how that power could be used. The Great Powers did not set aside the rules of procedure of the conference to force a solution on the others. Even when the sponsors threatened to withdraw from the UN project entirely, they never considered switching to the *overt* use of power to win approval of the draft, and the small states maintained their demand that the procedures of the con-

---

[81] Abbott and Snidal 2002.

ference be respected. The small states were well aware of these threats, but, as Russell reports, "the other delegations were not prepared to accept the ultimatum before having their say at several more meetings."[82] The value the small states placed on the rights of deliberation was, if anything, *increased* by the threats of the Great Powers. Once the coercive power of the sponsors was deployed, the opponents of the veto had no resources left except the publicity they could rally by having their opinions registered through open deliberation. This was all the more important to them once the substantive outcome was indeed a foregone conclusion. By carefully following the procedures, the strong states grounded their claim that the fight had been properly conducted and the result should therefore be respected.

## CONCLUSION

The proposals that the Great Powers brought to San Francisco had two qualities built into the design of the Council that set up the controversy to come: first, the Council was designed to institutionalize special rights for the Great Powers and to entrench those in international law; second, the Great Powers made it clear that no substantive changes were possible to this basic design. In dealing with the conflict inherent in these two qualities, the sponsors refused to make textual changes to the veto power and so instead had to find other ways to manage the small states and win their acceptance of these inequalities.

Seen in conventional bargaining terms, the San Francisco conference is quite empty. The small states gathered with the Great Powers and deliberated over a document that neither group expected to see changed. A great deal of discussion ensued that led to a unanimous vote and great relief upon the adoption of the treaty. The formal outcome of the treaty as it defines the Council is not materially different than would have obtained in the absence of the deliberative process; the Great Powers could have opened the Charter for signature in April 1945, without a meeting at all, and had the same result. The conference is puzzling in that it appears to be an expensive process that lacks any substance at all. In the context of American politics, Alexander Schuessler has described the paradox of voting in similar terms: "In the standard terms of incentives, the remarkable lack of any private instrumental returns to participation, together with the imposition of a very real cost of participation, makes this scenario a stark instance of the participation paradox." Seen in instrumental terms, both the paradox of voting and the San Francisco Conference

[82] Russell 1958, 736.

are intriguing precisely because, to borrow Schuessler's words, *"there is no outcome!"*[83]

The evidence presented in this chapter suggests that there was indeed an outcome to San Francisco. It is similar to the outcome Schuessler identifies for participation by American voters: by taking part in the process, the small states at San Francisco earned the right to express their preferences and have them noted in a public forum, and thus succeeded in reinforcing their identities as full citizens of international society. That these activities did not change the formal outcome is irrelevant; the participants had no expectation that major changes would occur. The Great Powers took advantage of states' desire to participate in the deliberative exercise by hosting a public conference, confident that the result, in the end, would be support for their text. Thus the small states did gain something valuable in the course of the deliberations at San Francisco. But this cannot be measured in terms of formal changes to the Charter.

Some of the legitimizing strategy of the Great Powers was based on providing informal reassurances to the rank and file about how the veto would be used. Although falling far short of legal concessions on the veto, we have seen how these verbal commitments were highly valued by some delegations at the conference. They served their purpose at the time of San Francisco in winning support for the draft, but they represented promises of future behavior that could prove costly for the Great Powers. The next two chapters examine how the legitimacy of the Council has affected both its day-to-day politics and its management of crises. The power of legitimacy to influence state behavior is evident in both these venues.

[83] Schuessler 2000, 24; italics in original.

# CHAPTER 5

# Blue Helmets and White Trucks

INTERNATIONAL POLITICS unfolds differently in the presence of legitimated international institutions than it would in their absence. The present chapter looks at some familiar patterns in state behavior at the Security Council to show the impact of the early legitimation of the Council discussed in the previous chapter. Emphasizing the connection between the legitimacy of an institution and the creation of useful symbols, I demonstrate the behavioral consequences for international politics of the legitimacy of the Security Council. The evidence supports the conclusion that states tailor their behavior to take into account legitimated institutions, although they do not cease being strategic actors. By creating new symbolic resources and altering the strategic context of international action, legitimated international organizations affect how states perceive their interests and the payoffs of available policy choices. This argument reinforces the general claim of the book that legitimacy plays an important role in international politics.

Much of the behavior of states in international politics cannot be understood without an awareness of the role of legitimacy in creating the resources over which states compete. As a result, there are two important gains to be made from this chapter. First, it shows more clearly the full range of effects of legitimacy in international politics, making more concrete the concepts discussed in chapter 2. Second, it makes conceptual sense of some common outcomes in international politics that are otherwise inexplicable. Linking the concept of legitimacy to an empirical examination of the symbolic content of contemporary politics at the Council carries forward the study of both IR theory and the UN Security Council.

The chapter examines three areas of state behavior around the Security Council that illustrate different elements of the strategic pursuit of the symbols of Council legitimacy. These are the politics of the Council's agenda, the elections to non-permanent seats in the Council, and the role of Council authorization for the use of force by states. In each of these three realms, the behavior of states is counterintuitive according to a purely materialist definition of states' goals and interests. The patterns they display appear irrational according to materialist notions of state interests, since they involve spending resources and energy in ways that are not sensible in non-symbolic terms. When symbolic politics enters the picture, however, things look different. This suggests that the domains of rational, strategic actors and of socially constructed decision contexts must be considered together in international relations.[1] The cases examined here provide evidence for reconsidering the debates over how legitimacy affects both strategic behavior by states and power politics among them. The Council's power over its symbols translates into a degree of autonomy for the organization from its member states, even its most powerful. Previewing chapter 6, this autonomy can, in some instances, mean that its symbols might be used against even the strongest states on the Council, further highlighting the independence of legitimized IOs from their member states.[2]

## THE SYMBOLIC POWER OF THE SECURITY COUNCIL

In this section I explore three areas in which states compete for symbolic rewards in and around the Security Council: first, with respect to the agenda; second, with respect to membership; and third, with respect to the use of force. In each, we see states attempting to pursue their particularistic, strategic interests by calling on symbolic resources that are the products of the community as a whole.[3] These resources are constituted by beliefs about their legitimacy. There are no compelling material reasons for the pursuit of Council symbols by states; the desire to be associated with the Council can only be understood by recognizing the power the Council has by virtue of beliefs in its legitimacy. In the third example, we also see how the Council gains power by being the gatekeeper for states seeking its symbols. Symbolic politics engenders many forms of competition. The examples all take the form of competition over the *use* of the symbols of the Council. Other kinds of competition would include struggles over the right to define new symbols or over the relative status of different symbols or over the right to interpret existing symbols.[4] Evidence of this last kind of competition around the Council is discussed in chapter 6.

### *The Agenda*

The symbolic power of the Security Council is evident in the energy that states expend on having the Council pay attention to issues of concern to

---

[1] Consistent with my state-centric approach, I treat in this chapter the use *by states* of legitimated symbols at the Council. This should not be taken to imply that these resources cannot be used by other actors. For the use of internationally legitimated symbols by domestic actors, see Bukovansky 2002; and for their use in civil wars, see Bob 2005; and Metelits 2004.

[2] Barnett and Finnemore (2004) discuss how the legitimacy of the goals and structures of IOs increase their autonomy.

[3] Hurd 2002.

[4] For a typology, see Harrison 1995.

them, even where there is little material payoff to be had. The bringing of
issues to the Council carries enormous symbolic weight but often little
material effect, and so perhaps nothing illustrates better the symbolic
power of the Security Council than the struggles over its agenda.

The agenda of the Council consists of two parts. First, there is the provisional agenda for each Council meeting, which is prepared by the Secretary General and contains the various current crises or issues that may be
the topics for the meeting. At the start of each meeting, the Council
members discuss and vote on the provisional agenda, making it the "official" agenda for that meeting. The second part consists of all the topics
which were once on the official agenda of an individual meeting but
which were not finally disposed of by the Council. This list is officially
called the *Summary Statement*[5] of the Security Council (also known informally as the Agenda) and is effectively a running tab of open issues
which the Security Council once discussed and may return to some day or
may just want to postpone dealing with but, for whatever reason, does
not want to formally close. At the start of 2005 it contained 147 items,
some almost as old as the UN itself. It is extremely rare that one of these
"stale" items is reopened for substantive discussion. The *Summary Statement* is a good location to observe the symbolic politics of the Council,
because although states often work hard to keep a favored issue on the
Agenda there is very little material payoff to its being there. The payoff
comes in the currency of symbol and recognition.

In the debates over the shape of the UN at San Francisco in 1945, the
medium and small states recognized that the right to bring matters to the
attention of the Security Council might be a valuable tool and should not
be exclusively reserved for Security Council members or, worse, for permanent members only.[6] The right of non-Council actors to bring issues to
the attention of the Council was enshrined in the Charter at several
points: in Article 35(1) for UN members without a Council seat, in 35(2)

[5] Its full title is *The Summary Statement by the Secretary General on Matters of Which the
Security Council Is Seized and on the Stage Reached in Their Consideration*. It was established
under Rule 11 of the *Provisional Rules of Procedure of the Security Council* (http://www.un
.org/Docs/sc/scrules.htm) and is now an annual document (rather than the weekly specified in the rules). The *Summary Statement* of 2005 is S/2006/10.

[6] See the histories given in Russell 1958, 650–654; and Goodrich, Hambro, and Simons
1969. In practice, the right to "bring a matter to the Council" is equivalent to placing it on
the agenda, since the latter happens more or less automatically as a result of the former.
The Council has occasionally rejected a proposed agenda item and, as master of its own
procedures, the proposing state has no legal avenue to pursue the matter. A Guatemalan
item was rejected in 1954 on the grounds that it should first have been treated by the Organization of American States (Goodrich, Hambro, and Simons 1969, 361), and Bailey
and Daws (1998, 89–91) discuss the informally substantive debate that usually precedes
this procedural decision.

for non-members of the UN, and in Article 99 for the Secretary General.[7] Since they cannot force the Council to act on an Agenda item, the small and medium states effectively fought for the right only to bring issues to the Council and leave them there.

No provision was made at San Francisco for how issues were to be removed from the Agenda, and items are removed much less readily than they are added. In practice, disposing of an item from the Agenda has been treated as a prerogative of the Council collectively (and not of the state that originally raised the matter)[8] and is accomplished in one of three ways: by resolutions or decisions that dispose of the matter, by the rejection of all proposals submitted, or by an explicit decision to remove it.[9] Each of these effectively requires an active decision on the part of the Council, but there are often reasons why the Council is unwilling to be particularly active and so, by default, matters have passed from the agenda of an individual meeting to the *Summary Statement*, where they accumulate. Once a question is on the *Summary Statement,* there is often little reason to return to it, absent some exogenous change in circumstances, but removing it from the *Statement* generally provokes a strong reaction. Usually at least one state feels a need to keep an issue alive, even if "alive" means practically moribund on the *Summary Statement*. With the right to place issues before the Council distributed among all UN members and no easy mechanism for the Council to remove them, the *Summary Statement* has become a catalogue of simmering arguments, increasingly divorced from the real work of the body. For instance, in the period of the most recent *Repertoire of the Practice of the SC* (which reaches only to 1984) *no* item was removed from the *Summary Statement*.[10] From an administrative point of view, this has become something of a joke as the *Summary Statement* has grown longer and longer, filled with items that are increasingly stale, with little chance of ever again becoming active in front of the Council.

[7] In addition to these formal channels, UN members often take advantage of informal means of alerting the Council to issues they find important. Pakistan, for instance, makes a point of sending letters to the Council president and the permanent members whenever it feels India has taken a provocative action over Kashmir. See, for instance, "Pakistan takes India bomb blast accusations to UN chief," *Agence France Press*, March 12, 1998; "Spokesman denies acquisition, deployment of missiles," *BBC Summary of World Broadcasts: Excerpt from Radio Pakistan*, June 16, 1997; *The Hindu*, June 14, 1997, p. 1; "Pakistan asks India to settle Kashmir dispute," *Reuters World Service*, May 16, 1996; "Pakistan says India preparing for nuclear test," *BBC Summary of World Broadcasts: Excerpt from Radio Pakistan*, March 17, 1996.

[8] The decisive interpretation on this came from the Iran-USSR dispute in 1946. See Bailey and Daws 1998; and Meisler 1995, 28–34.

[9] Bailey and Daws 1998, 79–81.

[10] *Repertoire of the Practice of the Security Council, 1981–84*, 1992, ST/PSCA/I/Add.9.

The rank-and-file membership of the UN has historically resisted efforts to rationalize this system, recognizing in its peculiarities one channel by which non-members of the Council can associate themselves and their problems with the authority of the Council. In a revolutionary move, and after some ad hoc pruning of the list in the early 1990s, the Security Council took unilateral action in 1996 to pass a new procedural rule which said that "matters that had not been considered by the Council in the preceding five years would be deleted from the list of matters of which the Council was seized."[11] This would have removed 42 of the 139 items on the *Summary Statement* at that time. However, even before this rule could take effect, the protests from the non-members of the Council were such that the Council (after a change in its presidency) amended the new rule so that any member of the UN could keep an item on the *Summary Statement* merely by notifying the Secretary General that "it wished an item to remain on the list."[12] This reprieve would last one year but was indefinitely renewable. Consequently, of the 42 items bound for deletion in early 1997, 29 were kept on at the request of member states. In October 1997, 5 more items were dropped and 1 was retained by request, leaving a *Summary Statement,* including new items, of 128 items.[13]

To digress, it is noteworthy that this power to request that an item remain on the Agenda is the right of any UN member; it is not reserved for members of the Security Council. Thus the peculiar organizational situation has been created in which non-members of an organization have a decisive voice over the organization's agenda. This extends the unusual arrangement agreed to at San Francisco and encoded in the Charter whereby non-members of the Council can introduce items to the Council agenda and the Council itself cannot veto their introduction. Now technically the Council cannot even remove those items once they are introduced except by a substantive resolution or decision resolving the matter. This is one area where the distinction between Council member and non-member is blurred.[14]

One leader in the agenda game has been Pakistan. The *Summary Statement* contains several ancient items relating to the India-Pakistan dispute in its various manifestations, and the government of Pakistan makes frequent reference to this fact in its international statements. In October 1998 a spokesperson tried to use the continuance of the dispute on the Council agenda to leverage greater attention to the issue at the UN. Call-

[11] The rule is contained in S/1996/603; the quote is from S/1997/40, 2–3. See the discussion in Bailey and Daws 1998, 81–83.

[12] S/1997/40, 3.

[13] See A/52/392, where the Secretary General notifies the General Assembly of issues before the Security Council.

[14] For others, see Hurd 1997.

ing the India-Pakistan question "the oldest issue on the UN agenda,"[15] the Deputy Permanent Representative of Pakistan to the UN said that the matter "deserved a more detailed reference in the UN Secretary General's annual report."[16] Not surprisingly, Pakistan has been very quick under the new procedures to protect its agenda items from falling off the *Statement* after five years of inactivity. For the past several years, when the *Summary Statement* is released each January or February listing which items are set to be deleted at the end of the year, it already contains a paragraph saying that a request has been made to retain the three India-Pakistan entries. In the January 1999 *Statement* the request had been made in November 1998, more than a full year before the deadline.[17]

A sense of the importance states attach to the *Summary Statement* is evident in their responses to the effort to streamline the process in 1996. At that time the president of the Council emphasized that the reforms would make no *material* change to the ability of states to bring matters to the Council: "The removal of a matter from the list . . . has no implication for the substance of the matter and does not affect the exercise by member states of [their] right to bring matters to the attention of the Security Council. . . . The Council may at any time decide to include any matter in the agenda of a meeting of the Council, whether or not it is mentioned in the list."[18] The reaction by some states was empassioned beyond what would be expected given the minimal material consequences of the change. The chair of the Arab Group called it a "fundamental error": "The norms proposed in the note [that is, S/1996/603*] ignore the historical importance of many of the matters that it is proposed to delete and that we regard as still of the utmost importance and as pertaining to the core of the Security Council's jurisdiction in the domain of the maintenance of international peace and security."[19] Pakistan said, "We regret to note that, in this case, the Council has decided to strike out items without taking into consideration the substantive merit of each issue in so far as the maintenance of international peace and security is concerned, and without prior consultations with the States concerned. This is unprecedented and carries serious political implications for the future work of the

---

[15] This is only partly true. The oldest India-Pakistan question on the *Summary Statement* dates from January 6, 1948, and the Palestinian question, which is also still on the Agenda, was introduced on December 9, 1947, but was postponed and first discussed on February 24, 1948. See S/7382.

[16] Radio Pakistan, October 6, 1998; cited by BBC Summary of World Broadcasts, October 8, 1998.

[17] S/1999/25 para. 8. The same generous advance notice was given in the 2000 document; see S/2000/40 para. 13.

[18] S/1996/603.

[19] S/1996/655.

Council, as well as for the position of the States directly concerned."[20] Pressing their chance to increase the visibility of old disputes in the Council, many stressed the view that a formal meeting of the Council should be held and an official decision made in order to drop an issue from the list.[21] Failing to do so would represent an attempt to "deal with substantive issues on the Council's list in a procedural manner."[22]

What is significant in the politics of the Agenda is the strength of the UN members attachment to their little piece of official Council attention, even when it is as far removed from obvious practicality as an entry on the *Summary Statement* that has not been considered for many years and has little prospect of ever again seeing the lights of the chamber. At stake here is more than the second-face, agenda-setting power noted by Bachrach and Baratz.[23] The second face of power is important because manipulating the agenda can have a substantive effect on whether decisions are taken in an organization. How this plays out depends on the decision rule of the body. Interest in the Agenda of the Security Council is different, because actors have enough experience to know an item remaining on the *Summary Statement* will likely never be raised again, nor, of course, any decision taken on it. This is clearly not a case of agenda setting in that sense. Instead, states at the Council appear to value *in itself* having an item of their concern placed on, or remain on, the agenda of the Council. They behave as if this is a valued good, independent of any action taken on the matter.[24] It provides some institutional acknowledgment that their problems are recognized by the international community, and states value such recognition.

Seen in this light, the behavior of non-members of the Council resembles what some anthropologists have noted about ceremonies and rituals in many domestic societies: to be allowed to participate in important ceremonies is a right worth fighting for. As Harrison says of ritualized contests, "the right to fight and compete for the important roles in these events is itself often a closely guarded prerogative. . . . Viewed sociologically, these struggles [over participation] are an integral part of the preparations for the ritual."[25] The right to participate in the contest is itself a valued good, even if one has no reasonable expectation of winning the

[20] S/1996/649.
[21] S1996/751 and S/1996/649.
[22] S/1996/649.
[23] Bachrach and Baratz 1962. See also Lukes 1974.
[24] The symbolism of Council attention may be important to a party in either a positive or a negative sense. When it is negative, the act of bringing a matter before the Council may be strenuously opposed by a state. But this opposition is itself evidence that Council attention is a significant matter for states.
[25] Harrison 1992.

contest itself. Thus merely by keeping a list of matters with which it is seized, the Council has created a new kind of prestige resource in international politics. The value states place on holding a space on the list is derived from the legitimacy they ascribe to the Council itself.

*Membership*

Recognizing the symbolic power of the Security Council also helps us understand another strange phenomenon surrounding the body: the continued strength of the desire to become a non-permanent member of the Council. The logic that drives states to seek non-permanent seats assumes that there is a payoff for the winning state, measured in terms of enhanced influence over Council decisions. However, the decision-making influence of non-permanent members is extremely low, and there are reasons to believe that it has been declining further in recent years. Therefore, the payoff to winning a non-permanent seat has been greatly reduced. However, the competition over seats has, if anything, increased. This leads to a puzzle in the motivation of states, for which new attention to symbolic politics provides a resolution.

To assess the value of a non-permanent seat, we need to compare the decision-making influence of non-permanent members in the Council to that of non-members. Recent changes in the Council's working methods have diminished the difference between the two, and this has come about by several means. As already noted, power over the agenda has been somewhat diffused to all members, but more important is the increase in consultation between the permanent members and states not formally involved with the Council at all.[26] The form of consultation that has been most institutionalized is that with the states that contribute material to peacekeeping missions. Extensive rules are now in place to regularize contact between the troop-contributing countries and the Council.[27] Other states that contribute exceptional resources to the UN, notably through the budget (i.e., Germany and Japan) have also developed something like "quasi-membership" on the Council by virtue of their frequent and substantial participation in Council consultations, whether or not they are in a non-permanent seat. In addition, certain groups of states, such as the Non-Aligned movement, have extensive consultations between their members that have a Council seat and the rest in the General Assembly. Still others participate less often but perhaps more visibly, in the shape of

---

[26] Hurd 1997.
[27] See S/PRST/1994/22, May 3, 1994; S/PRST/1994/62; A/49/621; A/RES/49/37; and S/PRST/1996/13.

being invited to Council debates without a vote when their interests are at stake. Such invitations are far more common today than in the past and have become routine. Perhaps one-third of all official Council meetings now involve the formal participation of non-Council members. Generally the greater participation by non-members has increased dramatically since the early history of the United Nations, and the special privileges of membership have been devalued (except, of course, for permanent members with vetoes).

In addition to the increased consultation between non-members and the Council, a second movement has widened the gap between the permanent five and the non-permanent members. The real work of the Council takes place more and more among the permanent five themselves in "informal sessions" (which, because they are not official Council meetings, do not need to be open to the non-permanent members or to the public and do not in a strict sense even exist as Council meetings).[28] Almost every formal Council meeting now is a pro forma affair, scripted in these advance informal consultations. The president of the Council now almost invariably notes when opening an official meeting that "the Security Council is meeting in accordance with the understanding reached in its prior consultations."[29] As the distance between the permanent five and the non-permanent members has grown, and that between the non-members and the non-permanent members has diminished, the distinction between non-members and non-permanent members has doubly declined. This reduces the value of a non-permanent seat to aspiring states.

In summary, the effective decision-making power in the Council is monopolized by the permanent five: substantive decisions cannot be made without their active or passive assent, and proposals not expected to win that assent are generally not even introduced. Where the permanent five choose to include others in this process, they do not exclusively choose from among the Council's non-permanent members. They also bring in non-members who have something to contribute to the decision, such as troops, money, or special interests. While the permanent members control both first- and second-face power in the Council, the difference in decision-making power between non-members and non-permanent members is declining. Thus we cannot look for the value of a non-permanent seat in terms of a state's ability to make or break Council decisions in accord with the state's interests.[30] Yet competition for access to these seats is increasing.

[28] For a good discussion, see Bailey and Daws 1998, chap. 2.
[29] This phrase appears in the opening paragraph of the provisional record of nearly every Council meeting. See, for instance, S/PV.3848, January 14, 1998.
[30] O'Neill 1997.

The energy and resources states spend trying to get elected to a non-permanent seat is considerable and apparently is increasing. Candidate states often announce their intentions to run years in advance, set aside other diplomatic appointments, and mount elaborate and expensive campaigns in New York and foreign capitals.[31] The enthusiasm to be a non-permanent member extends even to very small states that lack the diplomatic capacity or budget to fulfill its requirements.[32] The election of states in the "Western Europe and Others Group" (WEOG) category in 1998 marked a new intensity in competition, which has since spread through the other regional groups. The 1998 campaign, in which self-styled candidates Canada, Greece, and the Netherlands competed for one seat, was more brazenly laced with gift giving and lobbying for votes than was considered normal at the time. The Netherlands invited voting delegates to performances of the Royal Concertgebouw Orchestra of Amsterdam and took them on cruises of the East River; Canada, which ran a four-year campaign costing an estimated CDN$1.9 million, sent retired diplomats and academics to lobby governments in nearly a hundred countries and, at the end of the campaign, gave ambassadors free tickets to a performance of the Cirque du Soleil in New York; and Greece hosted a week-long cruise in the Aegean for 120 UN delegates and their families.[33] Earlier campaigns in this and other groups have also been extravagant, including "brown envelopes left in hotel rooms during junkets," but new levels appear to have been reached in 1998.[34] As one official put it, "Potential candidates for non-permanent seats seem undiscouraged by the apparent stranglehold exerted on Council business by its five permanent members . . . [and] membership in the Council is seen at the UN in the late 1990s as more of a prize than ever."[35]

Why is it a prize at all? What is the payoff to these election campaigns, particularly for states such as those in the WEOG that are already in a position to consult with the Council because of their roles in peacekeeping operations or elsewhere? On the Canadian campaign in 1998, David Malone has addressed the "Why bother?" question, and finds three main reasons why states pursue membership.[36] First, membership may provide an opportunity to influence the course of debate on an issue of concern. For example, Morocco, during its term between 1992 and 1993, was able to exert "considerable leverage" over the Council's position on the Western

[31] Malone 2000.

[32] Ibid.

[33] *Ottawa Citizen*, October 8, 1998, p. H4; *Financial Times*, October 9, 1998, p. 4; Malone 2000.

[34] *New York Times*, August 2, 1998, p. 4.

[35] Malone 2000, 3.

[36] Ibid., 5–7.

Sahara conflict because it had access unavailable to its rival, the Polisario Front. Malone believes, however, that it is generally unrealistic for states to expect to be active decision makers, given the distribution of power in the Council. Second, if concrete decision-making power is unavailable, states may attempt to press "themes" on the Council from the backbenches, such as Canada's theme of "human security" in the 1999–2000 term. "So far," Malone says, "striking results on this front have been few."[37]

Finally, there is the dominating motive of "prestige." Given the unsavory nature of much of the campaigning, Malone contends that "international prestige should almost certainly not be measured through the outcome of such contests, but to a considerable extent it is so assessed in New York."[38] Winning means that the status and prestige of the state's diplomats increases, in New York and around the world; the state enters into a position of prominence, even if not of actual power, should a world crisis arise; and the state knows that it is in a position that other states envy. This last point is important: the symbolic value of a seat comes precisely because it is sought by others; it comes from outside. O'Neill defines the term by saying that "someone possesses *prestige* if the members believe that the person is generally admired in the group. . . . One way to gain prestige is by winning a symbolic contest."[39] Leading the "space race" or hosting the Olympics, he suggests, is comparable to winning a non-permanent seat in the Council. This prestige also has an important domestic dimension. Winning a seat is a diplomatic success that can be useful to a government for domestic purposes. It implies that the government is internationally respected and prominent, and has the ear of the powerful. Of course, this carries the danger that a failed candidacy might become a domestic embarrassment. For this reason, Malone points out, governments tend to delegate the most strenuous and high-profile lobbying for votes—the "heavy slogging"—to their foreign ministers and officials, thus preserving a useful distance for the head of government should the campaign fail.[40]

What a Security Council non-permanent seat is to established states, a General Assembly seat is to "new" states: a source of authority by association. It confers prestige and recognition on an actor and allows it to appropriate some of the authority derived from the legitimacy of the institution. Even if a state's real gain in influence over decisions or access is minimal as a result of winning a non-permanent seat, the increase in its status and visibility is significant. The activities of non-permanent members are generally on the order of raising points of interest in discussions,

[37] Ibid., 7.
[38] Ibid., 18.
[39] O'Neill 1999, 193, 195.
[40] Malone 2000, 9.

learning about the views of others and the leanings of the Council on given issues, and enjoying the overall appearance of being at the center of important undertakings. The Canadian foreign minister said recently of the contribution of the non-permanent members, "Clearly the permanent five have a privileged position but it doesn't stop the other non-permanent members from saying what they want to say, being in the Security Council when the issues are discussed, and using that as a forum to reach out."[41] These are important not because they give states influence over outcomes but they provide an opportunity for states to enhance their status. The gap between the decision power in the Council, which is vested in the permanent members and those they choose to consult, and the enthusiasm among potential non-permanent members is bridged when one recognizes the symbolic power that accrues to the elected members.

The formal membership of the Council does not exhaust the opportunities for states to be participants in its debates and operations. Non-members of the Council make their influence felt in informal consultations with members and as invited speakers in formal deliberations.[42] The erosion of the distinction between members and non-members, encouraged by the increase in informal consultations prior to Council meetings, has provided an even greater opportunity for the views of non-members to be included.[43] The active presence of non-members in formal and informal Council deliberations makes it more difficult to sustain the criticism that the Council is losing its effectiveness because its membership no longer reflects the "realities" of the distribution of power among states. The power of this criticism only becomes clear when we distinguish between *membership* in the Council and *participation* in its work.[44] Measured in terms of participation, it is likely that Council decisions do indeed take into account, even if only informally, the views of the largest or wealthiest or most militarist states depending on the question at hand.[45] Formal membership provides something to a state which mere informal participation does not. To say that a non-member state is consulted by the Council so that its practical position is similar to that of a member of the Council is clearly insufficient for those lobbying for a seat in the chamber.

[41] *Ottawa Citizen*, October 9, 1998, p. A1.

[42] Non-members of the Council may request space to speak at Council meetings, and the request is generally approved as a matter of course. The "invitation" really comes from the invited, not the Council.

[43] Hurd 1997.

[44] On participation and legitimacy in the Council, see Picco 1995.

[45] The metric used to determine which states are the most "important" for a given decision, and thus which ones must be included for a decision to have legitimacy, is itself an interesting and flexible construction. See also Hurd 1997.

For non-permanent members, Security Council membership is a symbolic, not a formal, source of power. This distinction is crucial to any model that emphasizes the degree to which a non-member state is "satisfied" with the substantive outcomes of Council decisions.[46] As we saw with elections of non-permanent members, a state may still value a seat at the table even when it does not imagine that its presence will alter the substance of future decisions. Satisfaction with the outcome may be less important to a state in many instances than the symbolic status that goes with formal membership. The failure of the Council to be "representative," which is at the heart of most reform programs, is therefore only a failure to the extent that the audience accepts representativeness as important to legitimacy. Thus, if indeed the antiquated composition of the Council is an obstacle to its taking effective action, it is because representation is an element in legitimation.

Many discussions of Council reform miss this point and, as a result, become mired in contradiction. The most common premise for enlarging the Council is that reform is essential, as the Council no longer reflects the "realities" of international politics. Kofi Annan has said that "a change in the Council's composition is needed to make it more broadly representative . . . of the geopolitical realities of today, and thereby more legitimate in the world."[47] Others have similarly said that the Security Council "is indisputably out of date"[48] and, more generally, that "almost all of our institutions are structured for a world that has departed."[49] This thinking is sufficiently common, according to Edward Luck, "to qualify as conventional wisdom."[50] It rests on a materialist interpretation of Council membership which suggests that the composition of the Council should reflect the material distribution of power in the world. However, the expansion plans proposed by most reformers go beyond including states whose new *material* power makes them logical candidates (Germany and Japan) and look to including countries whose presence is thought to be *symbolically* important. On symbolic criteria, proposals often argue for regional or cultural diversity or for representativeness among Council members. These criteria suggest a distribution of seats that is at odds with any distribution which could be derived from examining changes in the material power of states. Thus, in practice, Council expansion proposals generally incorporate an unstated theory of the connection between membership and legitimation that contradicts the materialist assessment that geopolitical changes have left the Council looking like an anachronism.[51]

[46] For instance, O'Neill 1997.
[47] Annan 2005. Similarly, see Krause and Knight 1995, and the essays in Russett 1997.
[48] *New York Times*, "U.N. Tackles Issue of Imbalances of Power," November 28, 2004.
[49] Brent Scowcroft; cited in *Financial Times*, November 28, 2004.
[50] Luck 2005, 126.
[51] Hurd 2008.

## The Use of Force

A third application of Security Council legitimacy is evident in the legitimating effect of Council decisions on the use of force by states. Since the
Kuwait operation of 1990, the Council has been treated as the most relevant international institution for granting or withholding collective legitimation for international war, and we now have a broad spectrum of cases
of war authorization from which to draw generalizations. Two distinct
classes of case are evident, typified by the 1990 and 2003 operations
against Iraq and by the Russian "peacekeeping" missions in central Asia.
The two are very different in the controversies they generate and arise
based on different parts of the Charter. The former are extensions of the
self-defense and collective security provisions of the Charter (Articles 51
on self-defense and 39, 42, and 48, among others, on collective security),
whereas the latter combine elements of classic peacekeeping and regional
security into a novel variant. The previous cases in this chapter related
mainly to small states, but the "use of force" cases allow us to see similar
patterns of appropriating Council legitimacy acted out by Great Powers.
This subsection looks at how two Great Powers have tried to win international support for their uses of force by anchoring them in the Security
Council.

The United States led two international coalitions in war with Iraq, in
1990 and 2003. In both instances, the U.S. sought prior endorsement of
the wars from the Security Council and, also in both cases, acted as if it
believed that Council approval was a valuable good. It invested political
capital and credibility to make the case to Council members and other
states that its policy was in accord with the UN Charter, and indeed that
the Charter *demanded* a military response to Iraq. The capital included
incentives offered to states, sanctions threatened against them, and the
time that leaders devoted to making the case. That the 2003 appeal was
ultimately futile in relation to many important states added to the costs by
consuming American credibility and goodwill.

It is easy to show that, in both cases, the U.S. preferred to have the
Council's approval: the investments of capital make sense only if a return
was expected. This does not mean that the U.S. wanted approval *at any
cost*—clearly, at some level of cost and inconvenience, the U.S. was willing
to forego the benefits it would accrue from Council support. Also, the
willingness to bear costs was lower in 2003 than in 1990. But in both
cases U.S. behavior revealed a calculation that there were benefits to be
won by pursuing Council legitimation.

Explaining *why* the U.S. valued Council approval is more controversial.
Two versions are possible, with legitimacy playing a central but different
role in each. Either the U.S. genuinely believed that there was a legiti-

mate norm that Council authorization was required prior to using international force, or it did not believe this but knew that others did. The first version suggests that the U.S. had undergone the socialization process described in chapter 2 as central to developing a belief in legitimacy: the norm had entered U.S. beliefs about its interests and was an internal motivation to comply with the norm. The latter suggests that it had not done so but that it recognized a strategic interest in using the socialization of others as a tool to manipulate them and gain an advantage. Knowing which was the case requires making judgments about the true beliefs of the U.S., or of its leaders, and is therefore impossible to do conclusively; however, indications from the Bush administration in 2003 that it did not accept that Council approval was mandatory give strong reasons to doubt that internalization had taken place, at least internalization of a norm that wars cannot be started without Council approval. But other countries must have internalized the norm for this explanation based on manipulation to operate. Only if third-party states were genuinely socialized to the norm would it be possible for a U.S. strategy to make sense. Thus the two versions each rely on internalization of beliefs about legitimacy, but the actors for whom internalization has taken place differ. As I show in chapter 6, states that have internalized international norms may be open to manipulation by those who have not.

The Russian "peacekeeping" missions of the 1990s reveal a similar pattern of a Great Power seeking to manipulate third-party states by incorporating the legitimated authority of the Council into its policy. Rather than attempt to have Council approval for military missions abroad, Russia framed its policies in the symbols of UN peacekeeping. This took advantage of the broad support for peacekeeping in the international community and used it instrumentally to further Russian security interests.

Since the retreat from "conventional" UN peacekeeping after the American reaction to the Somalia mission, it has become more common for a regional power to intervene in local conflicts under the rubric of "peacekeeping." However, because these so-called regional peacekeeping missions often resemble the kind of overt regional imperialism that has lost much of its credibility in the international community, they leave the participants vulnerable to criticism as "neo-imperialists." Russia was derided from many quarters that its regional "peacekeeping" operations in Georgia, Moldova, Tajikistan, and elsewhere in its "near-abroad"[52] were a "fig leaf,"[53] merely covering up "the Kremlin's imperialistic recidivism,"[54]

[52] The term "near-abroad" itself inspires images of empire.
[53] *Financial Times* (London), December 2, 1993, p. 2.
[54] *Boston Globe,* January 6, 1994.

which signaled its desire to return to the Russian continental empire.[55] Similar doubts about the intentions of peacekeeping by former colonial powers have been raised with respect to most of the large states, even when involved in operations that originate at the UN, including France in Lebanon,[56] and the U.S. in Africa, Haiti, and elsewhere.[57]

The general response to these criticisms has been to invoke the legitimizing symbols of the United Nations, as Russia had done. This relied on the belief that the symbolic involvement of the UN changes the nature of the debate regarding military intervention, because, as Almond says, peacekeeping is now one "source of authority to use . . . coercion or force."[58] In a purely symbolic move, the Russian army painted its helmets blue early in its unilateral involvement in Moldova in the summer of 1992. At that time the UN had not approved the mission, but the Russians evidently saw this as a way to win local and international support for the idea that the mission was that of "peacekeeping."[59] They likewise painted their vehicles white, in UN style, during the conflict in Tajikistan. A colonel and spokesman for the Russian army in Tajikistan said, "We need to do this to show that we are proper peacekeepers."[60]

The symbolism of blue helmets and white trucks is available to any actor; access to it is not monitored by a gatekeeper as described in chapter 2. But because such symbolism can be appropriated at no cost, its social power is presumably reduced. Therefore the Russians also campaigned at the Commission on Security and Co-operation in Europe (CSCE) and at the UN to have these bodies recognize its operations as "official" multilateral peacekeeping missions, and to have the Commonwealth of Independent States accepted as a "regional peacekeeping organization."[61] These campaigns downplayed the Russian dominance of the operations, and emphasized their multilateralism and similarity to the UN model and standards for peacekeeping. Through this effort, Russia convinced the Security Council to support two of its missions as official peacekeeping missions, and gained support from the Organization for Security and Co-operation in Europe (OSCE) for its 1994–95 mission in Chechnya.[62] The two missions, in Georgia and

[55] See also *The Independent,* February 10, 1994; and the *Daily Telegraph,* October 30, 1993. The essays in Ra'anan and Martin 1995 adopt the imperialism perspective. For an explanation of Russian policy, see Shashenkov 1994, esp. 60–65.

[56] Interview with Timur Goksel, Yale UN Oral History Project, p. 42.

[57] Bennis 2000.

[58] Almond 1995, 34.

[59] *The Independent* (London), February 10, 1994, p. 23.

[60] *Financial Times,* December 2, 1993, p. 2.

[61] Jonson and Archer 1996. It did the same for its force in Georgia. See also *New York Times,* May 27, 1994, p. A3.

[62] Jonson and Archer 1996. On Chechnya in the early phase, see Pursiainen 1999.

Tajikistan, were sanctioned by the Council through the creation of small UN observer missions (UN Observer Mission in Georgia [UNIMOG] and UN Mission of Observers [UNMOT] in Tajikistan, respectively) and would ostensibly monitor the military missions organized by Russia.[63]

In exchange, the Russians accepted certain Council limits on their behavior: a requirement for reporting back to the Council and the presence of a nominal number of UN monitors in the field.[64] Russia also dropped its opposition to an U.S. military plan regarding enforcing sanctions on Haiti in order to win American support in the Council for its peacekeeping.[65] Despite these modifications, in the most important ways Russia's military operations still do not resemble peacekeeping as practiced or defined by the United Nations. A review of the four main missions up to 1996 (those in Moldova, Tajikistan, Georgia, and Nagorno-Karabakh) found that the planning and execution of the operations by the Russian military violated *all* the key requirements that the UN has established for peacekeeping.[66] First, Russian military operations generally include, in the mission, troops from one of the contending parties, which violates the rule of impartiality. Second, the recourse to military force tends to come sooner rather than later, so that military force is used as the *primary* instrument in achieving a political conclusion. Third, to the extent that the consent of the parties is sought in advance at all, it is sought in the context of military coercion.[67] Although the model of peacekeeping applied by the UN has changed significantly from the 1960s to the present, the three requirements of impartiality, force as a last resort, and consent of the parties are still central to its definition.[68] None of these principles was followed in the Russian peacekeeping missions.

The Russian efforts to earn the Council's approval for their operations only make sense if we appreciate the importance of symbols to international politics and the power of the Council to transfer its legitimacy to the acts of others. The label "peacekeeping" is treated similarly to a commercial trademark: its "owners" (the Security Council) guard it jealously, and "consumers" (the international community in general) see its presence

---

[63] Both missions are described on the UN Department of Peacekeeping Operations website: www.un/org/Depts/DPKO/missions. On Georgia, see Dale 1996; on Tajikistan, see Neumann and Solodovnik 1996.

[64] Barnett 1995.

[65] *New York Times*, August 1, 1994. See also Almond 1995, 39.

[66] Jonson and Archer 1996.

[67] For a discussion of consent in this context, see Almond 1995, 41.

[68] The various modes of peacekeeping are described in the *Agenda for Peace* and its *Supplement*. Variations on the theme are discussed in Sutterlin 1995. For empirical studies that contrast peacekeeping from other types of UN operations, see Paris 2004. The Somalia operation comes closest to what we might call the "Russian model" of peacekeeping missions, which may help explain its outcome.

in an operation as a signal of the operation's "contents." The benefit to the Russians from their effort is that states not involved in either the decision to grant recognition by the Council or the conflict on the ground end up responding differently toward the conflict if the Council attaches its "peacekeeping" trademark to it. Representing an operation as peacekeeping affords some insulation against its being labeled imperialism. However, the content the label refers to in this case is not fixed, which opens the possibility of competing interpretations. As demonstrated by the Russian cases, "the term and the concept of peacekeeping are ambiguous; they entail differing, opposing, and combative policies. This ambiguity permits creative actions that can be self-serving for the states involved."[69]

The behavior of Russia and others with respect to the label "peacekeeping" helps illuminate the structure of authority in the international system. The discursive power to apply the label "peacekeeping" lies not with Russia or any other individual state but with the Security Council as an entity with its own corporate identity. This is not a legal or academic judgment but one evident in the practice of the actors involved: states behave as if the Council is the legitimate authority for making these classifications. In material terms, Russia or others could simply use the label "peacekeeping" without any UN input, essentially appropriating the authority to make such classifications themselves. This would be acceptable linguistically but would not have the same practical effect in the world, as it goes against the intersubjective definition of the symbol to which states have been socialized. Anyone can use an object in ways that do not validate its accepted symbolic associations, but one cannot expect it to still retain its symbolic value.[70] Russia's activity shows that it, as much as anyone, recognized the Council as the legitimate institution to decide on the proper use of the term "peacekeeping." This poses problems for any model which suggests that states are actors that do not recognize any authority higher than themselves.[71] The Security Council is just one example of such a higher authority, revealed not by its Charter or any legal interpretation but by the practices of states themselves.

## "LAUNDERING" AND INSTITUTIONAL AUTONOMY

The behavior of the Great Powers with respect to the use of force suggests that they sometimes approach the Council with the intention of

[69] Almond 1995, 35.

[70] Although the "misuse" of symbols by unauthorized agents or in unauthorized ways generally brings a powerful backlash, it may still provoke a strong reaction.

[71] For instance, Waltz 1979 and the entire tradition that begins by positing an "international anarchy."

"laundering" their favored policies through the legitimating machine of the Council. Abbott and Snidal have found that other international organizations are involved in the same process. Generally, they say, "activities that might be unacceptable in their original state-to-state form become acceptable when run through an independent, or seemingly independent, IO."[72] A prime example of laundering is provided by recipient states that are reluctant to accept aid from donor states that is conditional on policy reforms but willingly accept aid from the same originating source with the same conditions when it is dispersed by an international financial institution like the World Bank or the IMF. "States may prefer development assistance from an independent financial institution over direct aid from another state, especially a former colonial power or one seeking political influence."[73] Similarly, these authors say, the monitoring function of the International Atomic Energy Agency is perhaps more readily accepted by subject states because it is performed by an apparently autonomous international organization, even though all are well aware that existing "nuclear states as a group dominate the agency."[74]

The success of a laundering operation requires that the perception of institutional autonomy separates the organization from its dominant members. In other words, the organization must have a corporate identity. "Organizations must be structured—from their organization of governance down to their personnel policies—to create sufficient independence for laundering to succeed."[75] The perceived separation of the institution from the strong states that either created it or dominate it is an essential feature of legitimation, and is evident in both the creation of the Council at San Francisco and in the operation of the symbols of the Council since then. There exists in social institutions an act of collective "misrecognition" by which individuals accept that a collection of practices will be considered to be a separate and meaningful entity.[76] An institution exists only where the audience recognizes that it does, and that recognition endows the institution with powers which distinguish it from mere "patterns of behavior." At this point it has a corporate identity.

Perceptions of corporate identity transform a hypothetical or "potential" institution into an actual, working institution that cannot be avoided.[77] The corporate identity of the Council can be seen in the extent to which the Security Council is viewed as the default location for collective

[72] Abbott and Snidal 1998, 18.
[73] Ibid.
[74] Ibid., 19.
[75] Ibid.
[76] On intentionality, see Searle 1995 and Gilbert 1989; on misrecognition, see Bourdieu 1991; and on collective identity generally in international relations, see Wendt 1999.
[77] Bourdieu 1991, chap. 11; Wendt 1999.

international action and the extent to which acts of international collective action that are *not* endorsed by the Security Council are seen, prime facie, as suspect and subject to criticism on those grounds. If a mission lacks Council endorsement, it is seen as needing justification, as with Russia's ostensible "peacekeeping" operations or the U.S. invasion of Iraq in 2003. The NATO bombing campaign against Serbia in 1999 was not subject to prior Council debate or resolution, and this was frequently raised by critics as a relevant fact for criticism.[78] The Secretary General used particularly strong language, saying, "unless the Security Council is restored to its preeminent position as the sole source of legitimacy on the use of force we are on a dangerous path to anarchy."[79] Defenders of the campaign were forced to make justifications to rationalize this absence.[80] The reaction of the Council to international incidents is generally expected, even actively sought and waited for, and its absence is a recognized signal that the permanent members strongly disagree on how to react.

The question of corporate identity is particularly significant in the field of IR, as there has always been much controversy over distinguishing between international organizations and their member states. It also has implications for theories of international organizations which deny that an international organization can (or that any actually *do*) possess corporate identity;[81] that is, the evidence of corporate identity in the Council contradicts the view that the effects of international organizations can always be accounted for entirely by the actions of participating individual actors. Such a view argues that the perceptions of individuals that a collective exists are either unimportant or impossible, and so talk of an international organization with an "independent" effect on outcomes is misguided. This is what Margaret Gilbert calls the concept of the "singular agent."[82] Notably this position in International Relations is not always allied to methodological individualism, as it generally is in sociology. It often takes as the relevant "individual actor" the collective entity known as the state. Thus international outcomes are described as the products of *state* intentions and behavior, in contrast to either individual persons or interna-

---

[78] For instance, Falk 1999. See also the British Parliament's Foreign Affairs Committee *Fourth Report*, June 7, 2000, which finds that the bombing campaign was illegal but morally justified. Available at http://www.publications.parliament.uk/pa/cm199900/cmselect/cmfaff/28/2813.htm (accessed June 7, 2000), HC 28-II.

[79] Kofi Annan, cited in *New York Times*, May 19, 1999, A11.

[80] For instance, Madeleine Albright's statements in an interview that was aired on the Public Broadcasting Service's *Newshour with Jim Lehrer*, May 7, 1999, recorded at http://secretary.state.gov/www/statements/1999/990507b.html. See also *USA Today*, May 21, 1999, 6A; and *New York Times*, May 19, 1999, A11.

[81] See, for instance, the essays in Brown, Lynn-Jones, and Miller 1995.

[82] Gilbert 1989.

tional institutions. The objection, then, is not to the philosophic possibility of corporate identity (which would be the more consistent methodological individualist position) but to the empirical fact of its existence in any institution other than the nation-state. The corporate identity of the state is taken for granted even while denying, a priori, corporate identity to any other collective actors.

Laundering entails relying on the symbols of the institution to do the work rather than doing it oneself, and this requires that the powerful lose some control over the process. The weak states, as the audience for the laundering or symbolism, must in some way "certify" that the separation is real or they will not subscribe to its symbolism. Thus the creation of independence that is required for "laundering" works against the image of powerful states using IOs cynically to mask their acts of power politics. A more apt situation in which to observe this masking might be among the weaker states as they appropriate the symbols created by the strong in order to achieve entirely different objectives. This is described in detail in chapter 6 with respect to Libya and the UN sanctions regime against it.

## IMPLICATIONS FOR THE THEORY OF LEGITIMATION

In chapter 3 I discussed the controversy over how legitimacy relates to strategic behavior in international relations. The three cases presented here provide useful resources for revisiting at least two of these, those on strategic behavior and on power politics. In each case states were pursuing what they saw as their interests, and using the symbols and legitimacy of the Council as tools in their power-politics competitions with other states. The legitimated symbols of the Council were instruments or resources in the hands of states striving for advantage over others. The combination of the normative and strategic thinking shown in the cases suggests that academic IR needs to adopt an approach in which legitimacy and strategic thought are not antithetical to each other. Schimmelfennig's assumption that states conduct "strategic action in a community environment" is a good beginning.[83]

### Strategic Behavior and Legitimacy

The cases in this chapter show two different ways in which states pursue strategic action in the context of symbolic resources derived from the legitimacy of the UN Security Council. First, the countries that pursued

---

[83] Schimmelfennig 2003b, 156.

non-permanent membership in the Council, and those that worked to have their issues placed on the Council's agenda, appear to have seen their association with the Council as a good that was valued in itself. They acted as if they believed that their association with the Council increased their social standing in the community of states, and they saw that making the most of that association would advance their interests. Without a clear material payoff to their strategies, it seems plausible that the small states involved in these efforts had internalized the prestige associated with the Council into their assessments of their own interests, and so were operating on the logic of legitimacy described in chapter 2. Second, the behavior of the United States and Russia suggests that these Great Powers thought that the international community would react differently toward the use of international force if they won prior approval from the Security Council. The type of approval they sought was different in the two instances, but the underlying interest-based motivation was the same: they believed that the costs of war would be reduced because third-party states would accept war with Council sanction in ways that they would not without it. Because a clear material gain could be had from using the Council in this way, the instrumentalism motivating their behavior is apparent. However, their strategies remain founded on a belief in the legitimacy of the Council insofar as they presuppose that other countries will behave differently toward the use of force when it is authorized by the Council.

The behavior of the small states and of the Great Powers in these cases was motivated by a belief in the legitimacy of the Council and a strategic assessment of how that legitimacy could be used instrumentally to further the national interest. We cannot make sense of the appeal to symbols in the pursuit of interests if we insist on a methodology that does not allow considering both logics simultaneously. Therefore separating state motives into distinct logics of "appropriateness" and "consequences" moves us away from an understanding of these cases rather than toward it.[84] Given my argument, it is counterintuitive. It is not possible, as Lewis would have it, "to test competing claims side by side and assess which image—rationalist or constructivist—more accurately accounts for the behavior of national officials."[85] Nor is it possible to consider sequentially and in isolation the effects of one logic and then the other, as is suggested by the "two-step" metaphor.[86] Both the constitution of interests and the behavioral pursuit of strategic advantage are influenced by the presence of legitimated international institutions.[87] The utility of the symbols around

[84] March and Olsen 1998.
[85] Lewis 2003, 99.
[86] Legro 1996.
[87] Finnemore 2004.

the Council suggests that the effects of Council legitimacy are important not just in the socialization process behind interest formation but also in the observed behavior of interest-maximizing states. The behavior of states, not just the constitution of interests, is affected by the presence of legitimated symbols from international organizations, and so treating them in isolation from each other means missing important elements of each.

The difference legitimacy makes to international politics is not that it supplants strategic thought with something else. Rather, the countries in the three cases above show a combination of the strategic pursuit of their interests and the recourse to internationally legitimated resources; they use the symbols of the Council as instruments by which to further their interests. We do not have enough information to decide whether internalization has happened in all cases,[88] but the orientation of strategic action around socially constructed resources makes clear that we cannot interpret the behavior without considering the effects of legitimation on strategic behavior.

### Power

Two novel kinds of power are on display in these cases: the power states get from associating themselves with the legitimacy of the Council and the power the Council gets from controlling the terms of that association. Far from replacing power politics, the legitimation of the Council changes the context of power politics by institutionalizing it.

The power a state accrues when seen as associated with the Council is appealing to both small states and Great Powers. Access to the Council agenda is of most interest to small states, presumably since it is among the few symbolic resources of the Council that they can "afford," whereas the legitimating capacity of the Council over the use of force is highly valued by Great Powers. The contests over access to non-permanent seats described above were mostly conducted by medium powers, but in the wider fight over Council enlargement there is ample evidence that a seat on the Council is valued by all categories of states: the most powerful states in today's system seek permanent seats, and smaller states seek membership rules that maximize their chances of having a turn in a rotating seat. The vehemence with which states pursue schemes for Council enlargement that they expect will increase their access to a seat is testament to the power that comes from being associated with the Council,

---

[88] Cf. Schimmelfennig (2003a, 284) who concludes his study of EU and NATO enlargement by concluding that "it is plausible to assume" that internalization was not at the root of state behavior toward international norms.

particularly in the absence of an expectation that a veto will accompany the seat. The pattern of regional rivals opposing each other's candidacy for seats is further evidence that they attach political power to membership. This power comes not from control over the decisions of the Council but from the prestige earned by associating with the legitimated Council.

When the Council acts as a gatekeeper, controlling access to the legitimating symbols under its authority, it gains some autonomy in the international system. In these cases the Council has something valuable to confer on states, and their desire for the good induces them to offer something in exchange, most often the promise of behavior that meets the Council's view of appropriate conduct. As a general rule, this increases the sense that the Council is a corporate actor, unitary and distinct from the states that are its members. But in all the cases there is also a countervailing tendency by which states seeking Council legitimation appeal directly to the individual states and make offers that might change their behavior in the Council. For instance, when Great Powers seek legitimation for the use of force, they approach the Council as a collective but also traffic heavily in bilateral pressure of Council members. In both the Iraq 2003 and the Russian peacekeeping cases, the "applicant" Great Power offered side payments to Council members to win their support. This is generally done discretely, but when it does enter into the open it undermines the corporate identity of the Council as an autonomous actor. The complex politics behind the maintenance and reinterpretation of legitimated institutions is the theme of chapter 6.

## CONCLUSIONS

This chapter discussed three sets of situations where we find states competing with one another using symbolic resources and tools that come from the UN Security Council. In each instance we saw that many states perceived (or at least acted as if they perceived) real value or benefit to be gained from an association with the Council. The form of the association was different in each situation—from official presence in the chamber to an unofficial presence through the Agenda to approval for the use of force—but, in each, states tried to improve their international standing by winning a symbolic payoff from the Council. These are "material" benefits, but mediated through symbols, and so are different than the kind of material payoff traditionally of interest to scholars of International Relations.

These symbols all ultimately draw their power from the legitimacy of the Security Council. It is the perception of legitimacy in the Council that invests its symbols with their value, their stock of "political capital" in the "moral economy" of international affairs. Both the users of symbols, and the audience for them, bring to mind the power of the institution, and the power of the institution comes at least in part from its legitimacy. In his very interesting study of changes in the Italian Communist Party (PCI), David Kertzer shows how the symbols of the party, including its name, remained powerful in the late 1980s because its members maintained long-standing and well-entrenched beliefs in its legitimacy. Even as European communism was in crisis, and the electoral fortunes of the party were low, the leadership found it extremely difficult to change the name and other symbolic products of the party, meeting fierce internal and popular opposition. The measure of the power of the name "PCI" was the loyalty it commanded in its audience—and not necessarily the electoral impact it could mobilize. Analogously the power of the symbols of the Council is derived from the power of the Council itself; behind the symbol is the legitimated institution.[89]

The pursuit of interests is set within the symbols and institutions of intersubjective society, not separate from them. States using the symbols of the Council as instruments of power are acting as strategic rationalists in a context populated by collective meanings. They are not required, as some theorists would have it, to choose between intersubjective meanings and rational behavior.[90] As Mary Douglas says about socialization and instrumentality in anthropology, "It is when making threats and offers that individuals often invoke the power of fetishes, ghosts, and witches to make good their claims."[91] Cajoling and scheming with and against others in the effort to come out ahead relies on a prior intersubjective understanding of the values and meaning of status symbols, objects, and hierarchies so that these can be offered, wielded, and withheld with conviction.[92]

The features of a social landscape which I have discussed in this chapter such as symbols and corporate entities have an existence as the tangible products of legitimated institutions, but they also have another existence as ongoing processes or the accumulation of practices and activities, rather than objects. Institutions are the product of patterned practices and interactions, and, as such, they are never settled or final or fixed, even if they represent themselves or are represented in terms of finality and fixity. In his excellent study of the role of identity, Calhoun says that "identity is no more than a *relatively* stable construction in an ongoing process

[89] In domestic politics legitimacy is not the only means by which institutions can gain power, and so legitimacy is not the sole foundation for their symbols. In IR, of course, IOs do not have coercive power with which to challenge the preeminence of most states, and thus must rely on their legitimacy for their power.

[90] For a review and critique, see Wendt 1999.

[91] Douglas 1986, 29.

[92] O'Neill 1999.

of social activity."[93] Searle makes the same point: "What we think of as social *objects*, such as governments, money, and universities, are in fact just
placeholders for patterns of *activities*."[94] In an analogy to the wave and
particle manifestations of atoms, social institutions may be seen as either
objects or practices depending on the circumstances of the observer. They
are objects when, as in this chapter, we see agents deploying physical symbols like the blue helmets of peacekeepers, but the importance of practice
is never far from the surface. The continuance of the symbol as an object
of power depends on its repeated use and recognition as such. On the
other hand, when we take institutions to be primarily practices, as the
next chapter does, at some point we must come to deal with the institution's accumulated history, which gives it somewhat settled meaning and
attributes, and thus with an objectification. New meanings cannot be as-
cribed at will to an existing institution, precisely because it has some
properties of an object. Perhaps we are best off seeing both object and
practice as metaphors rather than as precise descriptors. Each distorts the
discussion by prioritizing certain aspects of the social world over others.
They should therefore be used together so as to avoid the impression that
either is dominant over the other. In this spirit the next chapter emphasizes the procedural, active, and dynamic qualities of institutions in order
to balance the more object-oriented approach taken here. It examines
more explicitly how states often try to redefine the symbols of the Council in the pursuit of their interests. In its effort to undermine the Council's sanctions against it, Libya redeployed the same legitimated resources
that the United States and Britain sought to use to defend the sanctions
regime.

[93] Calhoun 1991.
[94] Searle 1995, 57.

# CHAPTER 6

# Libya and the Sanctions

As SHOWN IN THE previous chapter symbols associated with the Security Council can be politically powerful in international politics. States spend considerable effort in the pursuit of symbols associated with the Security Council, and the latter gains power as a result. The precise meaning of a symbol, and the uses to which it may be put, are largely but not entirely in the control of the legitimated institution that created it. The autonomy of the symbol, manifest in the moments when it is not fully under the control of the institution, makes it important to look at the process of contestation and revision that goes on among actors as they struggle for advantage through institutions. In this chapter I look at how the use of symbols by one actor can open the way to their use by others, and how along the way the symbols can have significant political impact on the behavior of states. The legitimacy of the Council emerges as a power resource that is at one and the same time valuable to states but also vulnerable to disruption, reinterpretation, and delegitimation.

This chapter explores the strategy of Libya between 1993 and 1999 as it sought to end the UN sanctions regime against it. It compares the arguments and reasoning presented by the pro-sanctions states in defense of the sanctions to the response by the Libyan government. It shows that Libya sought to undermine the legitimacy of the sanctions regime by reinterpreting the norms of the Council and the international community. Libya was both legitimating the sanctions regime while at the same time legitimizing its own alternative interpretation of procedural justice, international norms, and select international institutions. The compromise that eventually ended the sanctions regime in 1999 came about as dwindling third-party support for the sanctions was threatening to undermine the interests of the U.S. and the U.K. in a legitimated Council. I suggest that this shift in support was a result of the successful deployment of legitimizing arguments on the part of the Libyans. This is important in explaining the trajectory of one sanctions episode and also illustrates more generally how the legitimacy of an institution can be a resource of power for weak actors, and how it can constrain the behavior of the strong. It provides a complement to the traditional rationalist approach to sanctions in the well-known work of Lisa Martin among others.[1] Libya's appeal to

---

[1] See also Drezner 2003 and Smith 1996.

"liberal internationalist" norms in its own defense show how norms can be powerful tools in the service of rational goals.

The contestation over, and ambiguity of, norms are often overlooked in International Relations, even among constructivists. Constructivists and others in IR have sometimes failed to make clear that simply because international structures such as balances of power and arms races are socially constructed that does *not* mean they cease to exist as soon as one actor "changes its mind" about their meaning. Some critics imply that constructivism suggests that all is ephemeral and that "reality" rests on nothing more than an actor saying so.[2] This is a caricature of what it means for something to be socially constructed, and it underrates the perduring power of institutions and symbols in international politics. On the other hand, it is also the case that constructivists have a tendency to presume, for argument's sake at least, a greater degree of consensus over norms than is plausible. Inis Claude made the convincing case in 1966 that the power of the United Nations lies not mainly in the application of material power in order to change states' behavior but in the ability to confer or withhold the legitimation of the international community on states and their acts.[3] Claude argued that the General Assembly and the Security Council have influence in world politics through what look like unenforceable statements or rhetoric. He suggested they are powerful because they are based on an implicit grant of authority by states who behave as if these statements are important enough to fight over. However, Claude's image of legitimacy and authority was something of a one-way street where states cede authority to an interstate organization which then "stores" it and dispenses legitimation when called on to do so. Explanations for the spread of norms based in "epistemic communities" frequently take a similar approach. For instance, Martha Finnemore's study of the role of the UN Educational, Scientific and Cultural Organization (UNESCO) in the spread of national science policies among states sees the international organization as a supplier and views states as buyers, consumers, or learners of this single, central norm.[4]

The image of a central, legitimacy-supplying authority obscures two very important processes that are central to international relations. First, it overlooks that there are always competing interpretations and sources of authority and legitimacy. The social consensus about the meaning of an institution or norm is never absolute. In IR it is well established that there are overlapping norms, and overlapping institutions, and that a state will have plenty of opportunity to shop among them. Second, the process of

---

[2] For instance, Mearsheimer 1994–95.

[3] Claude 1967.

[4] Finnemore 1993. Levy's (1994) article on policy learning is notable for putting the learner's cognitive filters and theories ahead of the unmediated transfer of norms.

socialization *within* an individual is never complete; therefore the agent always experiences some turmoil and indecision with respect to legitimacy and authority, as well as susceptibility to arguments from different points of view. Somewhere between the neorealists' denial of the coherence of institutions and some constructivists' overestimation of it lies the important but missed terrain of conflict and contestation over interpretations of legitimacy in norms and institutions. This middle ground is important not just because it shows up the extremes of the two poles but more so because there is action going on in the middle that is not going on at the extremes. We miss the action of competing legitimizing narratives entirely if we accept the view of the world from either extreme.

Having discussed legitimacy in earlier chapters in somewhat monolithic terms, this chapter works in the other direction by recognizing that communities are never unanimous in their assessment of the legitimacy of institutions. There are always dissenting opinions within the society, and these are inevitably accompanied by struggles and contests to declare the legitimacy of one set of institutions over others. These struggles over institutional authority are perhaps the most interesting aspects of social affairs, and may lead to great violence, including civil war. This is equally true in international relations as in domestic societies, and so in examining the effects of the legitimation of the Security Council we should pay attention not only to the uses of its symbolic capital but to competing efforts to define it or assert its illegitimacy. If being perceived as legitimate is a source of power for the Council, then reinterpretations of that legitimacy by outsiders may be seen as a threat to its power. Moreover, the actors against whom that power is used would do well to try to deny or reduce the power of the institution by convincing the society that the institution has lost its legitimacy or never even had it. The best place to observe the workings of this symbolic power in IR is among those actors who have Claude's "collective legitimation" of the system applied against them, that is, those states that are ostracized by the society and where that ostracism is widely seen as legitimate and broadly enforced.

Instances of UN sanctions against states make up one set of cases where the international community sets itself against a state. States in this situation—for instance, Iraq from 1990 to 2003 and Libya from 1992 to 2003—are generally weak in material power relative to the social system mobilized against them and are often facing a society largely decided in its opposition to them. They have few powerful allies and only very limited access to the tools of military strength. As we will see, however, they are not completely without power resources: precisely because of the availability of the system's symbolic resources to pro-sanctions actors, the subjects of sanctions also have access to certain rhetorical and institutional devices that they can use to try to leverage changes to the regime of sanctions against them. Of course, this leverage does not fully compensate for the fundamental inequalities of power between, say, Libya and the United States. Libya remains the much weaker power. However, it does provide Libya with a tool that it would not have in the absence of the legitimated institution.

The following sections address the issue of contestation and opposition to authority in international relations, drawing on the history of Libya's foreign policy in response to the UN sanctions regime against it. The central theme is how Libya used the symbols, institutions, and practices current in the international system to try to achieve the opposite result from that preferred by the strongest actors in the system. The rearguard action by the U.S. and U.K. to maintain their preferred interpretation of these symbols was, ultimately, unsuccessful. The use of symbols as power by the strong states leaves the door open to subversion by the weak.

The chapter proceeds in five sections. The first examines general ideas regarding opposition to legitimated power, drawn from sources and concepts mostly outside the International Relations literature. These emphasize the force of using one's opponents' claims of legitimacy and justification against them. I then present an overview of the program of UN sanctions against Libya since 1992. The third and fourth sections examine, respectively, the reasons and justifications presented by the pro-sanctions coalition and by the Libyans in opposition. Libya's strategy against the sanctions relied on recycling, in opposition, the very claims to legitimation made by the strong states on behalf of the Security Council and the sanctions regime. The use of communal symbols by the sponsors of the sanctions was perforce a risky tactic in that it meant giving up some control over the process, but the nature of the legitimated power of the Council required that they present their claims as consistent with its norms. In the final section I examine the implications of the case for the three controversies over legitimation described in chapter 3.

## OPPOSITION AND SYMBOLIC POWER

The use of symbols, institutions, and authority in the service of a political cause can be, as discussed in chapter 5, a significant lever of power. The ability to successfully deploy symbols, interpretations, and meanings in a social context can mobilize political forces and change the nature of conflicts. However, it also generates forms of opposition that differ from opposition to direct coercive force, and leaves the powerful vulnerable to symbolic or institutional overturning. Social institutions are collective and intersubjective. They are inherently public in the sense that their existence depends on widespread popular acceptance. This collective feature is the source of their persistence and their "structuralness," but it is also the basis of their weakness for it means they remain vulnerable to disruption and reinterpretation in the process of their reproduction. The persistence of social structures by repeated reproduction through practice, even those one may oppose or find unjust, provides some hints at strategies for effective opposition against them, strategies that capitalize on their socially constructed nature.

The construction of a legitimate institution is never complete in the sense that all relevant actors accept the construction, or accept it in the same way, and that it is self-perpetuating. It is always "under construction." The incompleteness expresses itself in many ways. For instance, it requires that the institution be constantly reinforced by the supportive behavior and statements of actors. Absent this reinforcement, it will collapse. It also means that different individuals will hold different interpretations of the meaning of the institution and its requirements. A relatively solid institution is merely one where these interpretations overlap more than they do in a more fragmented institution. It also means that there might be competing tendencies within an actor itself. An actor might have attachments to several institutions or norms simultaneously which could require divergent or even opposite reactions to a situation. These inconsistencies in individuals can last for extended periods and culminate in a crisis only when the actor faces a situation that calls on both internalized beliefs at the same time. The incompleteness inherent in the authority of all social institutions is described by William Connolly in terms of the "ambiguous achievement" of all norms and standards:

> If there is no harmonious unity toward which individuals and societies tend, no state which, once reached, brings to unified fruition all of the ends and virtues worthy of our admiration . . . we must expect that every operative set of authoritative norms contains arbitrary elements within it. They are arbitrary in the sense that while indispensable to this way of life there are other forms of living, admirable in their own way, in which this specific set would not be necessary. . . . Any authoritative set of norms and standards is, at its best, an ambiguous achievement.[5]

The ambiguity of authority, its impermanence and instability, suggests room for challenging existing institutions, or at least challenging the dominant interpretation of existing institutions, by capitalizing on the fissures and contradictions that already exist within them. The need for constant reinforcement and for excluding contradictory interpretations, in society and in the individual, give to institutions their dynamic nature. Each reference to a legitimate institution as a means of securing compli-

[5] Connolly 1987, 20–21.

ance from others involves two implicit statements: the first is a contention that the current situation is a suitable one in which to invoke the symbol or institution, that it is sufficient analogous to the setting of past uses. The second is a promise that the agent who makes the reference will abide by its understood meanings and limits. Both statements open the possibility of dissent and reinterpretation.

James C. Scott has examined ways in which dissent is expressed in situations of tight control. He begins with the useful reminder that we cannot infer from the simple absence of open revolt anything about the penetration of dominant ideology into the consciousness of subordinates. Often, he says, observers and historians turn to the phrase "false consciousness" as a result of mistakenly taking at face value the statements of loyalty expressed by subordinates and reading them as expressions of internal commitment to the social order. In fact, a more common pattern is that subordinates, by definition, are successfully constrained from visible actions which challenge the order, but their ideology and thinking are not. Dissident ideology is expressed in other ways, notably in "hidden transcripts" of opposition performed away from the surveillance of the dominant power.[6] In public, dissent from the status quo is often presented in terms that appeal to a reading of the "basic" values professed by the dominant actors. However, this is not necessarily conservative or even a victory for the hegemon. Rhetorical and institutional efforts to overthrow an unjust rule or decision often take the form of a claim to be making a more truthful and historically accurate interpretation of the values underpinning the institution. In other words, claims about the injustice of an institution are often made in the language of the institution itself, and proposals for redress are made in the form of a return to the institution's "authentic" values. Frank Hearn uses the reliance on "nostalgic" language of "lost rights" and "customary obligations" by eighteenth-century English protesters to make several excellent points about the "imaginative reconstruction of the past."[7] The image of the past deployed by the protesters, he contends, was more an idealized version of what the future *should* be than a historical account of some kind of degeneration from the past to the present. Opposition movements commonly base their arguments for reform on claims that the existing order is being "untrue" to itself in this way. Scott argues that this, in fact, is the general pattern in the early stages of what turn out to be whole-scale revolutions as well as more minor reforms. It is a common strategy to mobilize reform by attaching one's cause to institutions or symbols that are already accepted as legitimate by the society in which one is working. The local "language," broadly de-

[6] Scott 1990.
[7] Hearn 1975, 201.

fined as the collection of established patterns and symbols, is the most powerful reference for both reformers and revolutionaries.

Subordinates who protest in such ways may actually believe in the primacy of the values they are appealing to (i.e., the values of the system as it exists), but more likely they do not.[8] They are playing a public game in which prudence and their position of weakness require that they continue to appear loyal to the powers that be. However, this is not just powerless fawning by the weak—these appeals are significant insofar as they actually contribute to their objective of realizing change in the structure of authority. It is, after all, the superiors, and not the subordinates, who are most committed to the myths and symbols of the order, and most constrained by their logic. This gives the subordinate some room to manipulate the superior. That these constraints are exercised through words and symbols and institutions gives an indication of the power of rhetoric and meaning to structure the social world, and to mobilize actors in response.

The UN Security Council is an excellent location to observe such mobilizations in international relations. The stronger states are more secure in their dominance to the extent that the Council is accepted as legitimate, and therefore it is in their interest to maintain the Council's legitimacy.[9] But, as we saw in chapter 4, the founding of the Council required the dominant states to fight against competing tendencies to egalitarianism and democracy, and to make certain promises regarding the compatibility of the Council in action and those competing values. In the case of the Libyan sanctions, a weak state pursued a strategy of calling back into question these commitments of the Big Three, and used the rhetoric of the U.S. and U.K. to undermine their preferred policy.

## UN SANCTIONS AGAINST LIBYA

The UN Security Council issued two resolutions containing sanctions against Libya, the first (Resolution 748) in March 1992 and the second (883) in November 1993. An earlier resolution, 731, provided the backdrop to these decisions in that it defined the changes in policy that were required of Libya which, when ignored, provoked the sanctions. The objective of all three resolutions was to induce Libya into greater cooperation with the West over the issue of two Libyan nationals identified by the U.S. and U.K. as being involved with the bombing of Pan Am flight 103,

[8] Kittrie (2000) attempts to distinguish "honest" political opposition from "mere" strategic use of political symbols.

[9] This interest in a legitimated Council competes with other interests, and there will be instances, as when the U.S. invaded Iraq in 2003, where a permanent member may defy the Council in favor of other goals.

which crashed near Lockerbie, Scotland, in 1988. Resolution 731 noted four demands, which were first spelled out in two statements issued in the United States, Britain, and France in November 1991 and later pressed with the enforcing resolutions 748 and 883. These were that the government of Libya surrender for trial all those charged with the bombing crimes and accept complete responsibility for the actions of Libyan officials; that the government disclose all it knew about the crimes, including the names of those responsible, and allow access to witnesses, documents, and other material evidence; that it pay appropriate compensation to the victims' families; and that it commit itself to cease all forms of terrorist action and support to terrorist groups. The first three demands were contained in a joint U.S.-U.K. statement, and the fourth in a U.S.-U.K.-France statement. The three resolutions of the Council did not spell out these demands but rather referred to the two statements and then expressed, in 731, that it "strongly deplores the fact that the Libyan government has not yet responded effectively to the above requests to cooperate fully" and then "determined," in 748, that Libya's "continued failure to respond fully and effectively to the requests . . . constitute[s] a threat to international peace and security."

The sanctions imposed by Resolution 748 prohibited air travel to or from Libya and arms sales to Libya, and asked other governments and international organizations to reduce the size of Libyan diplomatic delegations. Further, Resolution 883 froze some Libyan assets abroad and halted the transfer of oil technology with Libya. Significantly neither resolution included restrictions on the purchase of Libyan petroleum itself or affected assets abroad concerned with oil imports and exports. Even though the Libyan economy was heavily dependent on oil revenue—crude petroleum accounted for 85 percent of Libya's dollar-value exports in 1991—the Security Council did not interrupt this trade directly because of the significance of Libyan oil exports to several major European countries, notably Italy, Spain, Germany, and France.[10] Italy acquired about one-quarter of its oil imports from Libya. (Several governments, including the U.S. and U.K., imposed unilateral, national-level oil embargoes against Libya as early as the mid-1980s.)[11] With the absence of oil and oil revenue from the UN sanctions regime, the effect of the sanctions was not as comprehensively devastating to the Libyan economy as the post-1991 sanctions were to the Iraqi economy. However, they did impose significant costs on the Libyan government and population, and had

[10] Trade data from "International Trade Statistics Yearbook 1995," United Nations, 1996.

[11] Oil imports to the U.S. were banned in 1982, and comprehensive U.S. sanctions began with Executive Order 12543 on January 7, 1986. Britain imposed sanctions in April 1984, and the EU instituted a ban on arms transfers to Libya in 1986.

an enormous impact on the status and prestige of the government in its dealings with international organizations and other governments.[12] Removing the sanctions and returning to a more normal relationship with the major Western economies has been the central goal of Libyan foreign policy for nearly a decade. James Rubin, spokesman at the Department of State, said in 1998, "It is their only international diplomatic exercise, as far as I can tell . . . to go around and seek assistance from other governments in getting the sanctions lifted."[13]

### The Sponsors' Arguments

Security Council sanctions under Chapter VII of the Charter are legally binding on all member governments of the United Nations but in practice their legitimacy relies heavily on effective implementation by states. The Council cannot force governments to implement policies that would make sanctions effective, and so it must rely on the self-motivated compliance of states. Often the mere legal compulsion to obey the Council is insufficient to ensure that states comply, and the proponents of Council action go further in providing reasons for compliance. As noted in earlier chapters, one cannot expect automatic compliance from states simply by saying, "Do this because the Security Council says so." The authors of Council action generally deploy a variety of community resources in an effort to show that the Council's claim to be the collective spokesperson for the international community is justified and to persuade the relevant audience of third-party states that the activity is legitimate. As with all symbolic resources, the legitimacy of sanctions is carefully constructed by the Security Council, and is generally strategically attacked by the government that is the target. The "construction" of the legitimacy of sanctions takes place in and around the Security Council as the matter is debated and support rallied within and outside the Council. Here, the symbolic resources of the Council are put to use by the proposers of the sanctions to encourage support.

With respect to the first of the two Libyan sanctions resolutions, two periods of discussion are relevant, one regarding the debates around Resolution 731 on January 21, 1991, and the second the debates on the Chapter VII resolution, 748, of March 31, 1992. Resolution 731 essentially called on Libya to "immediately provide a full and effective response" to the earlier four demands made public by the U.S. and the

---

[12] Libya's claims of damage are reported in S/26139, *inter alia*. See a recent journalistic report in Viorst 1999.

[13] *Federal News Service*, July 21, 1998.

U.K. the previous autumn, which were, as noted more fully above, that Libya turn over the two suspects, that it disclose all it knows about the bombings, that it cease support for terrorism, and that it pay compensation.[14] The resolution made no mention of further action should Libya fail to comply, and it did not specify what Charter provisions it was relying on for its authority—although it did contain a statement that international terrorism "constitute[s] a threat to international peace and security," which is important Charter language for justifying Council involvement in an issue.

An important goal of the three sponsoring states—the U.S., the U.K., and France—was that the vote on Resolution 731 be unanimous to strengthen the symbolism of the decision. They delayed introducing the proposal to the Council from December 1991, when it was informally agreed upon, to January 1992, to allow the two-year terms of Cuba and Yemen on the Council to expire, thus removing two likely negative votes. Of course, the negative votes of non-permanent members such as Cuba and Yemen are inconsequential from a legal standpoint (unless they prevent the necessary nine affirmative votes for a decision), but unanimity is a powerful rhetorical tool in the effort to present the Council as embodying the voice of the "international community." Yemen, it is interesting to note, did figure in the process in the end. Under the procedural rules of the Council any UN member can ask to be heard in the chamber, a request that is almost automatically approved.[15] Yemen requested and was granted time to speak as a non-member of the Council during the debate on 731 and made a statement that closely paralleled Libya's own arguments against the sanctions. Presumably this was something like the same statement it would have made as a non-permanent member. The content of the statement mattered less to the United States and Britain than the fact that Yemen's institutional status had changed so that it no longer threatened the unanimity sought by the sponsors. That the vote was indeed unanimous became an important reference point in subsequent discussions of the resolution. Immediately after the vote, the U.S. representative to the UN stated that the unanimity showed that "the voice of the international community is clear and determined."[16] This was repeated in some form in most pro-sanctions statements thereafter.

---

[14] For details of the joint U.S.-U.K. statement of November 27,1991, giving the four demands, see *The Independent* (London), November 28, 1991, p. 1. The government of France did not join this statement but did back a separate statement with the United States and Britain in which the requirements of the Libyan government were stated more generally.

[15] See Bailey and Daws 1998, 154–159, for a discussion of Article 32 of the Charter and Rules of Procedure 37 and 39.

[16] S/PV.3033.

After weeks passed without the core demand of 731 being met—that of turning over the two suspects—the U.S. and U.K. drafted a resolution calling for mandatory limited economic sanctions against Libya, and invoked the legal force of Chapter VII of the Charter. Most sanctions programs in the prior history of the UN have not been explicitly founded on the authority of Chapter VII.[17] This draft provoked significantly more controversy than did Resolution 731 and required that the sponsors (the two drafting states plus France) lobby Council members and other states more strenuously. This lobbying centered on three rhetorical themes: the threat to international peace and security posed by the potential proliferation of terrorism; the adherence to well-established community standards on procedural justice; and the need to promote and enforce respect for legitimate international organizations. These three strands of discourse established the themes of legitimation that the defenders of the sanctions would subsequently refer back to in order to justify continuation of the sanctions.

The first theme of justification was important because a threat to international peace and security rationalizes the Council as the appropriate forum for dealing with the issue. Article 24(1) of the Charter states, inter alia, that "members confer on the Security Council primary responsibility for the maintenance of international peace and security" and, although the meaning of the qualifier "primary" is widely debated,[18] it is generally understood to indicate that the Council is empowered to act whenever (but *only* when) a threat to international peace and security can be found.[19] The U.S. representative argued in the Council that terrorism constitutes such a threat and therefore "fully justifies the adoption by this Council of measures pursuant to Chapter VII of the UN Charter."[20] Sir David Hannay for Britain emphasized the global nature of the threat by noting that the two airplane bombings killed citizens of more than thirty countries: "The whole world has an interest in combating terrorism."[21] Identifying a global threat to international peace and security was intended

---

[17] Bennett 1991, 138–139.

[18] For instance, this qualification was used to justify the Uniting for Peace resolution of the General Assembly in 1950, which claimed an implicit *secondary* obligation for the Assembly to act on matters of international peace and security as a result of the Council's *primary* responsibility.

[19] Of course, in the manner of institutionalized practices, the repeated use of this justification by the sponsors of the resolution has contributed to its legitimacy and institutionalization so that subsequent discussion of the purview of the Council has been cast in these terms. See, for instance, Reisman 1993.

[20] S/PV.3063. This began the precedent, used most notably by the Council after September 11, 2001, that "international terrorism" is automatically within the jurisdiction of the Council. For elaboration, see Kirgis 2001.

[21] S/PV.3063.

to preempt the arguments by Libya and others that the dispute was either a legal one (regarding extradition law, aviation treaty law, or conflict of jurisdictions), or a bilateral one between Libya and each of the sponsors. The British member made this explicit, suggesting that Libya's recourse to the International Court of Justice was, in fact, "directed at interfering with the exercise by the Security Council of its rightful functions and prerogatives under the UN Charter. . . . Any other view would undermine the primary responsibility for the maintenance of international peace and security."[22]

The second area of justification of the sanctions centered on the strict following of procedural justice in their formulation and implementation. Pickering, the U.S. representative, made clear the sponsors' contention that the sanctions met the relevant standards in international law and norms, namely, that they were proportionate, compassionate, and a last resort: "The means chosen in this resolution are appropriate; these sanctions are measured, precise and limited. They are a multilateral, nonviolent and peaceful response. . . . They are the response prescribed in the Charter as the appropriate next step. . . . They are tailored to fit the offence."[23] The British representative said that the "sanctions themselves are tailored precisely to [the] objective," and the French called them "balanced and appropriate . . . selective and fitting."[24] In addition to being "appropriate" the sponsors emphasized the humanitarian exemptions in the sanctions, including provision for permitting flights "on grounds of significant humanitarian need" if approved in advance by a committee of the Council. This was said by the sponsors to include flights for the pilgrimage to Mecca (the *hajj*).

Finally, the sponsors promoted the justification that whatever the substance of the original resolution, it had been duly passed by the Council and had the force of law, and that Libya was therefore flouting the collective will of the international community by ignoring it. This provided a lever to move those states that may have had doubts about the merits of the Council's case but nevertheless thought of themselves as being on the side of international norms and law. The Hungarian representative, for instance, said that the escalation to sanctions in Resolution 748 was needed to defend "the credibility and authority of the UN . . . [and] to ensure compliance with its own resolutions."[25] A state that is prepared to ignore the Council, as Libya was held to be doing, was in itself taken to be a threat to the international order, whatever the origins of the original dis-

---

[22] Ibid.
[23] Ibid. On sanctions in international law, see Bowett 1972.
[24] S/PV.3063.
[25] Ibid.

pute between the Council and the state. The sponsors later spoke of Libya's refusal to comply as "defiance of the will of the international community."[26] The U.S. representative brought in other international institutions, nodding at the "efforts by the Secretary-General, the League of Arab States and indeed many others to bring about Libya's compliance."[27] These references to respected international institutions reinforced the desired image that the international community in all its institutional manifestations was standing opposed to the government of Libya on this issue. It was here that the unanimous vote on Resolution 731 was heavily played by the sponsors of 748, as it strengthened the argument that the dispute set Libya against the rest of the "international community."

Also revealing in these arguments is the concern with establishing a reputation of resolve for the Council, or for its dominant members. The U.S. representative repeatedly emphasized the "important message" being sent by the Council in supporting sanctions: that the Council "is prepared to take concerted political action against the continuing defiance of international obligations," and that it is "prepared to back up its own words with action."[28] In a manner similar to the Hungarian statement above, Ambassador Pickering went on to say: "That message is the surest guarantee that the United Nations Security Council, using its specific, unique powers under the Charter, will preserve the rule of law and ensure the peaceful resolution of threats to international peace and security, now and in the future." The behavior of the sponsoring states was strongly conditioned by their attachment to certain preconceptions about how reputations work and are acquired.[29]

## Libya's Response

The sponsors' justifications for the sanctions centered on the threat to international peace and security, the unanimity of the international community, and the power of correct procedure to rationalize an outcome. The early strength of the sanctions points to the success of the U.S. and U.K. in winning acceptance for these reasons among the target audience of states. Libya's response, in turn, was to challenge each of these themes on its own terms by presenting an alternate image of the relation between the sanctions regime and the international community, one in which Libya was seen as the defender of liberal internationalism and the U.S. and U.K.

---

[26] A/48/314; also S/26304.

[27] S/PV.3063.

[28] Ibid.

[29] These are examined and criticized in Press 2005. On reputation, see also Mercer 1996; O'Neill 1999; and Sartori 2002.

were the "outliers." Libya sought to undermine the widespread belief that it was an "outlaw" by showing evidence of a scrupulous adherence to international standards, and by showing the sponsors' failings of those standards. In the end, the progress of Libya's campaign and the stress it elicited in the sponsors created a tension in the sponsors' position. The U.S. and U.K. increasingly had to choose between maintaining the legitimacy of the Council and pressing for support of the sanctions. Eventually a growing disrespect for the sanctions among third-party states threatened to delegitimize the Council as it continued to demand respect for its resolutions.

The history of the external relations of Libya since the sanctions were imposed shows a concerted effort to appeal to accepted international practices and associate them with the Libyan government, in the service of delegitimizing the sanctions in the eyes of influential states and organizations. The government attempted to reduce the appeal of the sanctions to other states by engaging in rhetoric that showed the Council's position to be unrepresentative of the will of the international community at large and unreflective of the community's professed values. Libya did not attempt to say that the Council resolutions against it were irrelevant or inconsequential, or that the Council itself was illegitimate or should be ignored. Instead, it used the language of liberal internationalism to provide a reinterpretation of each legitimizing claim by the U.S. and U.K., seeking to undermine the tendency of many to accept these two as the "spokespeople" for the international community. Where sanctions regimes are effective it is generally because states choose to enforce them, and they make that choice partly based on their perceptions of the sanctions' legitimacy or illegitimacy, which in turn is a function of their sense of the perceptions of others in the international community. As noted above, legitimacy and symbolism are intersubjective, social goods. They are relational and public, and have value for an individual *because* they appear to have value for others. Libya tried hard to show that the sanctions were generally seen in the community as illegitimate as a way of encouraging states that were on the fence to indeed *see* them as illegitimate.

Libya's "campaign" can be divided thematically into three specific efforts, directed at precisely the justifications given by the U.S. and U.K. in trying to legitimize the sanctions in early 1992. Libya's representatives contended, over the course of several years, that the sanctions regime violated norms of procedural justice recognized in international law and in the domestic legal systems of most states, including the U.S. and the U.K.; that supporting the sanctions constituted *disrespect* for accepted international organizations and the wishes of the international community, rather than respect for them; and, finally that such disrespect was itself a threat to international peace and security. On this last point, the Libyan position closely resembles that of the sponsors of the sanctions, except, of course, in identifying the content of the violation of international institutions. The repeated use of these arguments, and the manipulation of the procedural rules of international institutions, forced the U.S. and U.K. to respond continually in a variety of settings to the contention that the sanctions violated the very norms by which they were justified.[30] Eventually the desire to defend the legitimacy of the Council itself created the conditions for the compromise of 1998, which is discussed below.

## PROCEDURAL JUSTICE

The Libyan government made several arguments to undermine the sponsors' claims that procedural justice contributed to the legitimacy of the sanctions. Libyan statements referred repeatedly to the fact that punishment in the form of sanctions was imposed before the matter was fully investigated "through judicial channels,"[31] before the U.S. and U.K. had presented "supporting evidence or proof" to the Libyans, and even while the sponsors were asking Libya (in Resolution 731) to disclose the documents and witnesses in its possession (which implied that U.S. and U.K. investigators had not yet been able to consider all relevant documents).[32] Placing punishment ahead of comprehensive judicial hearing, the Libyan government argued, violated both the fundamental norms by which most domestic judicial systems operate as well as accepted international judicial practice. This was linked, in Libyan statements, with repeated references to the humanitarian costs of the sanctions program, emphasizing the toll that was being exacted prior to official judgment.[33]

The central violation of procedure on which Libya relied was the resolution's bypassing of the Montreal Convention on Civil Aviation.[34] This treaty, enacted in 1971 and ratified by all the major players in the conflict, was intended to "arrive at a generally acceptable method of dealing with alleged perpetrators of acts of unlawful interference with aircraft."[35] The Convention holds that a state that is in possession of an individual alleged to have committed an offense of air terrorism "shall, if it does not extra-

---

[30] I am mainly interested in how these arguments were directed at governments, but the Libyan tactics were also designed to appeal to the families of the victims and to an international interpretive community of international lawyers. These two other audiences might usefully be studied separately.

[31] A/48/PV.20, p.5.

[32] S/PV.3033.

[33] For instance, A/48/PV.20. Also S/26139, S/24428, and S/1994/921.

[34] Formally the *Montreal Convention on the Suppression of Unlawful Acts against the Safety of Civil Aviation*, September 23, 1971.

[35] Reser 1998, 819.

dite him, be obliged, without exception whatsoever . . . to submit the case to its competent authorities for the purpose of prosecution."[36] The choice on extradition lies with the state holding the suspect, and in the absence of an extradition treaty between a state holding a suspect and a state wishing to try the individual, the former "may at its option consider this Convention as the legal basis for extradition in respect of the offences." Further, "extradition shall be subject to the other conditions provided by the law of the requested State."[37] If a dispute arises about the interpretation of the Convention, Article 14(1) states: "Any dispute between two or more Contracting States concerning the interpretation or application of this Convention . . . shall . . . be submitted to arbitration." If that fails, the dispute may be referred to the ICJ.

Libya contended that it had fulfilled its obligations under the Montreal Convention by investigating the suspects itself, and thus that the Lockerbie conflict constituted a dispute under the terms of the Convention. It requested international arbitration, and then ICJ involvement, to certify its cooperation. The constant effort to cast the dispute in legal terms was an attempt to demonstrate to states considering complying with the sanctions that being "law-abiding" in the international context did not necessarily mean automatically following the Security Council, even in the face of Articles 24 and 25. Because the question was debatable on the law, they said, a legal forum should be used until it is resolved. This cleanly separated the responsibilities of the Council and those of the International Court of Justice. Libya said, in 1992: "If there is a conflict of jurisdiction, it is of a legal nature and international law and the relevant international conventions set out the concrete ways and means to solve it. . . . There can be no doubt that this is a purely legal question. Neither can there be any doubt that therefore the Security Council is a forum that is not competent to consider the question."[38]

The United States and Britain, on the other hand, sought to prevent the issue from taking on the rhetoric of a legal dispute. Protracted debate on legality and illegality would take the matter away from the Council, where the sponsors were relatively strong, and give it to institutions that, from the sponsors' point of view, were less "predictable." It is significant, however, that the sponsors were not free simply to ignore these Libyan appeals to international law: each challenge had to be met on its own terms and rebutted, since it was based on a rereading of the very norms and standards on which the U.S. and U.K. were relying to justify the sanctions. Thus the U.S. and U.K. participated in the ICJ cases, accepting

---

[36] *Montreal Convention*, Art. 7.

[37] Ibid., Art. 8(2).

[38] Libya at the Security Council prior to the vote on Resolution 741, S/PV.3033.

the risk of adverse judgments, because to ignore them would contradict the rhetoric of procedural justice which they sought to promote. Indeed, more generally, the United States has a very poor record of winning cases at the ICJ and yet continues vigorously to represent itself there.[39] This practice should be recognized as an effort by the U.S. to demonstrate its respect for the rule of law in international politics, as well as part of a response to particular claims made in specific cases.

## RESPECT FOR INTERNATIONAL ORGANIZATIONS

Libya made several efforts to show that its position was supported by, and in support of, various respected international organizations in order to establish that the U.S. and the U.K. were the parties out of step with the international community. This argument, that Libya was supported by the "mainstream" of international opinion, took several forms.

Libya played up its participation as a good international citizen in the effort to limit international terrorism. At each opportunity it publicized its condemnation of international terrorism, its steps to combat it, and its sympathy for the victims. In the debate on Resolution 731, Libya asserted that it condemned terrorism in all its forms and pledged its commitment to stamping it out from the world.[40] Each year it marked the "painful anniversary of the destruction of Pan Am 103" with memorials, even going so far as to write individually to the families of those who died at Lockerbie in order to explain its position.[41] In a 1999 speech Qaddafi repeated the following refrain: "We . . . feel the same [sympathy] for the families of all the victims of the aircraft. What I want to say here is that the [families of the] Lockerbie victims have not shown malevolence toward Libya. On the contrary, they have always supported us and have thanked us for our positive attitude and stances."[42] Qaddafi also regularly called for international conferences or special sessions of the General Assembly to "study the causes and dimensions of the [terrorism] problem."[43] To verify Libya's distance from terrorist groups, he invited the Secretary General to send missions to Libya to confirm that it was not supporting activities linked to terrorism.[44]

Second, Libya publicized its willingness to engage with a range of international organizations, as representatives of the international commu-

[39] Bekker 1998,
[40] S/PV.3033.
[41] S/1997/991.
[42] Speech on Libyan television in Arabic, March 2, 1999. Reprinted by *BBC Summary of World Broadcasts*, March 4, 1999.
[43] A/48/PV.20, p. 5.
[44] S/1996/609.

nity, to help resolve the particular conflict at the center of the resolutions. Libya requested international arbitration as mandated under the Montreal Convention on Civil Aviation to mediate legal points between it and the U.S. and U.K. On the question of the two suspects, Libya offered to produce the suspects to the UN Development Program office in Tripoli or to the secretary general or to the ICJ. In its willingness to cooperate with institutions other than the Security Council (and thereby the U.S. and U.K.), Libya hoped to convince its audience of third-party states that it was not being recalcitrant with respect to the international community, as was claimed by the U.S. and U.K., but rather had a bilateral dispute with these two states, one that should be resolved through legal channels or arbitration. In other words, its dispute was with the U.S. and U.K., and not with the Security Council or the community of states more generally.

Third, Libya also made public each indication that the sanctions were being disrespected by reputable actors, even while hiding other violations that might hurt its cause.[45] Every time a state or organization violated the sanctions or publicly questioned their justification, Libya broadcast the information to as wide an audience as possible as a means of showing that the Security Council was out of step with the community. By 1998 Qaddafi's speeches on Libyan television and radio, and the speeches of his diplomats at the UN and elsewhere, routinely included long lists of thank-yous and acknowledgments to the Organization for African Unity, the Arab League, the Gulf Cooperation Council, and individual states and leaders for their questioning of the sanctions regime.[46] The rhetorical power of violations and criticism was so potent that Libya, on occasion, reported events as violations when they were not, as in publicizing President Mubarak's visit with Qaddafi in July 1998 as a violation when in fact the trip had been approved in advance by the Security Council (although under the pressure of knowing that it would probably take place anyway).[47] This rhetorical power was understood by the sponsors, and at times the U.S. government chose to ignore certain violations for fear of increasing Libyan support by pressing the matter at the Sanctions Committee of the Security Council.[48] At the same time Libya sought to conceal other kinds of violations, such as its active smuggling program through

[45] One such violation was smuggling.

[46] See, for instance, Qaddafi's speech of March 2, 1999; reprinted by *BBC Summary of World Broadcasts*, March 4, 1999. See also BBC Report, June 11, 1998; BBC Report, August 6, 1998; and *The Guardian*, September 11, 1998. For speeches at the UN, see A/48/PV.20.

[47] *Agence France-Press*, July 9, 1998.

[48] One such instance is reported by the *Washington Post* with respect to Libya's sending pilgrims on the *hajj* to Saudi Arabia without first earning permission from the Committee (*Washington Post*, April 21, 1995).

willing foreign companies. Although this activity was no doubt useful materially, it did not serve the rhetorical goals that were achieved when other parties disrespected the sanctions—indeed, it worked against them. Thus violations by Libya were concealed, whereas violations by others were publicized.

Finally, Libya took careful advantage of the openings available to it under the procedures of the Security Council and other international organizations. The Council's operating rules on sanctions call for a review every four months by a Council committee. This provided Libya with a regular platform for making its case within the Council. It never failed to do so, and carefully submitted reports to the Council in advance of each meeting detailing each of the factors noted above: the absence of procedural justice, the damage caused by the sanctions, critical statements by "respected" voices (states, noted individuals, and international organizations), and cross-referencing all its previous reports.[49] In addition to the cases filed with the ICJ, Libya continued the legal theme with petitions for the arrest of American political and military officials over the 1986 bombing of Tripoli and Benghazi. Mirroring the domestic U.S. Grand Jury procedure which began the pressure to extradite the two Libyan suspects,[50] the Libyan prosecutor Mohammed Abdel-Wahab issued arrest orders in 1998 for the former director of the CIA William Casey, the National Security adviser John Poindexter, and seven others. Mirroring the process of American claims, Abdel-Wahab said that, if all else failed, Libya would "resort to the Security Council to get the accused."[51]

### INTERNATIONAL PEACE AND SECURITY

The language of threats to "international peace and security" is important in international law, since it is the enabling phrase used by the UN Charter to define the powers of the Security Council. It is generally included in Council resolutions to justify coercive measures. As such, it was vital to American and British justifications for sanctions against Libya: "Libya's involvement in these acts of terrorism indicates a serious breach of international peace and security."[52] However, the language is equally available to actors other than the Great Powers, and in these hands it can achieve very different ends. A central fact of the public quality of symbols and institutions is this: they cannot be entirely monopolized by the strong with-

[49] These and other Libyan communications to the Security Council and the UN Secretary General are documented in the annual *Yearbook of the United Nations*.

[50] The original indictment was issued by the District Court for the District of Columbia, November 14, 1991.

[51] *Boston Globe*, December 31, 1998, A4.

[52] US Ambassador Thomas Pickering to the Security Council, S/PV.3063.

out threatening the legitimacy on which they are based. Libya's speeches in the Council and elsewhere supported the Council's authority to take action against "threats to international peace and security," and thus supported the Council as an institution. These speeches also defined such threats in very traditional terms as any coercive action that did not have the support of the international community.[53] However, Libya then turned the tables on the United States and Britain by taking the two sets of evidence just described (the alleged lack of procedural justice and of community support) to represent the sanctions themselves as the threat to international peace and security, on the grounds that the resolutions were not widely and actively supported by the community. To the extent that this argument was persuasive to third parties, Libya could contend that the threat that should concerns the Council came from the sponsors of the sanctions resolutions, not from Libya itself.

## COMPLIANCE, DEFECTION, AND THE 1998 COMPROMISE

The sanctions on Libya were at first relatively well respected, even among states one might expect would not have supported them such as Egypt, Iran, and several North African states. There are several reasons for this. First, the sanctions regime itself was largely symbolic. It did not include controls on Libya's oil exports, which would have been the logical target had the international community wanted to seriously impinge on Qaddafi's interests. The ban on air travel and limits on diplomatic representation were undoubtedly an inconvenience, but the main goal of the Council was their symbolic effect in casting the Libyan government as an "outlaw." By contrast, the controls on Libya's overseas financial instruments did hit at resources of real consequence, but they took effect after Libya had had time to rearrange its finances in order to minimize the damage.[54] Second, the sanctions were respected in part because the sponsors were willing to use (or threaten to use) their leverage against third-party states to gain their acquiescence. Finally, the sanctions earned some respect in that they were duly promulgated by the Security Council, lending procedural legitimacy which in itself is an argument in favor of compliance. In all, international respect for the sanctions was judged to be relatively good in the early years.[55] Libya's international trade was disrupted: even without oil in the sanctions regime, Libya's total exports fell in the

[53] See, for instance, Libya's statements before the vote on resolution 731 in S/PV.3033, and on 748 in S/.PV3063.

[54] Rose 1998. See also *The Guardian*, February 27, 1994.

[55] Rose 1998. Bray (1996) calls the earlier unilateral U.S. sanctions "relatively ineffective" and says that the multilateral UN sanctions are "more likely to be effective."

years immediately after the sanctions, by 11 percent in 1992 and 24 percent in 1993.[56] Libya also ended up selling or drastically restructuring its foreign assets and firms.[57] In addition, pursuing the normal processes of diplomacy became difficult, and Libya came to rely on an informal network of middlemen, agents, foreign lawyers, and even some unknowing parties to communicate with other governments.[58] This intermediating collection of advisers and opportunists was blamed by the then UN Secretary General for making it more difficult to resolve the conflict.[59] Despite periodic U.S. and British complaints that some states were not abiding by the sanctions, for the first several years they were in fact well respected.[60]

Qaddafi's many proposals for various compromises were rejected by the sponsors, who insisted on what they considered the essence of the original demands: that the suspects appear before a British or American court. The consistency displayed by the sponsors was motivated in part by a concern for the reputation of the Council and its backers. The U.S. and U.K. were heavily invested in the rhetoric designed to legitimize the sanctions and were extremely reluctant to recognize any Libyan overtures for compromise. They feared that accepting any compromise would provide "face-saving for Qaddafi" and show that the sponsors were irresolute.[61]

The situation gradually changed as violations by third-party states began to accumulate, revealing an underlying discontent with the sanctions, particularly in Africa. Early on, for example, in 1995, Libya probed the limits of the flight ban by allowing its own airliners to transport pilgrims to Mecca for the *hajj*,[62] and in 1996 there were occasional flights from Tripoli to Egypt.[63] These violations increased in frequency throughout 1996 and 1997, although they remain isolated incidents. In May 1997 the U.S. State Department accused Niger and Nigeria of conducting unauthorized flights to Tripoli.[64] The pace of violations accelerated in 1998. Two Italian planes reportedly arrived in April 1998, marking the first European violation.[65] Then, in June 1998, the Organization of African Unity passed a resolution approving that its members

[56] International Monetary Fund, *Direction of Trade Statistics*, 1997.

[57] Vandewalle 1998, 146. See also *The Guardian*, February 27, 1994, p. 2.

[58] *Washington Post*, October 2, 1993, A12.

[59] Boutros-Ghali 1999.

[60] U.S. and U.K. complaints are documented in a 1996 report, S/1996/606, including that Libyan Airlines offices remained open in several cities and that Libyan diplomatic representation had in some locations increased since 1992.

[61] *International Herald Tribune*, August 1, 1998.

[62] *New York Times*, April 6, 1995; *Washington Post*, April 20, 1995.

[63] *New York Times*, July 6, 1996.

[64] U.S. Department of State, Press Statement, May 13, 1997. Accessed at secretary .state.gov/www/briefings/statements/970513a.html.

[65] *Washington Post*, April 25, 1998.

could ignore the flight ban as of that September.[66] This institutional dec-
laration spurred an increase in flight violations. Sudan, Chad, Niger,
Mali, and the Central African Republic each flew into Tripoli in September, to celebrate the anniversary of the Libyan revolution, and the Gam-
bia sent a flight a few days later. The Gambian flight was reported to
have been a "thank-you" for Libya having paid that country's back dues
to the UN.[67] President Mubarak of Egypt visited in July; he had secured
UN approval before his trip and so it was not a violation, but in the context of the other violations it was read as a signal of Egypt's impatience
with the ban.[68]

These violations of the flight ban did not contribute a real material
benefit to the government of Libya; there was no evidence that the flights
were carrying significant cargoes of prohibited industrial or military goods.
So, although they were real in that they contravened the literal prohibi-
tions in the resolutions, for the most part they were symbolic in that they
simply communicated the states' dissatisfaction with the sanctions. Of
course, symbolic status can turn into material benefit, and this is precisely
what happened. The significance of the decaying flight ban is that it put
pressure on the sponsors of the sanctions to somehow reconcile the position of the Council with the "facts on the ground." This pressure came
from below, from the rank and file of the UN, whose cooperation is essential for making sanctions regimes work.

The growing gap between the declared position of the Council and
the actions of many states became a threat to the perceived legitimacy of
the Council. There was a disconnect between the authoritative words of the
Council and the behavior of its audience. The Council could not force
states to participate in the sanctions regime and was increasingly seen as
holding a position that was out of touch with prevailing currents in the
international community, a very dangerous position for an institution to
occupy. In this case it threatened to reveal the Council as a surrogate for
the United States and Britain. If this were to happen, the Council's carefully constructed corporate identity would be undermined and, potentially, its power in other situations. This point was well made by the Canadian ambassador to the UN who said, in 1998, that for the Council to
exercise "leadership" it needs a "followership," and, in the case of the
Libyan sanctions, this was increasingly lacking.[69] The ambassador made

[66] This was communicated to the UN Security Council in S/1998/549 and S/1998/597.
[67] *The Guardian*, September 11, 1998. There was also a report that Libya paid Malawi's
back dues in 1999, after which Malawi made a public statement of support for Libya against
"U.S.-British intransigence" (*BBS Summary of World Broadcasts*, February 6, 1999).
[68] *The Guardian*, July 21, 1998.
[69] Remarks to the Security Council, cited in *International Documents Review* 9, no. 37,
October 26, 1998, p. 1).

clear that it would be dangerous for the Council's "credibility" if it insisted on maintaining the sanctions even after large sections of the UN membership had ceased to support them. Similarly the current Secretary General of the UN has said that he realized early in his tenure that Libya's strategy was gradually winning international support: "I realized that if we didn't find a way forward [the sanctions would lose all legitimacy]. [By] rejecting every Libyan proposal [the U.S. and U.K.] had boxed themselves into a situation of being the stubborn negative ones."[70]

The "way forward" was an agreement reached in 1998 under which the suspects would be tried in a third country where Scottish law would be applied. The basic formula that was adopted in the compromise was first proposed by Qaddafi as early as 1994. At that time, on the sixth anniversary of the Lockerbie explosion, Libya took out full-page ads in several leading newspapers to propose that a Scottish court conduct a trial of the two at the ICJ in the Hague.[71] The Arab League began championing the idea from May 1996 after its secretary general, Esmat Abdel-Meguid, visited Libya.[72] Other variants were advanced even earlier, for example, having Scottish prosecutors before the ICJ or at an *ad hoc* international tribunal.[73]

The U.S. and U.K. called this proposal a "non-starter" at the time of its first airing, and said, "We will not be satisfied with half measures [and] we reject offers to negotiate the extent of [Libya's] compliance with UN Security Council resolutions."[74] A senior State Department official said, "There can be no compromise on the need for trying the suspects in a Scottish court under Scottish law. We are absolutely opposed to any alternative trial venue."[75] Their position began to change as the rate of defections from the sanctions rose. By 1998 the cohesion of the pro-sanctions coalition was coming apart, leaving the Council in an institutionally dangerous position.

With the tenth anniversary of the bombing approaching, the U.S. and U.K. worried that their defense of the sanctions would appear to be a failure in light of the increasing number of states and organizations defecting from the regime. The U.K. was the more willing partner in the compromise, and it brought along a somewhat reluctant U.S. As a result, they

[70] Kofi Annan, cited in *New York Times*, April 7, 1999.

[71] *Washington Post*, December 22, 1994. The ad ran in the *Post* on December 21, 1994.

[72] *The Herald* (Glasgow), May 22, 1996.

[73] For the "Black Plan" of a Scottish prosecutor before the ICJ, see *The Independent* (London), January 24, 1994. Also see *Christian Science Monitor*, November 9, 1994.

[74] First quote unattributed in *Christian Science Monitor*, November 9, 1994; second quote by Michael McCurry, State Department spokesman, in the *Washington Post*, December 22, 1994.

[75] Unidentified official, *Christian Science Monitor*, November 9, 1994.

began calling the Scottish-law/Dutch-venue compromise their own and challenged Qaddafi to meet it. Once the U.S. and U.K. switched sides and began to support the compromise, they also began to cite its international support as contributing to its (and to their) legitimacy. In their letter to the UN Secretary General announcing their support for the measure, the permanent representatives of the U.S. and U.K. stated: "This initiative represents a sincere attempt by the Governments of the United Kingdom and the United States to resolve this issue, and is an approach which has recently been endorsed by others, including the Organization of African Unity, the League of Arab States, the Movement of Non-Aligned States and the Organization of the Islamic Conference."[76] This exactly mirrors Libya's earlier efforts to legitimize its position by refering to international community support.

The final version of the compromise specified that Scottish law would be applied at a court in a disused American military base in the Netherlands, Camp Zeist, which, for the purposes of the trial, would be transformed into Scottish territory.[77] The suspects were transferred in UN custody and protected by the UN while in the Netherlands. Three Scottish judges presided over the trial with no jury, according to Scottish procedures, and any prison time conferred was to be served in Scotland.[78]

The compromise rescued the sponsors from the worst aspect of their dilemma: their efforts to defend the Council's legitimacy even as the sanctions were being systematically violated. And it rescued Libya from the sanctions: they were suspended in April 1999 and removed by Resolution 1506 in 2003. Neither side had won a clear victory. Both were required to move from their initial positions and to accept provisions that they once had refused. In that, it was a classic compromise. Thus, although Libya's strategy cannot be said to have been entirely successful, it did provide third parties with an alternative interpretation of liberal internationalism and a principled defense for ignoring the sanctions. The sponsors' transition from "resoluteness" to "compromise" underlines the uncomfortable position they found themselves in as the defenders of the Security Council's legitimacy. Probably their first preference would have been to continue the sanctions until the demands of Resolution 731 were fully

[76] Letter dated August 24, 1998, from the acting permanent representatives of Britain and the United States to the United Nations addressed to the Secretary General, S/1998/795. See also Madeleine Albright's statement of the same day, cited in "Contemporary Practice of the United States," *American Journal of International Law* (1999) 93:174–179, and reproduced at http://secretary.state.gov/www/statements/1998/980824a.html.

[77] Details on the legal and security arrangements can be found at http://www.law.gla .ac.uk/lockerbie/index.cfm. Some colorful details on the transformation are provided in the *New York Times*, August 1, 2000, A4.

[78] Details in Niblock 2001.

met, as evidenced by their earlier rejection of the same compromise. Maintaining this position, however, when many smaller states showed signs of abandoning the sanctions coalition would impose a cost on the legitimacy of the Council. By 1998 the situation had moved beyond a threshold deemed unacceptable.

The foregoing suggests that there are two steps in the causal chain that links Libya's strategy to delegitimate the resolutions to the ultimate compromise that ended the sanctions. Both steps are crucial to understanding the eventual outcome. First, Libya's use of liberal internationalist rhetoric emboldened sympathetic states and encouraged them to violate the sanctions. Second, these violations induced the U.S. and U.K. to accept a more limited solution than originally demanded so that the Council would not be in the position of defending a program that existed on paper only.

Evidence for the first step in the process may be gleaned by observing the pattern of *which* states defected and which did not and the *manner* in which the former went about defecting. The initial states to defect were those with strong reasons to oppose the sanctions regime from the state. They had ideological, economic, or other internal reasons to prefer to stand with Libya than with the U.S. and U.K. Defections also emerged among states that originally appeared only weakly attached to the sanctions so that a small change in the structure of incentives they faced could be enough to tip the strategic calculus in favor of defection. For those governments, having a legal justification for defection reduced the political costs enough to change the balance. The manner in which violations were performed also supports the interpretation that Libya's strategy affected these states' behavior. The eagerness of the violators to publicize their actions suggests that they did not believe they were breaking important laws or norms; in fact, quite the opposite. They believed that, if pressed, they could justify their actions as legitimate under prevailing international norms. Libya's efforts helped to provide them with that justification.

The second step in the causal chain connects these violations with the change in policy of the U.S. and U.K. Evidence that the change came about because of concern with rising rates of defection is readily available in the contemporary accounts.[79] As Niblock reports, by 1997 "the sanctions were becoming unsustainable. With African, and possibly Arab, governments intent on flouting the sanctions . . . the sanctions regime might simply fall apart."[80] Decision makers were concerned that the rate of defection would continue to increase, and two moments in 1998 help to explain the particular timing of the policy change: the Italian violations in

[79] For instance, *New York Times*, November 1, 1998; July 25 1998.
[80] Niblock 2001, 52.

April and the anniversary in December of the bombing of Pan Am flight 103. Both occasions were interpreted as adding legitimacy to Libya's claims and thus further undermining the sanctions coalition, Italy because it signaled the leading edge of European impatience and the anniversary because it was expected to bring new calls from victims' families for more "flexibility" in the U.S.-U.K. position.[81] The compromise was settled in the fall of 1998, prior to the anniversary.

To be clear on the limits of my claims, let us consider two competing interpretations of the driving force behind the compromise. Each alternative takes issue with the argument presented here although at different levels: one disputes the very premise that there was a compromise at all and the other challenges the role of liberal internationalist norms.

First, on the existence of a compromise itself: comparing the 1998 outcome to the original demands of 1991, we see that the U.S. and U.K. got most of what they wanted—the two suspects in court, compensation, and a change in Libya's international behavior. This leads some to conclude simply that the U.S. and U.K. won and that the sanctions were a success. If this is the case, then Libya's strategic use of Council norms was at best a losing effort and certainly not worth much attention. My argument disagrees with this interpretation on the grounds that Libya made several valuable strategic gains by virtue of its tactics: first, in the end the suspects were not sent to the United States or Britain for trial; second, Libya forestalled turning the suspects over for several years, and this timing is valuable in itself; third, it bargained for, and won, written assurance that the judicial investigation would not go beyond the two suspects and so would not endanger superiors in the regime; and, fourth, it won enhanced social prestige among important international groups. This prestige came in two forms: for many states, Libya earned status for resisting Western pressure for so long, whereas, for others, it increased its respectability by agreeing to and carrying out a solution apparently based on international law and international organizations.[82] The ultimate result was much friendlier to Libyan interests than were the demands made in 1992, even though the damage from the sanctions was not negligible. In other words a compromise indeed occurred: both sides could claim a limited victory.

Second, on norms: one could accept that a compromise was made but still disagree with the causal story that I present. A strictly materialist version of events would suggest that Libya's reference to liberal internationalism made no difference to the outcome, and that the outcome would

---

[81] Ibid., 51–52.
[82] Many states may fall into both categories at once.

have been essentially the same in the absence of Libya's use of symbols around the Council. This line of reasoning centers on a hypothesis about the increase in costs to the U.S. and U.K. of maintaining the sanctions over time and is generalized in arguments about "sanctions fatigue." Haass, among others, has argued that sanctions regimes have a natural tendency eventually to erode and that the costs of maintaining an enforcing coalition increase.[83] This gives rise to a kind of natural life cycle for sanctions regimes, which is observable in this case: initial high compliance gradually declines and ultimately leads to a moment of crisis as the pro-sanctions states must reassess their commitment to the regime. Although the mechanisms by which this is believed to work are not well spelled out, one suggestion is that after a while policy-maker attention and public emotion wane, leaving would-be violators of the sanctions increasingly free to ignore the rules.

The evidence in this chapter partly supports this conclusion: rising costs to maintaining the sanctions regime were indeed decisive in pushing the pro-sanctions states toward a compromise. But the nature of and change in these costs cannot be explained except with reference to Libya's manipulations of international norms. By providing its allies with a set of arguments that liberal internationalism was on the side of violating the sanctions, Libya gave them the necessary tools to shift the onus back on the pro-sanctions states. Thus the pro-sanctions states, which valued above all their identity as liberal internationalists, were made responsible for responding to the reinterpretation of the norms. It is this response that grew costly and ultimately was not worth the sustaining investment. In the absence of Libya's actions, it would have been more damaging for countries in Africa to violate the sanctions; some might still have done so but at a greater cost to their reputations with the West. In the end, the changes in the costs of maintaining the sanctions regime were indeed crucial to the shift in American and British policy, but those costs were themselves driven by Libya's strategic manipulation of liberal internationalism.

## LEGITIMACY AND THE LIBYAN CASE

The Libyan case is conceptually complex for the theory of legitimacy developed in this book. It raises issues of hypocrisy and sincerity, and of multiple, competing, and layered sources of international legitimation. Both are unavoidable in international relations but also complicate the neat dichotomies presented in chapters 2 and 3.

[83] Haass 1998.

## *Hypocrisy, Sincerity, and Strategic Behavior*

It is entirely plausible that at least some of the states in this case were using liberal internationalist norms hypocritically. Between Libya's appeal to
the defecting states, their acceptance of these appeals, and the U.S. and
U.K. response in the Council, it is unlikely that all players were totally sincere in their rhetorical use of the norms. The strategic utility of hypocrisy
is conceptually interesting, for it relies on both a genuine commitment to
a norm among the audience and an instrumental manipulation of that
norm by the hypocrite. To explain the Libyan outcome, however, it is not
that we distinguish whether Libya's appeals and assurances were sincere—
in fact, that is beside the point. What matters is how the audience *reacted*
to the claims. Important states reacted sympathetically to Libya's use of
liberal norms, and their sympathy forced the U.S. and U.K. to respond by
altering their behavior, first by defending the sanctions against the new
rhetorical challenge, and second by accepting a compromise solution.
This is all the more interesting if the statements were indeed insincere,
since then we see the power of "mere rhetoric" to move governments.
Each of the government's steps involved trying to associate the Libyan
position with an international institution or practice that already enjoyed
wide legitimacy, in the expectation that the association would lead to a
change in the thoughts of the leaders of other states, much in the same
way that Russia capitalized on the power of the "peacekeeping" label to
change international reaction to its military operations, as discussed in
chapter 4. Both are strategic moves to take advantage of the "social
magic" of symbols, transferable from one user to another. Libya was not a
liberal state at the start of this episode, nor were those who began the
sanctions violations liberal states in their domestic affairs. But in liberal
internationalist symbols and institutions Libya found a powerful justificatory discourse that was significant to the self-identity of many influential
states in the system. This highlighted internal ambiguity in these liberal
states which they could not ignore.

The phenomenon of hypocrisy is important for understanding the relationship between constructivism and rational choice in IR theory. Where
constructivists generally focus on states that have internalized a norm,
and rationalists on states that have not, the successful use of hypocrisy
can only be explained by invoking both at once. For hypocrisy to "work,"
the actor must understand both its particular interests and the content
of the norm. This means that it cannot have fully internalized the norm.
But the actor must also expect the audience to respond only to its use of
the norm and not to the interests that it serves. The audience must therefore have internalized the norm. Unless we assume that the international
system is composed of two distinct types of states, some that can internalize

norms and some that cannot, then we must conclude that all states are potentially amenable to internalization even if some have not undergone the process for the norm in question. The constructivist ontology of the "social" state is therefore affirmed, and the rationalist ontology is disproved. But the constructivist must also account for the capacity of some states to apply strategic and instrumental calculations to their attitudes toward norms.

### Layered Sources of International Legitimation

The Libyan case invoked legitimacy and delegitimacy of three distinct institutional elements: the sanctions policy, the Council as a corporate entity, and a general set of liberal internationalist norms. Libya's strategy focused on undermining the Council's policy rather than the Council directly or the general norms of liberal internationalism. By basing its attack on showing that the sanctions were inconsistent with the general norms, it revealed its belief in a functional hierarchy between the three: the general norms stand at the apex of the pyramid, and were treated by all as the standard by which we measure the legitimacy of the Council and its policy; the policy itself had the lowest standing; and the formal organization of the Council was in between. The legitimacy of the formal organization was put in jeopardy to the extent that the Council committed itself to a policy which was being delegitimated. The threat to the Council was its continued association with the sanctions policy in the face of an apparently successful delegitimation drive against that policy. Libya succeeded in creating a zero-sum legitimacy contest between two opposite policies (pro-sanctions and anti-sanctions), and the Council's institutional legitimacy was in doubt if it was seen to be backing the "wrong" policy.

The case also speaks to the debate over proceduralism and legitimation. If the Council can be delegitimized by associating with a policy that many see as illegitimate itself, then we cannot account for institutional legitimacy entirely as a function of following correct procedures. The negotiation history of the Charter presented in chapter 4 emphasized a proceduralist origin for legitimacy, but the Libya case shows that even without states making claims about procedural violations the Council can face delegitimation based on the status of its outputs. The proceduralist conclusions of chapter 4 should be tempered by the acknowledgment that the legitimacy of the Council is in some measure controlled by the political uses to which states put its authority. Both the substance of these uses and the procedures followed to gain them have potential consequences for state beliefs about the legitimacy of the Council as an institution.

*Power*

The legitimacy of any of the three institutional levels can be used by states as instruments of power, but the existence of multiple levels suggests three interesting features about that power: these relate to autonomy, disruption, and forum shopping. First, those individuals who hold a genuine commitment to a symbol are often in a position of relative weakness next to others who do not but who are willing to manipulate them strategically.[84] In terms borrowed from above, there is greater freedom of action for the hypocrite than for the true believer, although we should remember that one does not *choose* which of these categories to belong to. Second, and as a consequence, once the dominant powers have come to rely in part on a legitimated institution to provide order in the international system, they have set a difficult task for themselves: their influence thereafter relies on a perpetual effort to maintain and police the legitimacy of the institution. This often requires action and statements they would rather have avoided. Once hitched to the rhetoric of due process and community support, the sponsors could not ignore Libya's statements and actions that appealed to these same principles but interpreted them differently. As Scott says, "Any ruling group, in the course of justifying the principles of social inequality on which it bases its claims to power, makes itself vulnerable to a particular line of criticism. . . . Every publicly given justification for inequality thus marks out a kind of symbolic Achilles heel where the elite is especially vulnerable."[85] This creates opportunities for subordinates to challenge the status quo. That an institution is a process that is never complete means there is "enabling power" for subordinate actors to intervene in the process and to shape the course of the reproduction of the institution.[86]

Power exercised through the mediating devices of institutions and language is vulnerable to disruption by strategies that employ those same devices and append new interpretations. Access to these resources is not necessarily distributed in the same proportion as material coercive resources. Actors that have little material power may have leverage in the symbolic and institutional fields against those that do. As a result, one may use the system's own institutional channels for opposition. This puts the onus on those working within the system to respond thoroughly to each challenge. Failure to respond or to respond without due process throws the charge of acting illegitimately back on those who have the strongest attachment to the rules in the first place, which can often help

[84] Schimmelfennig 2003a.
[85] Scott 1990, 103, 105.
[86] Judith Butler (1997, 94) develops this point with reference to openings for contestation in the construction of individual subjectivity.

the opponent's cause. The repeated legitimations required to justify the Council since its founding and to defend the Libyan sanctions resulted in the U.S. and U.K. having to commit to claims which were then available for others to use against them. The symbols which activate the authority of institutions are available to all participants, and their limits make claims even on the strong. When the strong cross those limits, they may damage the power of the institution. For this reason, to call the Council "a kingdom of words," as a former Lebanese ambassador to the UN did, is not to denigrate it or suggest its inferiority to other, presumed "kingdoms of action." The ambassador used that phrase as a term of respect for the Council, recognizing that symbols and language are at the bottom of political conflicts and that the Council is a key location for their use.[87]

The Libyan strategy conforms to what we know from other sources about resistance to legitimated authority. Sociologists and anthropologists report that resistance works best when presented in terms borrowed from the language of the authority. For instance, James Epstein has shown how the popular radicals in England in the late eighteenth and early nineteenth centuries relied on the established traditions of English constitutionalism to make their case for reform or revolution. The rhetoric of the new and competing idiom of Thomas Paine and the American and French revolutions was present but secondary to "the borrowed language of the past."[88] Epstein says, "What is striking about the early-nineteenth-century British political reasoning, both elite and popular, is how rooted debate remained within a discourse about the 'real' meaning of the English constitution."[89] In similar terms, the Puritans of the English Revolution first declared their grievances in a Petition of Right, recalling the Magna Carta.[90] The Libyan strategy could be used as a handbook for the modern internationalization of this advice: Libya tried persistently to show that the sanctions regime was at odds with certain professed values, namely the international community of procedural justice, respect for international organizations, and avoiding harm to innocents, and they presented themselves as upholding these values. Whatever the sincerity of the arguments, this strategy was extremely useful.

Finally, the evidence presented in this chapter suggests that there are multiple locations in the international system where actors might find legitimated institutions through which to press their interests. There is room for opposition to international authority precisely because, in the

---

[87] Interview with Ghassan Tueni by Jean Krasno for the Yale-UN Oral History Project, 1998. Transcript on deposit with Sterling Memorial Library, Yale University, New Haven, Conn. Inis Claude (1967, 88–90) made a similar point.

[88] Epstein 1994, 4.

[89] Ibid., 9.

[90] Hendel 1958, 12.

complex and fluid political structure of the international system (not to be mistaken with anarchy), many "official" channels are open for legitimating one's actions. Forum shopping is to be expected among them. These might include the Security Council, the International Court of Justice, regional groups, and citizen networks. Each has a specialization, which means that each has different costs and consequences and interpretations, and also invokes a different (but overlapping) network of symbols, rhetoric, and justifications. We see evidence, in the Libyan case, of a hierarchy among international sources of legitimation, and this could structure how forum shopping works. Appeals to superordinate institutions may trump lower ones, but the legitimacy of higher institutions may depend on avoiding connections to delegitimated lower-level policies.

Pluralism in the sources of legitimacy suggests that the "network" model of social organization might serve as a useful heuristic for the international system, and may counteract what we might call the "prejudice to centralize authority."[91] There is a tendency to favor unifying multiple centers of authority under a single institution, principle, or theme, leading to highly codified and centralized institutions, such as the state, and to centralizing ideologies and practices, such as high modernism.[92] International society, on the other hand, is not particularly centralized today (at least by most domestic standards) and therefore shows the possibility of a more pluralized system of authority, a one where competing visions have access to a greater diversity of legitimating institutions, even if each is less decisive than, perhaps, a single authority that sought to be comprehensive. This has peculiar advantages and disadvantages but avoids problems associated with centralizing ideologies and practices.[93]

## CONCLUSIONS

Two elements are particularly noteworthy in the interplay of Libyan and U.S.-U.K. justifications. First, Libya's campaign was addressed only indirectly to the Council itself, its putative opponent, and more directly to the "international community" on whose behalf the Council claims to speak and act. As discussed in earlier chapters, the Security Council is a significant player in the social field of international relations only to the extent that it is recognized as such by states. Its existence is predicated on its being seen as a legitimate representative of something like the "opin-

[91] In organization theory, see the essays in Powell and DiMaggio 1991; and also Emirbayer and Goodwin 1994; Thorelli 1986; and Powell 1990. In sociology and anthropology, the "social field" concept of Bourdieu (1991) is analagous.
[92] On centralization and high modernism, see Scott 1998.
[93] On the value of pluralism, see Connolly 1995.

ion" of the international community. In other words, the authority of the Council depends on the illusion of its "spokesmanship" for the international community, and so disrupting that connection became the imperative of Libyan foreign policy.[94]

Second, the tools the Libyan government used were the institutions and symbols of liberal internationalism. They were the rhetoric and referents of the current international order, appropriated to serve Libya's interests. Both sides were fighting with the same tools, and appealing to the same audience, using the rhetorics of procedural justice, community support, and institutional legitimacy to convince third parties that their side represented the values of the community.

These two elements reveal aspects of the political fight over sanctions that are not evident in analyses of sanctions that do not begin with the question of legitimacy. The work of Lisa Martin, for instance, is complementary to the analysis presented in this book and is not contradicted by it, but does leave open many important questions about the reasons for her findings. Martin presents a large-$n$ study of multilateral economic sanctions and many notable correlations: sanctions are more effective (in the sense of being more broadly accepted and enforced) when the lead "sender" of the sanctions bears large and public costs by engaging the sanctions, when an international institution calls for the regime as opposed to when it is championed by a single (even powerful) state, and when the number of other states participating is larger rather than smaller.[95] She treats these in terms of signaling games among rational actors, where states that are considering applying sanctions are anxious for credible evidence that others will also be participating in the sanctions regime. For Martin, community support for sanctions is important because it signals to others that the material costs of participating are widely shared.

The approach taken in this chapter complements and extends the materialist-rationalist model that Martin pursues, without assuming that the alternative to rational models are models of irrational behavior by "rogue states."[96] If we wish to impose a model of rational behavior on this process of attempting to delegitimize an institution, we might say that Libya was pursuing a rational interest in having the sanctions ended,

---

[94] On "spokesmanship," see Bourdieu 1991.

[95] Two variables, "declining American hegemony" and strong states ganging up on unstable and poor states, were found to be not significant to her model (Martin 1992).

[96] Margaret Doxey (1996, 45) begins her assessment of the Libyan case by noting that "Libya is a maverick state" and thereby infers that little can be predicted or understood about Qaddafi's motives or behavior. This would seem to presume that "irrationality" is the relevant alternative to Martin's rational-actor assumption. This misses out on more sophisticated approaches to what constitutes "rational" behavior.

and its behavior around the Council was a rational strategy for achieving that goal. This would accord with Martin's approach. However, the resources Libya used were provided by the international community in the form of meanings and symbols derived from the legitimacy of the United Nations. They were already constituted with the power to effect Bourdieu's "social magic." Libya's rational behavior took place in the context of these intersubjective power resources, and the strategy it employed can be used to say more about questions on which rational models are silent: Why was the Security Council the location for this dispute? Why did the sponsors anchor their goal of coercing Libya on the foundation of a Council resolution and the rhetoric of community support? Why did Libya's response take the form of claims to procedural justice and respect for international law? In other words, how were states' "interests" and the power resources available to them constructed?

Understanding Libya's response requires that we consider the socially constructed environment, and its intersubjective content of symbols, language, and institutions, alongside the strategic rational actor that is the state. The resources available to the state, the means at its disposal, and even the ends it pursues cross the conventional distinctions in IR between rationalist, realist, and constructivist concerns. The actions of states, and perhaps even the *existence* of states, depend on their participation in the creation and exchange of social goods with others. The tools that are available to a state in the pursuit of an objective depend on what others will recognize as appropriate means of conducting foreign policy, which in turn depends on a prior legitimization of certain institutions and practices as appropriate. The power of a Security Council resolution, and its utility in achieving a goal, is constructed out of the legitimacy of the body. As we have seen, this means that its power is also vulnerable to disruption by actions that reinterpret or challenge that legitimacy.

# CONCLUSIONS

# CHAPTER 7.

# Legitimacy and Sovereignty

THIS CHAPTER REVIEWS the arguments and evidence of the preceding chapters. It revisits the controversies about legitimacy presented in chapter 3 and considers how the evidence about the Council can help resolve them, and then draws implications from the project for both IR theory and for the practice of international diplomacy and institutional design. These two strands combine to show that the presence of a legitimated Security Council implies that sovereignty exists in the international system in a location other than the traditional form of the sovereign state.

The three controversies on legitimation involve how legitimation takes place; what effect legitimation has on strategic behavior; and how legitimation affects the power relationship between strong and weak actors. The findings from previous chapters allow us to conclude that legitimation does not simply turn strong states into hegemons and weak states into passive followers. Rather, legitimation can simultaneously strengthen the rules by which strong states seek to govern while also putting constraints on the freedom of action of both the strong and the weak. The findings also suggest that it was the deliberative procedure of the San Francisco conference and not favorable outcomes or fairness that legitimized the Council in its formative stage. Finally, the evidence shows that legitimacy in international relations cannot be adequately studied by approaches that adopt either the "logic of consequences" or the "logic of appropriateness" model. Instead, it supports an empirical research program that applies Wendt's work on agent structure to the study of states and international norms.[1]

All this points to important issues that can be addressed in future research. First, we have seen that strong states can gain by clever manipulation of legitimated rules but they must attend to the possibility that the rules may be reinterpreted by other actors in unfavorable ways. This is important for the design of new international organizations, and below I consider the special case of international courts. Second, the findings suggest that international organizations exhibit sovereignty when states see them as legitimate. Sovereignty is a category usually reserved to describe states and their right to noninterference by other states. But since the concept rests on the idea of legitimated authority over territories and populations, when nonstate institutions are in a position to wield such authority

[1] Wendt 1987.

it is a signal that the powers the term refers to are not exclusively contained within states. Sovereignty can be found at multiple locations in the international system, including at the Security Council.

## CONTROVERSIES

### *The Making of Legitimacy in the Council*

The legitimation problems of new organizations are notoriously challenging. Without a track record of success to give it a reputation, a new organization has a great need to be seen as legitimate but lacks the institutional power to establish itself. The Security Council was no exception, and, indeed, it presented its sponsors with a doubly hard case for legitimation: for one thing, all the powers of the Council depended on others seeing it as legitimate, as it possessed no independent means of coercion; for another, its structure contained an essential contradiction between the principle of equality and the reality of an unequal voting structure. The tension between formal equality and voting inequality was a problem for the sponsors, and how they approached that problem is instructive for students of legitimation.

Chapter 3 outlined several positions in the general debate about how legitimation is accomplished for institutions, and the evidence from San Francisco sheds light on these arguments. The episode provides some support for the claim that procedural correctness is a strong legitimizing force but little support for the "fairness" school. However, it can provide no conclusive answer about the relative impact of favorable outcomes and procedural correctness, because the case does not allow for cleanly separating the two.

First, the very design of the conference is a strong indication that the Great Powers believed that legitimation was crucial to establishing the new organization. The sponsors conceived of the San Francisco conference partly as a way to generate the belief among the rank-and-file states that the new organization, and the Council within it, was legitimate and therefore deserved their respect. Chapter 4 demonstrated that the Great Powers arrived at San Francisco committed to avoiding any significant changes to the draft Charter. They successfully resisted every pressure to weaken their broad powers of veto over all collective actions on international security. Given that they knew they would not concede on the substance of the matter, and given that their pre-conference intelligence told them that concessions would likely be unnecessary,[2] the best explanation

---

[2] Daws 2004; Schlesinger 2003.

of their motivation in holding the conference was to give the small states a chance to air their views. The sponsors were eager to encourage deliberation over the draft Charter as long as they controlled its terms so that no substantive changes were possible; the rules of procedure of the meetings were designed to allow debate but to make changes very difficult. Legitimation was the main purpose of the conference.

Second, the hypothesis that "fairness" generates legitimacy finds little support in the evidence from San Francisco. Neither the ground rules of the conference nor the contents of the draft Charter were seen as particularly "fair" in the sense of treating all participants equally, but this did not produce much controversy. The sponsors had special privileges in the procedures of the conference, and the Great Powers were guaranteed special powers in the Council itself. The complaint of "unfairness" of procedure or of substance was rarely made in the course of the conference. Complaints about *inequality* were raised from time to time but not in the language of fairness.

Finally, the role played by the conference procedures is important at San Francisco. The small states used the openings available to them under the rules of procedure of the conference to express their opposition to the veto, but once these openings were exhausted the small states shifted from opposition to support. The opponents of the veto allowed their opposition to be contained within the procedural bounds set by existing understandings about how international conferences should be organized. They did not continue to pursue their preferences through other channels. That the substantive interests of the small states in reducing the veto were not satisfied and yet these states embraced the outcome works against the favorable-outcomes hypothesis on legitimation presented in chapter 3. What legitimized the outcome was not any substantive concession to the interests of the opponents on the part of the Great Powers.

It is implausible that the opposition expressed by the small states at the conference was merely a ploy to win a better deal on Council voting. There is no evidence that the small states were insincere in their public statements against the veto or in the amendments they proposed. They were not playing a game by holding up the conference to see if the Great Powers would concede. Rather, in all likelihood the small states were sincerely expressing their preferences for a Council with a more limited veto right for permanent members, but when this proved impossible they accepted the draft as it was presented to them. The difference is important because had their opposition been sincere, then their eventual support for the Charter would have to be accounted for by something other than their realization that they would not win a better deal. The best interpretation available from the evidence in chapter 4 is that the small states valued the opportunity to voice their opinions and, whether or not they won on the substance, they were prepared to respect the results of the conference. This was true even though the procedures of the conference favored the sponsoring states, and even though the Great Powers enhanced their own advantage by threatening to use their political leverage to scuttle the whole process if their veto was diminished.

That said, the San Francisco evidence is not strong enough to distinguish definitively between the procedural and favorable-outcomes hypotheses. In that regard, the main debate from chapter 3 remains unresolved. Because many small states were eager to see the United Nations established as an institution, we cannot neatly isolate the relative contribution to the ultimate agreement of the legitimizing effects of the deliberative process from the overriding desire of delegations to see the conference succeed. Apparently both effects were important in the process that led to approval of the UN Charter: it was significant that the substance of the document was compatible with the basic demands of the participating states, but all participants felt that the opportunity to deliberate on the document, even without the expectation of significant concessions, was crucial to having it accepted by the delegations.

Intertwining these strands of evidence, we can conclude that it was essential to the legitimation of the Council that the rank-and-file states were offered a public forum at which they could debate the draft Charter according to conventional procedures of conference diplomacy. The San Francisco conference provided opponents of the veto the opportunity to express their opinions, propose changes, and vote on amendments. These deliberative mechanisms were valued by the small states, even in the absence of any real expectation that they would lead to substantive changes in the draft. This does not mean that other factors were not important to the outcome, but it does show that we cannot understand the process of negotiation, or the changes in the positions of the small states, without attention to the decisive role played by the legitimation that resulted from it and the prior legitimacy of the conference procedures. In this case of international institutional design, legitimation was central to the outcome.

### The Use of Legitimacy in the Council

The Council's legitimacy is a tool that states and others compete for the right to use. This has given rise to a series of interesting phenomena around the Council that can only be understood in relation to the Council's legitimacy. The cases examined in this book show several ways that states have sought to associate themselves with the Council as a means of legitimizing their actions, decisions, and identities.

Notable here are the efforts of states to win collective legitimation for the use of force, the desire by states to be elected as non-permanent members of the Security Council, and the value seen in having one's issues kept on the agenda of the Council. In each of these cases, great energy is spent to associate one's cause with a symbol of the Council, with no expectation that this association will change the material facts of a dispute, but a strong expectation that a change in symbolism alters the way others will act toward the situation. Since this change is a result of the underlying legitimacy of the institution, we can use it to explore how legitimacy operates to change actors' interests and behavior. In addition to showing how legitimacy works in IR in an empirical case, this reaffirms the central constructivist insight that material factors can only be understood within their ideational setting.[3]

Institutional legitimacy creates new resources of power for states. A powerful institution generates symbols associated with it, and these are of interest to actors in the pursuit of their goals. For international organizations, legitimacy is the main source of institutional power, and so it is a source of the symbolic resources available to states. In several ways, states tailor their behavior to take into account the symbolic resources that follow from legitimated international institutions, as when states strategically change their behavior in order to gain access to a powerful symbol, or when they use those symbols in a way that causes other states to alter their behavior. The first is illustrated by the Russian pursuit of the label "peacekeeping" for their former-Soviet area military operations, and the second by the American efforts to use the symbols of the Council to win greater international support prior to the invasion of Iraq in March 2003. There, the U.S. knew that Council approval of the operation would induce a number of third-party states to shift from a neutral stance to one that supported the American plans. The symbolic power of a Council resolution in favor of the mission had the potential for altering not just the reactions of other states to the operation but the American behavior in advance of it (evident in the diplomacy required to pass the resolution), the status of the UN in the eyes of member states, and the outcome of the mission itself. The failure of the U.S. to win a resolution authorizing the Iraq invasion signals another important feature of legitimacy: it is always subject to multiple interpretations, and these may be used for competing, even incompatible, purposes. Legitimation is a process.

### Contestation over Legitimacy in the Council

The political contestation that takes place around legitimacy is a sign that legitimation is never complete and never unanimous; it is inevitably sub-

[3] Wendt 1999; Barnett 2005.

ject to controversy, undermining, and competitive reinterpretation. These issues were illustrated in chapter 6 around the UN's sanctions against Libya from 1992 to 1999 over the Lockerbie suspects. The Libya case centers on the competing appeals to the Council's legitimacy made, on the one hand, by the U.S. and U.K. in defense of the sanctions and, on the other, by Libya in opposition to them. Each side attempted to borrow the language and symbols of the Council's legitimation for its own purposes. By tracing the negotiations between the two camps, and monitoring the shifting positions of third parties, we saw how the Libyan appropriation of the Council's legitimacy affected the strategic calculations of even the strongest states in the system. Ultimately, as the sanctions regime broke down, the U.S. and U.K. sensed a threat to the Council from widespread noncompliance with the sanctions, and at that point conceded to a compromise solution which they had rejected years earlier.

The Libyan episode demonstrates two important insights about legitimation and political conflict around international organizations: first, we see that the desire of the U.S. and U.K. to defend the Council's legitimacy ultimately trumped their initial policy preferences regarding Libya; second, we see how the use of legitimating resources from the Council can be a constraint on both superpowers and rank-and-file states. Great powers, when they rely on legitimacy to reduce their reliance on coercion in managing the system, become vulnerable to unexpected consequences. Legitimacy is subject to reinterpretation, with effects that are not always supportive of the interests of the strong. When this happens, the strong must decide whether to respect the new prevailing interpretation or break from the system and impose their interests either through force or with a newly targeted strategy of legitimation. In the Libyan case, they followed the former course, with the result that they reaffirmed the legitimacy of the Council's intermediating position. On Iraq, we see evidence perhaps of the latter course, the use of both force and redefined conceptualizations of legitimacy, with potentially important effects on the further development of the rules in question.[4] I consider the Iraq case further below.

The Libyan diplomacy provides useful evidence for assessing the debate in chapter 3 regarding the relationship between legitimation and hegemonic power. As predicted by those who suggest that legitimated institutions are important to achieving hegemony, the approval of the Council was useful for lowering the costs for the U.S. and U.K. of making the sanctions regime work. The collective legitimation provided by the Council helped increase third-party states' compliance with the sanctions and this added to the power of the strong states. Multilateralism made the

---

[4] Hurd 2006.

sanctions more efficient; indeed, it made them into a *regime*.[5] However, it also opened up new vulnerabilities in that power; once the behavior of third parties began to change under the influence of the Libyan counter-attack, the power position of the U.S. and U.K. deteriorated and they were forced to accept an unfavorable trade-off between defending the legitimacy of the Council and defending the sanctions regime. The use of legitimacy by the strong states to defend their interests presented to the Libyans a new channel for resistance: reinterpreting the legitimated norms of the Council became a useful tactic for undermining the sanctions. In sum, legitimate institutions may indeed reinforce the power of the strong, but this is not their only effect. They also add new forms of weakness and vulnerability to their domination. The strong are stronger by virtue of legitimation but only within bounds defined by the terms of the legitimation, and these terms cannot be entirely within the control of the strong.

## IMPLICATIONS

### Theoretical Implications

My findings, and how they were attained, suggest several promising new avenues for research in IR theory. First, my research advances the debate between constructivist and rational choice by moving beyond the dichotomy suggested by the twin "logics" of appropriateness and consequences. Second, the evidence of legitimacy around the Council encourages research on other international organizations to see whether this evidence is generalizable or, if not, what is peculiar about the Council relative to other IOs. Finally, it suggests that the Security Council is one location for sovereignty in the international system. Sovereignty is not only located in states; it appears wherever there is legitimated power in the international system. As a result, the metaphor of "international anarchy" among states is not a useful description of the areas of the international system under the authority of the Council. The structures of global governance do not just exist in the context of anarchy; they transcend it.

### Rationalism and Constructivism: Implications for Theory

This book contributes to theoretical debates in the field of academic International Relations in that it is based on a methodology that combines

---

[5] On efficiency, see Martin 1992; on the broad effects of multilateralism, see Ruggie 1993.

both rationalist and constructivist elements. This was necessitated by the characteristics of the problem investigated, and it raises important issues about how these two paradigms relate to each other. I suggest a relation between constructivist and rationalist approaches that is different than the "two-step" sequence proposed by Legro.[6] Since this relation is increasingly at the heart of controversies in IR theory, it is worth making explicit my contribution.[7]

The conventional wisdom in IR theory separates the study of state behavior onto the logic of consequences and the logic of appropriateness, and then maps rationalism and constructivism on the two, respectively. Rationalism, it is said, relies on a belief in individualist micro-foundations in social science and, moreover, a belief in a particular *kind* of individual—one that acts *rationally* in the sense that "individuals act rationally when they choose the best available means to achieve what they understand to be in their interest."[8] Groups of such individuals interacting create the complex patterns of society, including possibly some of its enduring institutions.[9] They also create the strategic environment in which individuals do their rational choosing, and so these patterns and institutions are added back into the analysis in the form of the constraints on action in future interactions. By contrast, constructivism is generally said to entail the belief that actors' interests, and thus actors themselves, are malleable in the process of social interaction, and therefore it directs attention to studying how identities, ideas, and interests are made, remade, and stabilized.[10] This, on a small scale, is the implication of the more general constructivist interest in examining "how the objects and practices of social life are "constructed.' "[11]

This book suggests that what March and Olsen present as two distinct logics can instead be recast as the "agent" and "structure" poles in a relationship of mutual constitution.[12] The effects that are generated as the two interact with each other are important, and are missed when the two are treated either as separate kinds of explanation or as arranged hierarchically with one controlling the other. Libya's efforts at the Council to legitimize an alternative reading of liberal internationalism, described in chapter 6, shows some of these effects. When the U.S. and U.K. deployed

---

[6] Cf. Legro 1996.

[7] See, for instance, the essays in Katzenstein, Keohane, and Krasner 1998; Risse 2000; Barnett 2005; and the special issue of *International Organization*, vol. 59, on socialization in 2005.

[8] Chong 2000, 12.

[9] See the essays in Koremenos, Lipson, and Snidal 2001.

[10] Wendt 1999.

[11] Fearon and Wendt 2002, 57.

[12] Wendt 1987. See also Dessler 1989.

the structure of international norms to influence how states behaved, Libya intervened with a competing interpretation of the meaning of the norms that carried a different behavioral injunction for states. The states to which these claims were directed were neither fully socialized by the structure of norms to accept them unquestioningly nor radically autonomous individual agents capable only of calculating material payoffs. Rather, both agents and structures were in flux: the meaning of the norms was being reworked, with implications for the practices that states engaged in, which then reinforced or undermined specific meanings of the norms and the actors' identities. Similarly, in chapter 5, the existence of the UN Security Council meant that the Russian army in Moldova had an *interest* in being seen as a peacekeeping force rather than as a force of the Russian Empire, and it created a set of procedures at the Council by which that interest could possibly be achieved. At the same time it limited the Russians by raising the costs of unilateral action without Council approval, which is simply the obverse of lowering the costs of action with Council approval. The rational interest states have in securing Council approval for their policies is a product of the legitimation of the Council. It is an exercise of sovereignty by the Council. Neither interests nor symbols can be understood without attention to the legitimation that constitutes them.

The politics around the legitimation of the Security Council provides little support for distinguishing either empirically or conceptually between the logics of consequence and of appropriateness, or for concluding that either legitimacy supplants strategic thought or strategic thought trumps legitimacy. There is no evidence in the preceding chapters that states abandon their strategic calculations about advantage, power, and status when they operate in the currency of symbols and legitimated institutions. Instead, there is abundant evidence that they take these institutions into account when acting. Strategic incentives remain important in motivating the behavior that we observe around the Council. At the Council we observe the hypocritical and instrumental use of legitimated international institutions and symbols in the same way as Krasner noted in his observations about state sovereignty.[13] But, contrary to Krasner, that power politics between states is partly carried out by the instrumental use of institutions should lead us to conclude instead that legitimizing and strategic behavior are mutually constituted rather than mutually exclusive. In this way the book relies on both constructivist and rationalist approaches. It treats states as goal-seeking actors that aim to achieve their interests in situations of constraint, but where the actors' interests, their resources, and their strategic calculations are all affected by the presence of legitimated international organizations.

[13] Krasner 1999.

### Generalizing to Courts and Other International Institutions

The empirical conclusions identified in the previous chapters are not unique to the United Nations or to the Security Council. They are relevant to other organizations that share with the Council two fundamental conditions: a heavy reliance on self-motivated compliance for their effects and an issue area of high political salience. These two factors combine in the Security Council and in international courts but not in organizations that control their own coercive leverage, such as the IMF or the World Bank, or those in non-security areas such as UNESCO.

International courts are among the IOs most heavily reliant on legitimacy. Courts, perhaps as much as the UN Security Council, are in a position where their influence depends on encouraging states to comply with decisions that cannot be enforced against recalcitrant states. The ICJ, for instance, has no enforcement capability and requires that disputing parties *choose* to implement its decisions, but its role in interstate disputes potentially brings it into conflict with states on matters they care a great deal about. This means that the ICJ is a heavy user of legitimation and a prime candidate for future research on both legitimacy and sovereignty. Maintaining the legitimacy of the Court requires a balance between a formal reading of the law and a sensitivity to the effects of its judgments. Though the Court has a general reputation for integrity, the long-term interests of the institution require that it pay attention to the latter. The ICJ and its predecessor, the Permanent Court of International Justice (PCIJ), are not blind to the greater political implications of their decisions, and some decisions show the hallmarks of a political concern with legitimation on the part of the judges, notwithstanding the Court's "powerful pull towards principled public discourse."[14] In the famous *Customs Union* case regarding the nature of state sovereignty, the PCIJ saw in a proposed free-trade area between Germany and Austria the potential for a full-fledged political union between the two and, recoiling at the implications, read an old treaty between Austria and Germany as prohibiting the free-trade area.[15] That reading, in the words of Rosenne, "was widely regarded as an attempt by the Permanent Court in a case of high political content to base its decision on political considerations clothed in legal guise."[16] Later cases show a general tendency in the ICJ to shy away from cases that appear to offer nothing but political trouble for the Court, sensitive as it is to the legitimation problems created by unhappy losers.[17] Also, since the early

[14] Franck 1995, 320
[15] Harris 1991, 105–108.
[16] Rosenne 1989, 233.
[17] Singh (1989, 132–133) sees the *Northern Cameroons* and *Nuclear Tests* cases in this light, and Franck (1995, 331) adds the *Western Sahara* advisory and the *Nicaragua* cases.

1980s the Court has in effect allowed the parties to a dispute to choose a subset of judges for hearing the case, designed as a way to make recourse to the Court more attractive to disputants. The use of these "Chambers," first put into practice in the U.S.-Canadian *Gulf of Maine* case in 1982, trades away some of the Court's autonomy in favor of an increase in traffic; the Court's rate of compliance is increased, and thus perhaps its legitimacy, but at the cost of reducing its institutional sovereignty over proceedings.[18]

The legitimation strategy of the ICJ in these cases is mirrored by the instrumental use of ICJ decisions by states. Claude noted that, "even when states resort to the International Court of Justice, they often appear to seek a judicial contribution to the success of their cause in the political forum" and noted the initiation of the *Certain Expenses* case and the *South West Africa* case as examples.[19] If these cases reflect a systemic use of the ICJ for instrumental purposes, then its usefulness is precisely a signal that it has been successfully legitimated, at least for some states.[20] Further investigation is warranted of the Court's place in the political economy of symbols in international relations, alongside that of the Security Council.

A very different kind of legitimation effort surrounds the International Criminal Court (ICC). Here, the legitimation problem is one of founding: how to create power in a new institution by convincing an audience that they should see the institution as legitimate.[21] For instance, according to the Lawyers Committee on Human Rights, "the authority of the International Criminal Court, like all international tribunals, will depend largely on its perceived legitimacy."[22] This problem occupied the attention of the NGOs that lobbied for the creation of the Court, and continued through the selection process for its judges. At the founding, the Rome Conference of the ICC followed a model similar to the San Francisco Conference of the United Nations, but with a few significant differences reflecting the different legitimation problem faced by the ICC. The conference setting maximized the opportunities for deliberation among the potential treaty signatories, but (as at San Francisco) within limits defined in the private negotiations among the most powerful states. The main difference between Rome and San Francisco was the much broader

---

[18] On this trade-off, see Franck 1995, 326–327.

[19] Claude 1967, 85.

[20] Franck agrees with Claude and goes further, concluding: "that a losing party in a World Court case will become the victim of bad publicity is often the only expectation motivating resort to the court" (1995, 330).

[21] "On the Legitimacy of the International Criminal Court," *Wall Street Journal*, March 7, 2003.

[22] Press release accessed at http://www.lchr.org/international_justice/icc/election/nomination/icc_nom.pdf.

inclusion of elements of civil society in the ICC process. This was necessitated by the greater contribution of NGOs to pushing the cause of the ICC in the first place, and perhaps also to changes in the "globalizing" world of international politics with new demands for the participation and inclusion of non-state actors. The NGO presence changed the legitimation exercise somewhat, in the sense that popular opinion was more important at Rome than it had been at San Francisco, but only a few of these groups had real power to derail the process, and so, like at San Francisco, the main deliberative opportunities were reserved for the states themselves.

An institution that has direct leverage over states, such as the IMF, may still require a foundation of legitimacy, but observing the role of legitimation will be more difficult because of the confounding effects of coercion.[23] Both the IMF and World Bank have paid a great deal of attention to perceptions of their legitimacy,[24] but the deference they induce among applicant countries is no doubt influenced by the loans they may make, and the effects of this leverage makes it harder to study the effects of legitimacy on state behavior. Like the Security Council, the International Financial Institutions (IFIs) have high political salience, but because they can leverage compliance by states through their control of loans rather than by their legitimacy, the workings of legitimacy are different and perhaps less evident. Other IOs, such as UNESCO, share with the Security Council the need to elicit self-motivated compliance, but their relatively low political salience makes them less likely locations to observe the play of legitimation.

These issues of interest to other international institutions signal that the kinds of international politics that characterize the Security Council are likely also to be found around other international organizations, most readily where the conditions of high politics and low institutional leverage exist. The drive for legitimation and the use of symbols derived from it are evident in many corners of the international system. Courts stand out as one such corner where further research into the bases of legitimation and delegitimation would surely pay dividends.

### Sovereignty after Anarchy

The existence of legitimacy in international organizations is important, because it reveals fundamental features about the constitution of the pres-

---

[23] The IMF's leverage is over states that borrow from the Fund. It has little influence over other members, but see Barnett and Finnemore 2004.

[24] For instance, the IMF's managing director said recently that the "Fund's credibility with its members rests as importantly as anything on the Fund's perceived legitimacy" (Rodrigo de Rato, "Globalization and the New Priorities of the IMF," October 20, 2005, http://www.imf.org/external/np/speeches/2005/102005a.htm).

ent international system. Sovereignty, understood as the exercise of legitimate authority in international relations, is not located exclusively in states. Sovereignty exists wherever processes of legitimation create powerful institutions of authority in world politics. Sovereignty can be found in some international institutions, including the Security Council.[25]

It is conventional to describe the international system as an "anarchy," where anarchy is understood to mean that there is no overarching government in a position of authority to dispense ultimate rulings that are binding on states. The anarchy problematique is sustained by scholars of IOs with the observation that none of the international organizations claims to be a supra-national power, and those that come closest have crucial legal limitations that keep them from attaining among states the authority exercised by domestic governments over citizens. For instance, the ICJ's power to judge on interstate legal disputes is subordinate to the consent of the states themselves. Even though the Court's rulings can be legally binding, there is nothing in the Statute of the ICJ that requires states to submit their disputes to the Court except voluntarily.[26] States retain the right to decide which disputes will reach the ICJ and so retain their monopoly over authority in this aspect of the international system. Similarly the World Trade Organization (WTO) has the power, through its Dispute Settlement Body, to decide authoritatively on trade disputes between members, and to approve punishing tariffs against states in violation of their WTO concessions. However, this power is limited in a number of ways, not least by the fact that states *consent* to membership in the organization and thus agree to the terms of the dispute settlement provisions in the WTO treaty. The WTO has power only by virtue of state consent and so does not formally trump state sovereignty. The ICC is equally the product of state consent in that it is binding only on states that choose to ratify the Rome Statute, although its powers to rule as invalid or insincere criminal investigations conducted by domestic courts comes much closer to the exercise of sovereign authority than exists in either the WTO or the ICJ.[27]

The key question is whether there are international organizations that possess legitimated social power. As Barnett and Finnemore have noted,

[25] Barnett and Finnemore (2004) find authority present in the bureaucracies of some international organizations by virtue of the perceived legitimacy of the organizations' goals and the organizational form of bureaucracy itself. They do not make the connection between authority and sovereignty.

[26] Article 36(1) of the ICJ Statute defines the jurisdiction of the Court as comprising "all cases which the parties refer to it," and Article 36(2) allows for a general prior commitment by states to use the ICJ for their legal disputes. See Gill 2003.

[27] The authority is final and binding, and without appeal by states. See Schabas 2004, 85–89.

where this exists one will find a relationship of authority between the IO and states.[28] Belief in the legitimacy of an organization's power creates authority in the organization. This undermines the classic dichotomy, from Waltz and others, between a sphere of domestic politics governed by authority and an international sphere governed by self-help.[29] The claim that sovereignty resides exclusively in states is foundational in all IR theory work that is premised on the anarchy problematique. My study suggests instead that the distribution of sovereignty is a variable rather than a constant in the international system. It changes based on historical and political conditions and practices. It may sometimes be highly centralized in states, but it can never be completely monopolized by states and indeed may often be highly decentralized among the various institutions and practices of the international system.

Finnemore traces changes in the legitimating justifications for international intervention from the nineteenth century, and finds that these justifications affected how even strong states conceived of the limits between them and other states. "Like any intellectual framework," she contends, "this set of normative orientations about what was desirable and how best to achieve those things enabled certain kinds of action and discouraged others."[30] Similarly recent histories of the development of sovereignty as an institution from Ian Clark and Mlada Bukovansky emphasize the influence of international legitimation on the development of domestic constitutional change.[31] Habermas argues that problems of self-legitimation for nation-states are leading toward new bases for legitimating political authority. These might arise from the interplay of NGO networks, business contracts, and the remnants of the nation-state creating a "post-national constellation" of power for "creating, generalizing, and coordinating global interests."[32] In all this scholarship there is an acknowledgment that the sovereign nation-state is embedded in a broader system of political authority, a "constitution" according to Philpott, the existence of which is essential to sustaining the interstate system.[33]

---

[28] Barnett and Finnemore 2004. Also see Barnett 2001.

[29] Waltz 1986.

[30] Finnemore 2004, 107. See also Deborah Avant 2005, 264: "The market for force has undermined states' collective ability to monopolize violence in the international system. This has not made states, per se, less important, but opened the way for changes in the roles states and other actors play in controlling force on the world stage."

[31] Clark 2005; Bukovansky 2002.

[32] Habermas (2001, 80) believes that the United Nations lacks the democratic credentials and grass-roots participatory opportunities that he thinks are the foundations of legitimacy, and so the UN is not a likely location to find legitimated international governance. My evidence suggests otherwise, in part because it focuses on state-centric legitimation rather than public opinion.

[33] Philpott 2003.

This broader context includes legitimated institutions of international power such as the Security Council. These institutions are locations of international sovereignty. The "global dimension of sovereignty" is, according to William Connolly, a more persuasive interpretation of recent international developments than is suggested by accounts that treat international sovereignty as zero-sum with state sovereignty.[34] He says instead that "sovereignty itself becomes more complex today . . . [with] both an additional level of sovereignty and new sites of citizen action appropriate to it."[35] He discusses Hardt and Negri who, in Connolly's words, chart "the migration of sovereignty to a layered global assemblage" made up of diverse institutions and actors, and comprising together what Hardt and Negri call "Empire."[36] These institutions are decentralized and so fail to qualify as "world government," but they operate as governing authorities in the international political system. The conventional conceptualization of international anarchy cannot be sustained in the face of "global governance" of this kind. Sovereignty in the international system is located in, and exercised by, both states and international organizations; in other words, sovereignty exists in international organization.

The Security Council is part of that set of institutions, and this book argues that, as a result, world politics unfolds in a significantly different way from what anarchy prescribes. States behave as if they acknowledge the sovereignty of the Council, and their behavior is changed by their efforts to accommodate and exploit it in the pursuit of their interests. The Council's presence changes the incentives faced by states and pervades international politics in ways that states have not consented to and from which they cannot simply choose to free themselves. Because perceptions of legitimacy rely on gradual processes of socialization rather than choice, states are not in a position to choose to abandon them abruptly and pick up some other perceptions. States can of course choose to act in ways that they believe will undermine or redefine the legitimacy of the Council, but they cannot *choose* to see the institution in a new way. Similarly states that do not perceive the Council to be legitimate must still live in a world alongside others who do, and they cannot simply choose a different world. As a result, the Council is in a position of authority in the international system with a power over states to which the states have not consented.

The presence of sovereign authority in the Council means that the system cannot be described as an anarchy. It does not satisfy the basic definition of international "anarchy" provided for IR by Helen Milner and others.[37]

[34] Connolly 2005, 148.
[35] Ibid.
[36] Ibid., 148–149.
[37] Milner 1991.

The system, instead, is *governed*, in a formal sense, by at least one institution that embodies Ruggie's "fusion of power with a legitimate social purpose" and that is located outside any individual state.[38] Finding authority and sovereignty in international organizations upends all models of IR theory founded on the assumption of international anarchy.

A system of "distributed" or "layered" sovereignty is one metaphor for describing this international system. Other possible metaphors include Bull's "new mediaevalism," Rosenau's "turbulence," and "Empire" from Hardt and Negri.[39] The approach advanced here differs from the anarchy problematique in three ways. First, it accounts for the fact that sovereign authority can and does exist in the international system beyond the level of the state, and that once lodged in legitimized international institutions, and for as long as it remains authoritative, it has decisive power over states in some situations. Second, it recognizes that such institutions do not govern the *entire* international system, and perhaps not even a majority of it—some aspects of world politics are "anarchical" and may remain so. That sovereignty exists beyond the state does not mean that it has been removed from states entirely. Third, it recognizes that, since sovereign authority is built out of legitimacy and legitimacy is itself unstable, the organizing principles of the international system are themselves inherently fluid. Because the anarchy problematique cannot accommodate the evidence in this book that sovereignty is decentralized and multilayered, the dynamics of the international system "after anarchy" stand high on the research agenda of theorists of the international system.

### *Policy Implications*

These theoretical conclusions are valuable to some, but, as Christopher Gelpi notes, findings of interest to academics may be of little concern to policy makers. This is not because the findings are irrelevant but rather because they often deal with the causal effects of variables that policy makers cannot manipulate.[40] In Gelpi's case, concerning crisis bargaining in international relations, academics may find it interesting that one strong factor in making crises more peaceful is the quality of the democracy of the protagonists; to policy makers dealing with a crisis, however, this is not compelling information if it does not indicate a lever they might use to increase their chances of prevailing peacefully. With this in mind, I elaborate on two

[38] Ruggie 1998, 64.

[39] Bull 1995; Rosenau 1990; and Hardt and Negri 2000. Others include the "international state" (Wendt 1994a), "private authority" (Cutler 1999), and "international political culture" (Bukovansky 2002).

[40] Gelpi 2003.

implications of my research that are relevant to policy and tuned to variables that policy makers have some control over and feel strongly about: one concerns delegitimizing unfavorable institutions, and the other concerns the status of the Council in the aftermath of the U.S.-Iraq war.

## STRATEGIES FOR DELEGITIMATION

The cases presented here suggest how political players might pursue a delegitimation strategy against an international institution they oppose. "Resistance," more generally, is an enormous topic and cannot be covered here. But having come this far, it is worth repeating that the perception that an institution is legitimate does not necessarily mean that it either serves the real interests of its audience or meets outsiders' sense of justice. Thus a readiness to question legitimized structures is always needed, as well as a willingness to undermine them when necessary. The continuation of a legitimated institution involves an ongoing social reproduction in which meanings are redefined, opposition deflected, and the institution buttressed; it is this reproduction that opponents must interrupt. The importance of social reproduction is what brought Pierre Bourdieu to the study of the French educational system.[41] From an abstract concern with the nonviolent but coercive power of social norms, Bourdieu turned his attention to the crucial role of pedagogy in supporting that power. Education, he said, "in reproducing culture in all its arbitrariness, also reproduces the power relations" which sustain the status quo.[42]

Two elements of a subversive strategy for international relations suggest themselves from the preceding chapters, both centered on the role of symbols in supporting structures of power. First, opposition should be presented in the language of the powerful. The symbols of the powerful can be deployed by any actor, as we saw in chapters 4 and 5, and can be used by the weak to discourage "cheating" by the strong—in other words, to coerce the strong by mobilizing existing norms in ways not favored by the strong. This was the heart of the Libyan strategy in the Lockerbie case, where the Libyans aimed to achieve their policy goals by convincing others that the strong states were disrespecting the basic institutions of international society. When the weak use the symbols of the strong in the pursuit of their own interests, the strong must decide whether to accept that use (and thus concede to the behavior of the weak) or reject it (and thus abandon its investment in the symbol). This is a technique that alters the behavior of the strong without changing the existing basis of legitimation of the social order as a whole.

---

[41] Bourdieu 1987.
[42] Jenkins 1992, 105.

Second, the symbols can be given new meaning. This is more openly subversive than simply discouraging hypocrisy since it changes the basis of legitimation, but because it is more obvious it is perhaps less dangerous to those in power. In his study of the symbolic politics that motivate ethnic civil wars, Stuart Kaufman discusses how recasting the meanings of symbols can be a useful strategy for preventing ethnic wars; however he also shows how power-seeking elites, in Moldova and elsewhere in the post-Soviet world, have redefined nationalist symbols in exclusivist terms to *provoke* ethnic cleansing and war.[43] At the Council recent shifts in how powerful states understand the key clause "threats to international peace and security" have shifted the scope and depth of the Council's legitimated power. The Council is now generally accepted to be authorized by the Charter to act in areas which once were the protected domain of domestic politics, such as terrorism, humanitarian disaster, and mistreatment of domestic populations. Redefining terms and symbols alters the power of the institution directly. This is more easily done by powerful players than by challengers; thus it is difficult to employ as a delegitimizing strategy but remains possible owing to the social foundation of legitimacy and power.

THE COUNCIL BEFORE AND AFTER IRAQ 2003

These chapters suggest an interpretation of the Council in the aftermath of the 2003 Iraq War that differs significantly from the prevailing view. Far from undermining the Council, the spectacular diplomatic confrontations and failures pre- and postwar *enhanced* the Council by reinforcing its basis of legitimation. The key to this understanding is a realistic sense of the original purposes and the legal mandate of the Council, recalled from chapter 4.

The critics of the Council over Iraq fell into two main categories: those who felt that the Council had failed in its purpose of defending the Charter against unilateral state aggression and should have acted more forcefully to stop the United States from deposing Saddam Hussein, and those who felt that the Council had failed to defend international peace and security by not authorizing the U.S. mission to enforce the resolutions against weapons of mass destruction. The two sets disagreed on a wide number of issues regarding international law, the interpretation of threats, and the utility of the inspections regime, but they agreed that the Council failed an important test by not acting forcefully to overcome the disagreements among the permanent members.[44] Many critics even concluded

[43] Kaufman 2001,
[44] See Hurd 2006.

that the Council's failure was evidence of a deeper and probably fatal condition brought on by the shift to U.S. unipolarity and the rise of terrorism.[45]

The evidence in this book suggests that this analysis is wrong, both in its starting premise and its policy implications. It is based on a fundamental misunderstanding of the nature of the Security Council, one that endows the Council with legal powers far beyond those that exist in the Charter, and it leads to wrong advice to policy makers regarding the UN. It is ironic that such neoconservative critics of the Council as Richard Perle and Charles Krauthammer should share with the progressive idealists an overinflated sense of the Council's power, purpose, and function in the world. The threat to the legitimacy of the UN brought on by the Iraq case is, as I discuss later, based on Articles 2(4) and 51, rather than with the Council.

A more "realistic" consideration of the Council's role in international security is possible based on the evidence in chapter 4 of the UN's founding. As we saw, the Security Council was seen from its inception as a political pact among the Great Powers to keep the peace among themselves. The principle that the strong states should manage the system on behalf of the rest was accepted without great disagreement at San Francisco, and was at the heart of the sponsors' design of the veto. There was never any serious suggestion that this was a system for emancipating the small states, nor that the Council should have the capacity to force a collective outcome on a reluctant Great Power. The veto is the key to this system. That the veto works negatively, in permitting Great Powers to kill resolutions with which they disagree, means that it biases the Council in the direction of inaction. The veto ensures that no collective action can be taken against the wishes of a permanent member, and so it guarantees that the Council will be paralyzed at precisely those moments of greatest tension between the Great Powers. This brake on collective action was expressly designed into the structure of the Council, and without it the UN would never have been supported by the strongest states.

Thus to dismiss the Council as a failure in the Iraq case because it did not force a collective outcome in the face of Great Power disagreement is to misunderstand the basic powers and authority of the Council.[46] The Council is not now empowered, and was never intended, to stop Great Powers from intervening in smaller states, and it contains no obligation of collective action except when the permanent members choose it. The real objectives of the Council are more modest than the critics suggest, and the Council's successes and failures should be assessed in terms that appreciate its powers more realistically. Its contribution was not negligible,

[45] For instance, Glennon 2003 and Krauthammer 2003.
[46] See also Price 2004.

even if it was less than what the neoconservatives were afraid of and also less than what some other activists aspired to.

Within the constraints of this basic inaction, the Council managed to contribute in three ways to its general goals of maintaining international peace and stability. These were based in the legitimate authority that some states perceived in the Council, and it was the wish to accommodate that authority that motivated the Great Powers to alter their international behavior.

First, the legitimacy of the Council made it worthwhile for the U.S. to seek Council approval for its preferred policy on Iraq. This produced the first round of diplomatic maneuvering and reopened the debate over how to deal with Saddam in the fall of 2002. It also forced the U.S. to justify its position, particularly on weapons of mass destruction, and it has subsequently found itself trying to live up to its public claims. In addition, the existence of the previous resolutions that found Iraq to be a threat to international peace and security was an important resource for the U.S. in constructing its case that Hussein was an international outlaw who had fewer rights of autonomy than rule-respecting leaders had. Second, many third-party countries, such as Canada and Turkey, looked to the Council to signal whether it was appropriate to support the mission. When the Council failed to approve the military solution to the Iraq problem, these countries (and a wide swath of public opinion) chose to stay on the sidelines. Had the Council acted differently, many countries and publics would likely have acted differently as well, and both the military and diplomatic challenges faced by the U.S. would have been lessened.[47] Third, the Council, by refusing to approve the operation, accomplished both of its (realistic but more modest) goals when Great Powers disagree: it reinforced the legal principles of the Charter on the use of force, and it raised the political costs of unilateralism for the hegemon. This is the most the Council was designed to do relative to the Great Powers.[48]

The critics of the Council are right that the Council was not strong enough either to block the U.S. action or approve it in the face of dissensus. Neither is indicated in the Charter as a realistic goal, and, indeed, the negotiating history of the Charter at San Francisco makes clear that the sponsors were adamantly opposed to both. Glennon maintains that the UN represented "a grand attempt to subject the use of force to the rule of law," but the veto makes abundantly clear that this was not the case, at least not as applied to the Great Powers.[49] What is important, from the

[47] Tharoor 2003.
[48] See Krisch 2005 more generally on the power of international law relative to a hegemon. See also Simpson 2005.
[49] Glennon 2003, 16.

point of view of the power of legitimacy is that the existence of the Council materially altered the political calculations of the U.S. in pursuing its preferred policies, and, more generally, when state officials mobilize the legitimacy of the Council behind their interests, they find it easier to win support and deflect criticism.[50]

There are threats to the legitimacy of the UN in the Iraq case, but these are located in the Charter in Articles 2(4) and 51 rather than arising through the Council. Article 2(4) commits member states to "refrain in their international relations from the threat or use of force," and Article 51 reaffirms the "inherent right of individual or collective self-defense if an armed attack occurs against a member." Together, these two articles provide a legal frame for international action that prohibits the use of force except in self-defense. Only the Council can authorize international war other than for self-defense as defined in Article 51. This frame of reference was readily accepted by both the supporters and critics of the 2003 invasion of Iraq, and they justified their different policy conclusions on different understandings of the terms of the two articles. The strength of these justifications, and the closeness of fit between the interpretation and the language of the Charter, may delegitimize the United Nations as a whole.[51]

The evidence in this book suggests that whole-scale delegitimation of the UN is highly unlikely. The "collective legitimation" that the Council can provide is extremely valuable to states, and the political contestation that takes place around the Council tends to reinforce rather that undermine the belief among states in its legitimacy.

---

[50] Chapman and Reiter 2004. On the role of domestic public opinion, see Taubman 2004.

[51] This would be consistent with Franck's argument about the weakness of Article 2(4) in Franck 1970. See also Franck 2003.

THE POWER OF the UN Security Council, and other international organizations, depends on being seen by states as a legitimate actor in world politics. This legitimacy is a complex phenomenon that is difficult to measure empirically. Nevertheless it has significant effects on the international system and on state behavior, even if the causal mechanisms behind these effects are indirect. Legitimacy gives strength to rules set down by international institutions that have little or no capacity to enforce them; it affects how states think about complying with or violating rules; and it affects how states react to instances of violation or compliance by others. The sovereign power gained by international organizations from legitimation is fragile. It can be damaged by mismanagement by the organization and by strategies of delegitimation backed by a competing power. The Security Council is unlikely to face whole-scale delegitimation in the near future, but the terms of its power are subject to reinterpretation by states, just as the terms of state power are subject to reinterpretation in "domestic" politics. Cases of extreme controversy at the Council, such as over the Lockerbie sanctions or over the 2003 U.S.-Iraq war, are opportunities for actors to promote new interpretations of the Council's legitimacy, and, if new interpretations take hold, they provide a new set of limits and powers for the institution. The boundaries around Council power shift as the terms of its legitimation are reconstructed by states and others. Institutions cannot avoid this process of evolution, and international organizations are no different in this way than either public or private institutions in domestic life. This is the consequence of the basic logic that gives the organization legitimated power in the first place.

The preceding chapters have shown several ways that the behavior of governments is changed because of the legitimacy of the UN Security Council in international affairs. We have seen that states compete for the Council's attention, compete to be associated with it, and compete to influence its pronouncements on issues like peacekeeping and sanctions. At times states seek to legitimate the Council, as the Great Powers did in 1945, and at other times to delegitimate it, as Libya threatened in the 1990s and the U.S. in 2003. At still other times states react to Council legitimacy not as active agents but as consumers, as when they compete with one another to be associated with it. We can also observe states pursuing their parochial, strategic goals using tools and instruments created by the Council. This is not a matter of states being socialized to act for common rather than individual goals. For instance, when the Russian military mimics the conventions of UN peacekeeping in its own operations, it is using symbols derived from the legitimated Council to make a powerful political point. These are all phenomena that provide circumstantial evidence of the legitimacy of the Security Council. They also simultaneously contribute to reinforcing that legitimacy, even while recasting it.

In chapter 6 we saw how the legitimacy of the Council was a valued goal and motivated the U.S. and U.K. response to Libya's campaign of reinterpretation. Because legitimacy is a quality that can never be fully settled, weaker states have opportunities to exploit the interests strong states have in maintaining the legitimacy of the institution. Such competition is not necessarily a sign of weak or declining legitimacy. It can actually be a sign that the institution is working and is powerful in that it attracts the attention of actors seeking to deploy it to their own ends. The loss of legitimacy comes instead when the institution fails to attract such attention and is ignored. This might occur if the institution is perceived to be dominated by one member or if it consistently fails to live up to the ideals and principles which justify it. Both problems, independence and hypocrisy, make the institution less useful to those trying to invoke its power-by-association, and may contribute to its marginalization.

The legitimacy of an international institution affects power politics among states in three ways. First, when states are socialized to believe in the legitimacy of a rule or organization, that state's conception of its own interests is altered. Internalizing supra-state sovereign authority affects the states' perceptions of their needs and wants, and how they conceive of important national goals such as security, status, and role. Consequently what appears to the state as a rational strategy to pursue these goals is changed from what existed previously. Second, when a number of states in the system share a common belief in the legitimacy of a rule or institution, there is a structural change in the international system. The condition that Weber called the "validity" of the system is created: the pattern of actor compliance with the legitimated norm affects the expectations of all states, not just those that have internalized it. Rational states should take into account the probability that the norm will be defended by the "believers," and in this way legitimacy can restructure the entire international system. Finally, the symbols associated with a legitimized international organization are powerful tools. States work to deploy them in the defense of their interests. Their power depends on the prior existence of a belief in the institution's legitimacy among at least some important states, but in practice we see that this can be significantly less than complete universal agreement. The tools can be used by states that have not internalized the belief in the legitimacy of the originating institution, and so come to be valuable instruments of foreign policy across the entire system.

The most important finding for international relations is that sovereignty exists in multiple locations in the international system, and is exercised by institutions beyond the state. This study documented this finding empirically and developed its implications conceptually. States invest the UN Security Council with legitimacy and then, as a result, they find themselves and the interstate system fundamentally changed.

# References

Abbott, Kenneth W., and Duncan Snidal. 1998. "Why States Act through Formal International Organizations." *Journal of Conflict Resolution* 42 (1): 3–32.

———. 2002. "Filling in the Folk Theorem: The Role of Gradualism and Legalization in International Cooperation to Combat Corruption." Paper presented at the annual meeting of the American Political Science Association, 2002.

Adler, Emmanuel, and Michael Barnett. 1998. "A Framework for the Study of Security Communities." In Emmanuel Adler and Michael Barnett, eds., *Security Communities*. Cambridge: Cambridge University Press.

Agulhon, Maurice. 1985. "Politics, Images, and Symbolism in Post-Revolutionary France." In Sean Wilentz, ed., *Rites of Power: Symbolism, Ritual, and Politics since the Middle Ages*. Philadelphia: University of Pennsylvania Press.

Albin, Cecelia. 2001. *Justice and Fairness in International Negotiation*. Cambridge: Cambridge University Press.

Almond, Harry H. 1995. "Peacekeeping: Russia's Emerging Practice." In Uri Ra'anan and Kate Martin, eds., *Russia: A Return to Imperialism?* New York: St. Martin's.

Alvarez, Jose E. 1995. "The Once and Future Security Council." *Washington Quarterly* 18 (2): 5–20.

Annan, Kofi. 2005. *In Larger Freedom: Towards Development, Security, and Human Rights for All.*" A/59/2005. New York: United Nations.

Associated Press. 2003. "Marines Topple Saddam Statue in Baghdad Square," April 9, 2003.

Avant, Deborah D. 2005. *The Market for Force: The Consequences of Privatizing Authority*. Cambridge: Cambridge University Press.

Axelrod, Robert. 1984. *The Evolution of Cooperation*. New York: Basic Books.

Axelrod, Robert, and Robert O. Keohane. 1985. "Achieving Cooperation Under Anarchy." *World Politics*. 38 (1): 226–254.

Bachrach, Peter, and Morton S. Baratz. 1962. "The Two Faces of Power." *American Political Science Review* 56:947–952.

Bailey, Sydney D., and Sam Daws. 1998. *The Procedure of the United Nations Security Council*. Oxford: Clarendon.

Baldwin, David A. 1993. "Neoliberalism, Neorealism, and World Politics." In David A. Baldwin, ed., *Neorealism and Neoliberalism: The Contemporary Debate*. New York: Columbia University Press.

Barber, Benjamin. 1995. *Jihad vs. McWorld*. New York: Ballantine Books.

Barnett, Michael. 1995. "Partners in Peace? The United Nations, Regional Organizations, and Peacekeeping." *Review of International Studies* 21:411–433.

———. 1997. "Bringing in the New World Order: Liberalism, Legitimacy, and the United Nations." *World Politics* 49:526–551.

———. 2001. "Authority, Intervention, and the Outer Limits of International Relations Theory." In Thomas Callaghy, Ronald Kassimir, and Robert Latham, eds., *Intervention and Transnationalism in Africa: Global-Local Networks of Power*. Cambridge: Cambridge University Press.

Barnett, Michael. 2005. "Constructivism." In John Bayliss and Steve Smith, eds., *The Globalization of World Politics: An Introduction to International Relations*, 3rd ed. Oxford: Oxford University Press.

Barnett, Michael, and Raymond Duvall. 2005. "Power and International Politics." *International Organization* 51 (1): 39–75.

———. 1999. "The Politics, Power, and Pathologies of International Organizations." *International Organization* 53 (4): 699–732.

Barnett, Michael, and Martha Finnemore. 2004. *Rules for the World: International Organizations in Global Politics*. Ithaca: Cornell University Press.

Baumann, Zygmunt. 1989. *Modernity and the Holocaust*. Ithaca: Cornell University Press.

Beetham, David. 1991. *The Legitimation of Power*. Houndsmill, Hamps.: Macmillan.

Beitz, Charles R. 1979. *Political Theory and International Relations*. Princeton, N.J.: Princeton University Press.

Bekker, Peter H. F. 1998. "Questions of Interpretation and Application of the 1971 Montreal Convention Arising from the Aerial Incident at Lockerbie." *American Journal of International Law* 92 (3):503–508.

Bennett, A. LeRoy. 1991. *International Organizations: Principles and Issues*. 5th ed. New York: Prentice Hall.

Bennis, Phyllis. 2000. *Calling the Shots: How Washington Dominates Today's UN*. Interlink Publishing.

Berger, Peter L., and Thomas Luckmann. 1966. *The Social Construction of Reality: A Treatise in the Sociology of Knowledge*. New York: Anchor Books.

Berkeley, Bill. 2001. *The Graves Are Not Yet Full: Race, Tribe, and Power in the Heart of Africa*. New York: Basic Books.

Biersteker, Thomas J., and Cynthia Weber. 1996. "The Social Construction of Sovereignty." In Thomas J. Biersteker and Cynthia Weber, eds., *State Sovereignty as a Social Construct*. Cambridge: Cambridge University Press.

Blau, Peter M. 1963. "Critical Remarks on Weber's Theory of Authority." *American Political Science Review* 57 (2): 305–316.

Bob, Clifford. 2005. *The Marketing of Rebellion: Insurgents, Media, and International Activism*. Cambridge: Cambridge University Press.

Bodansky, Daniel. 1999. "The Legitimacy of International Governance: A Coming Challenge for International Environmental Law?" *American Journal of International Law* 93 (3):596–624.

Bothe, M. 1993. "Les limites des pouvoirs du Conseil de sécurité." In *The Development of the Role of the Security Council*. Dordrecht: Hague Academy of International Law and Martinus Nijhoff.

Bourdieu, Pierre. 1987. *Distinction: A Social Critique of the Judgment of Taste*. Cambridge, Mass.: Harvard University Press.

———. 1990. *The Logic of Practice*. Cambridge, Mass.: Harvard University Press.

———. 1991. *Language and Symbolic Power*. Cambridge, Mass.: Harvard University Press.

Boutros-Ghali, Boutros. 1999. *Unvanquished: A US-UN Saga*. New York: Random House.

Bowett, D. W. 1972. "Economic Coercion and Reprisals by States." *Virginia Journal of International Law* 13 (1): 1–12.

Bowett, D. W. 1982. *The Law of International Institutions.* 4th ed. London: Stevens and Sons.

Bray, John. 1996. "Sanctions: Sticks to Beat Rogues With." *The World Today* (London) 52 (8–9): 206–208.

Brilmayer, Lea. 1994. *American Hegemony: Political Morality in a One-Superpower World.* New Haven: Yale University Press.

Brown, Michael E., Sean M. Lynn-Jones, and Steven E. Miller. 1995. *The Perils of Anarchy: Contemporary Realism and International Security.* Cambridge, Mass.: MIT Press.

Brysk, Allison. 1995. "Hearts and Minds: Bringing Symbolic Politics Back In." *Polity* 27 (4): 559–585.

———. 2000. *From Tribal Village to Global Village: Indian Rights and International Relations in Latin America.* Stanford: Stanford University Press.

Buchanan, Allen. 2002. "Political Legitimacy and Democracy." *Ethics* 112:689–719.

———. 2003. *Justice, Legitimacy, and Self-Determination: Moral Foundations of International Law.* Oxford: Oxford University Press.

Buchanan, J., and Tullock, G. 1962. *The Calculus of Consent.* Ann Arbor: University of Michigan Press.

Bukovansky, Mlada. 2002. *Legitimacy and Power Politics: The American and French Revolutions in International Political Culture.* Princeton, N.J.: Princeton University Press.

Bull, Hedley. 1995. *The Anarchical Society.* 2nd ed. New York: Columbia University Press.

Butler, Judith. 1997. *The Psychic Life of Power.* Stanford: Stanford University Press.

Caldeira, Gregory A., and James L. Gibson. 1995. "The Legitimacy of the Court of Justice in the European Union: Models of Institutional Support." *American Political Science Review* 89 (2): 356–376.

Calhoun, Craig. 1991. "The Problem of Identity in Collective Action." In Joan Huber, ed., *Macro-Micro Linkages in Sociology.* Newbury Park, Calif.: Sage.

Cameron, Maxwell A., Robert J. Lawson, and Brian W. Tomlin. 1999. *To Walk without Fear: The Global Movement to Ban Landmines.* Oxford: Oxford University Press.

Cameron, Maxwell A., and Brian W. Tomlin. 2000. *The Making of NAFTA: How the Deal Was Made.* Ithaca: Cornell University Press.

Caplan, Richard. 2004. "International Authority and State Building: The Case of Bosnia and Herzegovina." *Global Governance* 10 (1): 53–65.

Caron, David D. 1993. "The Legitimacy of the Collective Authority of the Security Council." *American Journal of International Law* 87 (4):552–588.

Carr, E. H. 1946. *The Twenty-Years Crisis.* 2nd ed. London: Macmillan, St Martin's.

Chapman, Terrence L., and Dan Reiter. 2004. "The United Nations Security Council and the Rally 'Round the Flag Effect." *Journal of Conflict Resolution* 48 (6): 866–909.

Chayes, Abram, and Antonia Handler Chayes. 1995. *The New Sovereignty: Compliance with International Regulatory Agreements.* Cambridge, Mass.: Harvard University Press.

Chong, Dennis. 1995. "Rational Choice Theory's Mysterious Rivals." *Critical Review* 9 (1–2): 37–57.

Chong, Dennis. 2000. *Rational Lives: Norms and Values in Politics and Society.* Chicago: University of Chicago Press.

Citrin, Jack, and Donald P. Green. 1990. "The Self-Interest Motive in American Public Opinion." *Research in Micropolitics* 3:1–28.

Clark, Ian. 2005. *Legitimacy in International Society.* Oxford: Oxford University Press.

Claude, Inis, Jr. 1967. *The Changing United Nations.* New York: Random House.

Coase, Ronald H. 1937. "The Nature of the Firm." *Economica* 4:386–405.

Coicaud, Jean-Marc. 2001. "Conclusion: International Organizations, the Evolution of International Politics, and Legitimacy." In Jean-Marc Coicaud and Veijo Heiskanen, eds., *The Legitimacy of International Organizations.* Tokyo: United Nations University Press.

———. 2002. *Legitimacy and Politics: A Contribution to the Study of Political Right and Political Responsibility.* Cambridge: Cambridge University Press.

Connolly, William. 1984. "Introduction: Legitimacy and Modernity." In William Connolly, ed., *Legitimacy and the State.* New York: New York University Press.

———. 1987. "Modern Authority and Ambiguity." In J. Roland Pennock and John W. Chapman, eds., *Authority Revisited: NOMOS XXIX.* New York: New York University Press.

———. 1995. *The Ethos of Pluralization.* Minneapolis: University of Minnesota Press.

———. 2005. *Pluralism.* Durham: Duke University Press.

Cortell, Andrew P., and James W. Davis Jr. 1996. "How Do International Institutions Matter? The Domestic Impact of International Rules and Norms." *International Studies Quarterly* 40 (4): 451–478.

Crandall, Christian S., and Ryan K. Beasley. 2001. "A Perceptual Theory of Legitimacy: Politics, Prejudice, Social Institutions, and Moral Value." In John T. Jost and Brenda Major, eds., *The Psychology of Legitimacy: Emerging Perspectives on Ideology, Justice, and Intergroup Relations.* Cambridge: Cambridge University Press.

Crawford, Neta. 2002. *Argument and Change in World Politics: Ethics, Decolonization, and Humanitarian Intervention.* Cambridge: Cambridge University Press.

Cronin, Bruce. 1999. *Community under Anarchy: Transnational Identity and the Evolution of Cooperation.* New York: Columbia University Press.

———. 2001. "The Paradox of Hegemony: America's Ambiguous Relationship with the United Nations." *European Journal of International Relations* 7 (1): 103–130.

Cutler, A. Claire. 1999. "Locating 'Authority' in the Global Political Economy." *International Studies Quarterly* 43:59–81.

Dahl, Robert, and Charles E. Lindblom. 1992. *Politics, Markets, and Welfare.* 2nd ed. New Brunswick, N.J.: Transaction.

Dale, Catherine. 1996. "The Case of Abkhazia (Georgia)." In Lena Jonson and Clive Archer, eds., *Peacekeeping and the Role of Russia in Eurasia.* Boulder, Colo.: Westview.

Daws, Sam. 2004. "The Path to Agreement at San Francisco." Unpublished manuscript, chap. 2b.

Derrida, Jacques. 1986. "Declarations of Independence." *New Political Science* 15:7–15.

Dessler, David. 1989. "What's at Stake in the Agent-Structure Debate?" *International Organization* 43 (3):441–473.

Deutsch, Karl, et al. 1957. *Political Community in the North Atlantic Area.* Princeton, N.J.: Princeton University Press.

Douglas, Mary. 1986. *How Institutions Think.* Syracuse: Syracuse University Press.

Doxey, Margaret P. 1996. *International Sanctions in Contemporary Perspective.* 2nd ed. New York: St. Martin's.

Doyle, Michael W. 1997. *Ways of War and Peace.* New York: Norton.

Drezner, Daniel W. 2003. "The Hidden Hand of Economic Coercion." *International Organization* 57 (3):643–659.

Edelman, Murray. 1988. *Constructing the Political Spectacle.* Chicago: University of Chicago Press.

Edkins, Jenny, and Véronique Pin-Fat. 1999. "The Subject of the Political." In Jenny Edkins, Nalini Persram, and Véronique Pin-Fat, eds., *Sovereignty and Subjectivity.* Boulder, Colo.: Lynne Rienner.

Eisenach, Eldon J. 1981. *Two Worlds of Liberalism: Religion and Politics in Hobbes, Locke, and Mill.* Chicago: University of Chicago Press.

Ellis, Desmond P. 1971. "The Hobbesian Problem of Order: A Critical Appraisal of the Normative Solution." *American Sociological Review* 36 (4): 692–703.

Elster, Jon. 1998. "Deliberation and Constitution Making." In Jon Elster, ed., *Deliberative Democracy.* Cambridge: Cambridge University Press.

Emirbayer, Mustafa, and Jeff Goodwin. 1994. "Network Analysis, Culture, and the Problem of Agency." *American Journal of Sociology* 99 (6): 1411–1454.

Epstein, James A. 1994. *Radical Expression: Political Language, Ritual, and Symbol in England, 1790–1850.* New York: Oxford University Press.

Evatt, H. V. 1946. *Australia in World Affairs.* Sydney: Angus and Robertson.

Eyre, Dana P., and Mark C. Suchman. 1996. "Status, Norms, and the Proliferation of Conventional Weapons: An Institutional Theory Approach." In Peter J. Katzenstein, ed., *The Culture of National Security.* New York: Columbia University Press.

Falk, Richard. 1999. "Reflections on the War." *The Nation* 268 (24): 11–15.

Fassbender, Bardo. 1998. *UN Security Council Reform and the Right of Veto: A Constitutional Perspective.* The Hague: Kluwer Law International.

Fearon, James, and Alexander Wendt. 2002. "Rationalism versus Constructivism: A Skeptical View." In Walter Carlsnaes et al., eds., *Handbook of International Relations.* London: Sage.

Ferejohn, John, and Debra Satz. 1995. "Unification, Universalism, and Rational Choice Theory." *Critical Review* 9 (1–2): 71–84.

Finnemore, Martha. 1993. "International Organizations as Teachers of Norms: The United Nations Educational, Scientific, and Cultural Organization and Science Policy." *International Organization* 47 (4): 565–597.

———. 1996. *National Interests in International Society.* Ithaca: Cornell University Press.

———. 2004. *The Purpose of Intervention: Changing Beliefs about the Use of Force.* Ithaca: Cornell University Press.

Flathman, Richard E. 1993. "Legitimacy." In Robert E. Goodin and Philip Pettit, eds., *A Companion to Contemporary Political Philosophy*, pp. 527–533. Oxford: Blackwell.

Franck, Thomas M. 1970. "Who Killed Article 2(4)? or: Changing Norms Governing the Use of Force by States." *American Journal of International Law* 64:809–837.

———. 1990. *The Power of Legitimacy among Nations.* New York: Oxford University Press.

———. 1992. "The Emerging Right to Democratic Governance." *American Journal of International Law* 86 (1):46–91.

———. 1995. *Fairness in International Law and Institutions.* Oxford: Clarendon.

———. 2003. "What Happens Now? The United Nations after Iraq." *American Journal of International Law* 97 (3): 607–620.

Gaventa, John. 1982. *Power and Powerlessness: Quiescence and Rebellion in an Appalachian Valley.* Urbana: University of Illinois Press.

Gelpi, Christopher. 2003. *The Power of Legitimacy: Assessing the Role of Norms in Crisis Bargaining.* Princeton, N.J.: Princeton University Press.

Gibson, James L., and Gregory A. Caldeira. 1998. "Changes in the Legitimacy of the European Court of Justice: A Post-Maastricht Analysis." *British Journal of Political Science* 28:63–91.

Gilbert, Margaret. 1989. *On Social Facts.* London: Routledge.

Gill, Stephen, and David Law. 1988. *The Global Political Economy: Perspectives, Problems and Policies.* Baltimore, Md.: Johns Hopkins University Press.

Gill, Terry D. 2003. *Rosenne's The World Court: What It Is and How It Works.* 6th ed. Leiden: Martinus Nijhoff.

Gilpin, Robert. 1987. *The Political Economy of International Relations.* Princeton, N.J.: Princeton University Press.

Gintis, Herbert. 2001. "The Puzzle of Prosociality." Working Paper of the Santa Fe Institute.

———. 2002. "The Hitchhiker's Guide to Altruism: Gene-Culture Coevolution, and the Internalization of Norms." Working Paper of the Santa Fe Institute.

Glennon, Michael J. 2003. "Why the Security Council Failed." *Foreign Affairs* 82 (May/June): 16–35.

Goldstein, Judith, and Robert O. Keohane. 1993. "Ideas and Foreign Policy: An Analytical Framework." In Judith Goldstein and Robert O. Keohane, eds., *Ideas and Foreign Policy: Beliefs, Institutions, and Political Change.* Ithaca: Cornell University Press.

Goodrich, Leyland M., Edvard Hambro, and Anne Patricia Simons. 1969. *Charter of the United Nations: Commentary and Documents.* 3rd, rev. ed. New York: Columbia University Press.

Green, Donald P., and Ian Shapiro. 1994. *Pathologies of Rational Choice: A Critique of Applications in Political Science.* New Haven: Yale University Press.

Grewe, Wilhelm G. 1994. "The History of the United Nations." In Bruno Simma, ed., *The Charter of the United Nations: A Commentary.* Oxford: Oxford University Press.

Grieco, Joseph M. 1993. "Anarchy and the Limits of Cooperation: A Realist Critique of the Newest Liberal Institutionalism." In David A. Baldwin, ed., *Neo-*

*realism and Neoliberalism: The Contemporary Debate.* New York: Columbia University Press.

Gruber, Lloyd. 2000. *Ruling the World: Power Politics and the Rise of Supranational Institutions.* Princeton, N.J.: Princeton University Press.

Haas, E. 1990. *When Knowledge Is Power.* Berkeley: University of California Press.

Haass, Richard N. 1998. "Economic Sanctions: Too Much of a Bad Thing?" Policy Brief 34. Washington, D.C.: Brookings Institution.

Habermas, Jürgen. 1975. *Legitimation Crisis.* Translated by Thomas McCarthy. Boston: Beacon.

———. 1979. *Communication and the Evolution of Society.* Translated by Thomas McCarthy. Boston: Beacon.

———. 1984. "What Does a Legitimation Crisis Mean Today? Legitimation Problems in Late Capitalism." In William Connolly, ed., *Legitimacy and the State.* New York: New York University Press.

———. 2001. "The Postnational Constellation." In Jürgen Habermas, *The Postnational Constellation: Political Essays.* Cambridge, Mass.: MIT Press.

Hall, Rodney Bruce. 1999. *National Collective Identity: Social Constructs and International Systems.* New York: Columbia University Press.

Hall, Rodney Bruce, and Thomas J. Biersteker, eds. 2002. *The Emergence of Private Authority in Global Governance.* Cambridge: Cambridge University Press.

Halliday, Terrence, and Bruce Carruthers. 2004. "Institutional Lessons from Insolvency Reforms in East Asia." Paper presented to the Forum on Asian Insolvency Law Reform, New Delhi, India.

Hardt, Michael, and Antonio Negri. 2000. *Empire.* Cambridge, Mass.: Harvard University Press.

Harper, Norman, and David Sissons. 1959. *Australia and the United Nations.* New York: Manhattan Publishing, for Australian Institute of International Affairs and Carnegie Endowment for International Peace.

Harris, D. J. 1991. *Cases and Materials on International Law.* 4th ed. London: Sweet and Maxwell.

Harrison, Simon. 1992. "Ritual as Intellectual Property." *Man* 27:225–244.

———. 1995. "Four Types of Symbolic Conflict." *Journal of the Royal Anthropological Institute* 1 (2): 255–272.

Hart, H. L. A. 1961. *The Concept of Law.* Oxford: Oxford University Press.

Hartmann, Frederick H., ed. 1951. *Basic Documents of International Relations.* New York: McGraw-Hill.

Hayward, Clarissa Rile. 2000. *De-Facing Power.* Cambridge: Cambridge University Press.

Hearn, Frank. 1975. "Remembrance and Critique: The Uses of the Past for Discrediting the Present and Anticipating the Future." *Politics and Society* 5 (2): 201–227.

Hechter, Michael. 1987. *Principles of Group Solidarity.* 4th ed. Berkeley: University of California Press.

Held, David. 1995. *Democracy and the Global Order.* Stanford, Calif.: Stanford University Press.

Helfer, Laurence R., and Anne-Marie Slaughter. 1997. "Toward a Theory of Effective Supranational Adjudication." *Yale Law Journal* 107:273–391.

Helms, Jesse. 1996. "Fixing the UN." *Foreign Affairs* 75 (5): 2–7.

Hendel, Charles W. 1958. "An Exploration of the Nature of Authority." In Carl J. Friedrich, ed., *NOMOS I: Authority*. Cambridge, Mass.: Harvard University Press.

Hilderbrand, Robert C. 1990. *Dumbarton Oaks: The Origins of the United Nations and the Search for Postwar Security*. Chapel Hill: University of North Carolina Press.

Hobbes, Thomas. 1968 [1651]. *Leviathan*. Edited by C. B. Macpherson. Harmondsworth, U.K.: Penguin.

Hoopes, Townsend, and Douglas Brinkley. 1997. *FDR and the Creation of the U.N.* New Haven: Yale University Press.

Howse, Robert. 2001. "The Legitimacy of the World Trade Organization." In Jean-Marc Coicaud and Veijo Heiskanen, eds., *The Legitimacy of International Organizations*. Tokyo: United Nations University Press.

Huntington, Samuel P. 1991. *The Third Wave: Democratization in the Late Twentieth Century*. Norman: University of Oklahoma Press.

Hurd, Elizabeth Shakman. 2004. "The Political Authority of Secularism in International Relations." *European Journal of International Relations* 10 (2): 235–262.

Hurd, Ian. 1997. "Security Council Reform: Informal Membership and Practice." In Bruce Russett, ed., *The Once and Future Security Council*. New York: St. Martin's.

———. 1999. "Legitimacy and Authority in International Politics." *International Organization* 53 (2): 379–408.

———. 2002. "Legitimacy, Power, and the Symbolic Life of the UN Security Council." *Global Governance* 8 (1): 35–51.

———. 2003a. "Too Legit to Quit." *Foreign Affairs* 82 (July/August): 204–205.

———. 2006. "The Great Powers and the UN Security Council: The Futile Search for Collective Security at San Francisco 1945 and Iraq 2003." In Harvey Starr, ed., *Approaches, Levels, and Methods of Analysis in International Politics: Crossing Boundaries*. New York: Palgrave Macmillan.

———. 2008. "Security Council Expansion and Institutional Legitimacy: Five Hypotheses in Search of a Test." *Global Governance* 14 (2). Forthcoming.

Ikenberry, G. John. 1992. "A World Economy Restored: Expert Consensus and the Anglo-American Postwar Settlement." *International Organization* 46 (1): 289–321.

———. 1999. "America's Liberal Hegemony." *Current History* 98 (January): 23–28.

———. 2001. *After Victory: Institutions, Strategic Restraint, and the Rebuilding of Order after Major Wars*. Princeton, N.J.: Princeton University Press.

Ikenberry, G. John, and Charles A. Kupchan. 1990. "Socialization and Hegemonic Power." *International Organization* 44 (3): 283–315.

Jackman, Mary R. 2001. "License to Kill: Violence and Legitimacy in Expropriative Social Relations." In John T. Jost and Brenda Major, eds., *The Psychology of Legitimacy*. Cambridge: Cambridge University Press.

James, Scott C., and David A. Lake. 1989. "The Second Face of Hegemony: Britain's Repeal of the Corn Laws and the American Walker Tariff of 1846." *International Organization* 43 (1): 1–29.

Jencks, Christopher. 1990. "Varieties of Altruism." In Jane Mansbridge, ed., *Beyond Self-Interest*. Chicago: University of Chicago Press.

Jenkins, Richard. 1992. *Pierre Bourdieu*. London: Routledge.

Johnston, Alastair Iain. 2001. "Treating International Institutions as Social Environments." *International Studies Quarterly* 45 (4): 487–515.

Johnstone, Ian. 2003. "Security Council Deliberations: The Power of the Better Argument." *European Journal of International Law* 14 (3): 437–480.

Jonson, Lena, and Clive Archer. "Russia and Peacekeeping in Eurasia." In Lena Jonson and Clive Archer, eds., *Peacekeeping and the Role of Russia in Eurasia*. Boulder, Colo.: Westview.

Jost, John T., and M. R. Banaji. 1994. "The Role of Stereotyping in System-Justification and the Production of False-Consciousness." *British Journal of Social Psychology* 33: 1–27.

Kahler, Miles. 1998. "Rationality in International Relations." *International Organization* 52 (4): 919–942.

Kant, Immanuel. 1984 [1795]. *Perpetual Peace and Other Essays on Politics, History, and Morals*. Indianapolis: Hackett.

Katzenstein, Peter J., Robert O. Keohane, and Stephen D. Krasner. 1998. "*International Organization* and the Study of World Politics." *International Organization* 52 (4): 645–686.

Kaufman, Stuart. J. 2001. *Modern Hatreds: The Symbolic Politics of Ethnic War*. Ithaca: Cornell University Press.

Kaufmann, Johan. 1996. *Conference Diplomacy: An Introductory Analysis*. 3rd ed. New York: St Martin's.

Keck, Margaret E., and Kathryn Sikkink. 1998. *Activists beyond Borders: Advocacy Networks in International Politics*. Ithaca: Cornell University Press.

Kelman, Herbert C. 2001. "Reflections on Social and Psychological Processes of Legitimation and Delegitimation." In John T. Jost and Brenda Major, eds., *The Psychology of Legitimacy: Emerging Perspectives on Ideology, Justice, and Intergroup Relations*. Cambridge: Cambridge University Press.

Keohane, Robert O. 1984. *After Hegemony*. Princeton, N.J.: Princeton University Press.

Keohane, Robert O., and Joseph Nye. 2001. *Power and Interdependence*. 3rd ed. New York: Addison Wesley Longman.

Kertzer, David I. 1988. *Ritual, Politics, and Power*. New Haven: Yale University Press.

———. 1996. *Politics and Symbols: The Italian Communist Party and the Fall of Communism*. New Haven: Yale University Press.

Kirgis, Fredric. 2001. "Terrorist Attacks on the World Trade Center and the Pentagon." *ASIL Insights*, no. 77. American Society of International Law: http://www.asil.org/insights/insigh77.htm.

Kissinger, Henry. 1964. *A World Restored: Castlereagh, Metternich, and the Restoration of Peace, 1812–1822*. New York: Universal Library.

Kittrie, Nicholas N. 2000. *Rebels with a Cause: The Minds and Morality of Political Offenders*. Boulder, Colo.: Westview.

Koremenos, Barbara, Charles Lipson, and Duncan Snidal. 2001. "The Rational Design of International Institutions." *International Organization* 55 (4) (special issue).

Knight, W. Andy. 1998. "Establishing Political Authority in Peace-Maintenance." *Global Governance* 4 (1): 19–40.

Krasner, Stephen D. 1993. "Westphalia and All That." In Judith Goldstein and Robert O. Keohane, eds., *Ideas and Foreign Policy: Beliefs, Institutions, and Political Change*. Ithaca: Cornell University Press.

——. 1999. *Sovereignty: Organized Hypocrisy*. Princeton, N.J.: Princeton University Press.

Kratochwil, Friedrich. 1984. "The Force of Prescriptions." *International Organization* 38 (4): 685–708.

——. 1989. *Rules, Norms, and Decisions*. Cambridge: Cambridge University Press.

Krause, Keith. 2002. "Multilateral Diplomacy, Norm Building, and UN Conferences: The Case of Small Arms and Light Weapons." *Global Governance* 8 (2): 247–263.

Krause, Keith, and W. Andy Knight. 1995. "Introduction: Evolution and Change in the United Nations System." In Keith Krause and W. Andy Knight, eds., *State, Society, and the United Nations System: Changing Perspectives on Multilateralism*. Tokyo: United Nations University.

Krauthammer, Charles. 2003. "UN R.I.P." *Washington Post*, January 31.

Krisch, Nico. 2005. "International Law in Times of Hegemony: Unequal Power and the Shaping of International Legal Order." *European Journal of International Law* 16 (3): 369–408.

Lagoni, Rainer. 1994. "The Economic and Social Council." In Bruno Simma, ed., *The Charter of the United Nations: A Commentary*. Oxford: Oxford University Press.

LeBuffe, Michael. 2003. "Hobbes on the Origin of Obligation." *British Journal for the History of Philosophy* 11 (1): 15–39.

Legro, Jeffrey W. 1996. "Culture and Preferences in the International Cooperation Two-Step." *American Political Science Review* 90 (1): 118–137.

Leheny, David. 2006. *Think Global, Fear Local: Sex, Violence, and Anxiety in Contemporary Japan*. Ithaca: Cornell University Press.

Levy, Jack S. 1994. "Learning and Foreign Policy: Sweeping a Conceptual Minefield." *International Security* 48 (2): 279–312.

Lewis, Jeffrey. 2003. "Institutional Environments and Everyday EU Decision-Making: Rationalist or Constructivist?" *Comparative Political Studies* 36 (1/2): 97–124.

Lipschutz, Ronnie D., and Cathleen Fogel. 2002. " 'Regulation for the Rest of Us?' Global Civil Society and the Privatization of Transnational Regulation." In Rodney Bruce Hall and Thomas J. Biersteker, eds., *The Emergence of Private Authority in Global Governance*. Cambridge: Cambridge University Press.

Locke, John. 1980 [1690]. *The Second Treatise of Government*. Indianapolis: Hackett.

Lohmann, Suzanne. 1995. "The Poverty of Green and Shapiro." *Critical Review* 9 (1/2): 127–159.

Luard, Evan. 1982. *A History of the United Nations: The Years of Western Domination*. New York: St Martin's.

Luck, Edward C. 1999. *Mixed Messages: American Politics and International Organization, 1919–1999*. Washington, D.C.: Brookings Institution.

Luck, Edward C. 2005. "Rediscovering the Security Council: The High-Level Panel and Beyond." In Ernesto Zedillo, ed., *Reforming the United Nations for Peace and Security*. New Haven: Yale Center for the Study of Globalization.

Lukes, Steven. 1974. *Power: A Radical View*. London: Macmillan.

Lynch, Marc. 1999. *State Interests and Public Spheres: The International Politics of Jordan's Identity*. New York: Columbia University Press.

Malone, David M. 1998. *Decision-Making in the UN Security Council: The Case of Haiti 1990–1997*. Oxford: Clarendon.

———. 2000. "Eyes on the Prize: The Quest for Nonpermanent Seats on the UN Security Council." *Global Governance* 6 (1): 3–23.

March, James G., and Johan P. Olsen. 1998. "The Institutional Dynamics of International Political Orders." *International Organization* 52 (4): 943–970.

Martin, Lisa L. 1992. *Coercive Cooperation: Explaining Multilateral Economic Sanctions*. Princeton, N.J.: Princeton University Press.

Martin, Lisa L., and Beth Simmons. 1998. "Theories and Empirical Studies of International Institutions." *International Organization* 52 (4): 729–758.

Marx, Anthony W. 2003. *Faith in Nation: Exclusionary Origins of Nationalism*. Oxford: Oxford University Press.

Mattern, Janice Bially. 2004. *Ordering International Politics*. New York: Routledge.

Mearsheimer, John J. 1994/95. "The False Promise of International Institutions." *International Security* 19 (3): 5–49.

Meisler, Stanley. 1995. *The United Nations: The First Fifty Years*. New York: Atlantic Monthly Press.

Mercer, Jonathan. 1996. *Reputation and International Politics*. Ithaca: Cornell University Press.

Metelits, Claire. 2004. "Reformed Rebels? Democratization, Global Norms, and the Sudan People's Liberation Army." *Africa Today* 51 (1): 65–82.

Milgram, Stanley. 1974. *Obedience to Authority: An Experimental View*. New York: Harper Collins.

Milner, Helen. 1991. "The Assumption of Anarchy in International Politics: A Critique." *Review of International Studies* 17 (1): 67–85.

———. 1997. *Interest, Institutions, and Information: Domestic Politics and International Relations*. Princeton, N.J.: Princeton University Press.

Morgenthau, Hans J. 1960. *Politics among Nations: The Struggle for Power and Peace*. 3rd ed. New York: Knopf.

Müller, Harald. 1993. "The Internalization of Principles, Norms, and Rules by Governments: The Case of Security Regimes." In Volker Rittberger, ed., *Regime Theory and International Relations*. Oxford: Clarendon.

Murphy, Sean. 1994. "The Security Council, Legitimacy, and the Concept of Collective Security after the Cold War." *Columbia Journal of Transnational Law* 32:201–288.

Neumann, Iver B., and Sergei Solodovnik. 1996. "The Case of Tajikistan." In Lena Jonson and Clive Archer, eds., *Peacekeeping and the Role of Russia in Eurasia*. Boulder, Colo.: Westview.

*New York Times*. 2003. "Frisson of Unease among the City's French." March 23.

New Zealand. 1945. *United Nations Conference on International Organization*. Wellington: Department of External Affairs.

Niblock, Tim. 2001. *"Pariah State" and Sanctions in the Middle East: Iraq, Libya, Sudan.* Boulder, Colo.: Lynne Rienner.

Notter, Harley. 1949. *Postwar Foreign Policy Preparation, 1939–1945.* Department of State. Reprinted 1975. Westport, Conn.: Greenwood.

Nye, Joseph. 2004. "Soft Power: The Means to Success in World Politics." Carnegie Council Books for Breakfast interview, April 13, 2004. Transcript at http://www.cceia.org/viewMedia.php/prmTemplateID/8/prmID/4466 (accessed 5/8/2006).

Odell, John S. 2000. *Negotiating the World Economy.* Ithaca: Cornell University Press.

O'Neill, Barry. 1999. *Honor, Symbols, and War.* Ann Arbor: University of Michigan Press.

Onuf, Nicholas, and Frank F. Klink. 1989. "Anarchy, Authority, and Rule." *International Studies Quarterly* 33 (2): 149–73.

Paris, Roland. 2004. *At War's End: Building Peace after Civil Confict.* Cambridge: Cambridge University Press.

Pauly, Louis W. 2002. "Global Finance, Political Authority, and the Problem of Legitimation." In Rodney Bruce Hall and Thomas J. Biersteker, eds., *The Emergence of Private Authority in Global Governance.* Cambridge: Cambridge University Press.

Pearson, Lester B. 1972. *Mike: The Memoirs of the Rt. Hon. Lester B. Pearson.* Vol. 1. Toronto: University of Toronto Press.

Perrow, Charles. 1986. *Complex Organizations: A Critical Essay.* 3rd ed. New York: McGraw-Hill.

Philpott, Daniel. 1999. "Westphalia, Authority, and International Society." *Political Studies* 47 (3): 566–589.

———. 2001. *Revolutions in Sovereignty: How Ideas Shaped Modern International Relations.* Princeton, N.J.: Princeton University Press.

Picco, Giandomenico. 1995. "The UN at Fifty: Reforming Institutions or Individuals?" *The World Today* 51:206–207.

Plomin, Robert, et al. 2001. "Why Are Children in the Same Family So Different? Nonshared Environment a Decade Later." *Canadian Journal of Psychiatry* 46:225–233.

Powell, Walter W. 1990. "Neither Market nor Hierarchy." *Research in Organizational Behavior* 12.

Powell, Walter, and Paul DiMaggio. 1991. *The New Institutionalism in Organizational Analysis.* Chicago: University of Chicago Press.

Press, Daryl G. 2005. *Calculating Credibility: How Leaders Assess Military Threats.* Ithaca: Cornell University Press.

Price, Richard. 1995. "A Genealogy of the Chemical Weapons Taboo." *International Organization* 49: 73–104.

———. 2004. "The League of Nations Redux?" In Richard M. Price and Mark W. Zacher, eds., *The United Nations and Global Security.* New York: Palgrave.

Pursiainen, Christer. 1999. "The Impact of International Security Regimes on Russia's Behavior: The Case of the OSCE and Chechnya." In Ted Hopf, ed., *Understandings of Russian Foreign Policy.* University Park: Pennsylvania State University Press.

Ra'anan, Uri, and Kate Martin, eds. 1995. *Russia: A Return to Imperialism?* New York: St. Martin's.

Rawls, John. 1971. *A Theory of Justice.* Cambridge: Belknap.

Raz, Joseph. 1990. Introduction to *Authority.* Edited by Joseph Raz. New York: New York University Press.

Reid, Escott. 1989. *Radical Mandarin: The Memoirs of Escott Reid.* Toronto: University of Toronto Press.

Reisman, W. Michael. 1993. "The Constitutional Crisis in the United Nations." *American Journal of International Law* 87 (1): 83–100.

Reser, Heather E. 1998. "Airline Terrorism: The Effect of Tightened Security on the Right to Travel." *Journal of Air Law and Commerce* 63: 819–858.

Reus-Smit, Christian. 1997. "The Constitutional Structure of International Society." *International Organization* 51 (4): 555–590.

Risse, Thomas. 2000. "'Let's Argue!' Communicative Action in World Politics." *International Organization* 54 (1): 1–40.

Rose, Gideon. 1998. "Libya." In Richard N. Haass, ed., *Economic Sanctions and American Diplomacy.* New York: The Council on Foreign Relations.

Rosenau, James N. 1990. *Turbulence in World Politics.* Princeton, N.J.: Princeton University Press.

———. 1992. *The United Nations in a Turbulent World.* Boulder, Colo.: Lynne Reinner.

Rosenne, Shabtai. 1989. *The World Court: What It Is and How It Works.* 4th ed. Dordrecht: Matinus Nijhoff.

Ruggie, John Gerard, ed. 1993. *Multilateralism Matters: The Theory and Praxis of an Institutional Form.* New York: Columbia University Press.

———. 1998. *Constructing the World Polity: Essays on International Institutionalization.* London: Routledge.

Russell, Ruth B. 1958. *A History of the United Nations Charter: The Role of the United States, 1940–1945.* Washington D.C.: The Brookings Institution.

Russett, Bruce, ed. 1997. *The Once and Future Security Council.* New York: St. Martin's.

Russett, Bruce, and John Oneal. 2001. *Triangulating Peace: Democracy, Interdependence, and International Organizations.* New York: Norton.

Russett, Bruce, and James S. Sutterlin. 1991. "The U.N. in a New World Order." *Foreign Affairs* 70 (2): 69–83.

Sabel, Robbie. 1997. *Procedure at International Conferences.* Cambridge: Cambridge University Press.

Sartori, Anne. 2002. "A Reputational Theory of Communication in Disputes." *International Organization* 56 (1): 121–150.

Schabas, William A. 2004. *An Introduction to the International Criminal Court.* 2nd ed. Cambridge: Cambridge University Press.

Scharpf, Fritz W. 1999. *Governing in Europe: Effective and Democratic?* Oxford: Oxford University Press.

Schimmelfennig, Frank. 2003a. *The EU, NATO and the Integration of Europe.* Cambridge: Cambridge University Press.

———. 2003b. "Strategic Action in a Community Environment: The Decision to Enlarge NATO to the East." *Comparative Political Studies* 36 (1/2) : 156–183.

Schimmelfennig, Frank. 2005. "Strategic Calculation and International Socialization: Membership Incentives, Party Constellations, and Sustained Compliance in Central and Eastern Europe." *International Organization* 59 (4): 827–860.

Schlesinger, Stephen C. 2003. *Act of Creation: The Founding of the United Nations.* Boulder, Colo.: Westview.

Schuessler, Alexander. 2000. *A Logic of Expressive Choice.* Princeton, N.J.: Princeton University Press.

Schumpeter, Joseph. 1942. *Capitalism, Socialism, and Democracy.* New York: Basic Books.

Scott, James C. 1990. *Domination and the Arts of Resistance: Hidden Transcripts.* New Haven: Yale University Press.

———. 1998. *Seeing Like a State: How Certain Schemes to Improve the Human Condition Have Failed.* New Haven: Yale University Press.

Searle, John. 1995. *The Construction of Social Reality.* New York: Free Press.

Sennett, Richard. 1980. *Authority.* New York: Norton.

Shapiro, Ian. 1986. *The Evolution of Rights in Liberal Theory.* Cambridge: Cambridge University Press.

Shapiro, Ian. 2001. "The State of Democratic Theory." In Ira Katznelson and Helen Milner, eds., *Political Science: The State of the Discipline.* Washington, D.C.: American Political Science Association.

Shashenkov, Maxim. 1994. "Russian Peacekeeping in the 'Near Abroad.'" *Survival* 36 (3): 46–69.

Simmons, A. John. 2001. "'Denisons' and 'Aliens': Locke's Problem of Political Consent." In A. John Simmons, ed., *Justification and Legitimacy: Essays on Rights and Obligations.* Cambridge: Cambridge University Press.

Simpson, Gerry. 2004. *Great Powers and Outlaw States: Unequal Sovereigns in the International Legal Order.* Cambridge: Cambridge University Press.

Singh, Nagendra. 1989. *The Role and Record of the International Court of Justice.* Dordrecht: Martinus Nijhoff.

Slater, Jerome. 1969. "The Limits of Legitimization in International Organizations: The Organization of American States and the Dominican Crisis." *International Organization* 23 (1): 48–72.

Soper, Philip. 1984. *A Theory of Law.* Cambridge, Mass.: Harvard University Press.

Smith, Alastair. 1996. "The Success and Use of Economic Sanctions." *International Interactions* 21 (3): 229–245.

Smith, Gaddis. 1994. *The Last Years of the Monroe Doctrine: 1945–1993.* New York: Hill and Wang.

Spears, Russell, Jolanda Jetten, and Bertjan Doosje. 2001. "The (Il)legitimacy of Ingroup Bias: From Social Reality to Social Resistance." In John T. Jost and Brenda Major, eds., *The Psychology of Legitimacy: Emerging Perspectives on Ideology, Justice, and Intergroup Relations.* Cambridge: Cambridge University Press.

Spruyt, Hendrik. 2005. *Ending Empire: Contested Sovereignty and Territorial Partition.* Ithaca: Cornell University Press.

Steffek, Jens. 2003. "The Legitimation of International Governance: A Discourse Approach." *European Journal of International Relations* 9 (2): 249–275.

Strange, Susan. 1996. *The Retreat of the State: The Diffusion of Power in the World Economy.* Cambridge: Cambridge University Press.

Suchman, Marc C. 1995. "Managing Legitimacy: Strategic and Institutional Approaches." *Academy of Management Review* 20 (3): 571–610.

Sutterlin, James S. 1995. *The United Nations and the Maintenance of International Peace and Security: A Challenge to Be Met.* Westport, Conn.: Praeger.

Tannenwald, Nina. 1999. "The Nuclear Taboo: The United States and the Normative Basis of Nuclear Non-Use." *International Organization* 53 (3): 433–468.

Taubman, Jarrett. 2004. "Towards a Theory of Democratic Compliance: Security Council Legitimacy and Effectiveness after Iraq." *Journal of International Law and Politics* 37:161–224.

Tharoor, Shashi. 2003. "Why America Still Needs the United Nations." *Foreign Affairs* 82 (5): 67–80.

Thielemann, Eiko R. 2003. "Between Interests and Norms: Explaining Burden Sharing in the European Union." *Journal of Refugee Studies* 16 (3): 253–273.

Thorelli, Hans B. 1986. "Networks: Between Markets and Hierarchies." *Strategic Management Journal* 7:37–51.

Thucydides. 1954. *History of the Peloponnesian War.* Translated by Rex Warner. Harmondsworth, U.K.: Penguin.

Tilly, Charles. 1992. *Coercion, Capital, and European States, AD 990–1992.* Cambridge: Blackwell.

Tsebelis, George. 2002. *Veto Players.* Princeton, N.J.: Princeton University Press.

Tyler, Tom R. 1990. *Why People Obey the Law.* New Haven: Yale University Press.

———. 2001. "A Psychological Perspective on the Legitimacy of Institutions and Authorities." In John T. Jost and Brenda Major, eds., *The Psychology of Legitimacy: Emerging Perspectives on Ideology, Justice, and Intergroup Relations.* Cambridge: Cambridge University Press.

———. 2006. "Psychological Perspectives on Legitimacy and Legitimation." *Annual Review of Psychology* 57:375–400.

*United Nations Conference on International Organization [UNCIO],* 1945, Volume 11.

Vandewalle, Dirk. 1998. *Libya since Independence: Oil and Statebuilding.* Ithaca: Cornell University Press.

Van Oudenaren, John. 2003. "What Is Multilateral?" *Policy Review* 117.

Vaubel, Roland and Thomas D. Willett. 1991. *The Political Economy of International Organizations: A Public Choice Approach.* Boulder, Colo.: Westview.

Viorst, Milton. 1999. "The Colonel in his Labyrinth." *Foreign Affairs* 78 (2): 60–75.

Voeten, Erik. 2005. "The Political Origins of the UN Security Council's Ability to Legitimize the Use of Force," *International Organization* 59 (3): 527–558.

Waltz, Kenneth N. 1979. *Theory of International Politics.* Boston: Addison-Wesley.

———. 1986. "Anarchic Orders and Balances of Power." In Robert O. Keohane, ed., *Neorealism and Its Critics.* New York: Columbia University Press.

Walzer, Michael. 1977. *Just and Unjust Wars: A Moral Argument with Historical Examples.* New York: Basic Books.

Walzer, Michael. 1983. *Spheres of Justice: A Defense of Pluralism and Equality.* New York: Basic Books.

Warrander, Howard. 1957. *The Political Philosophy of Hobbes.* Oxford: Clarendon.

Weber, Max. 1978. *Economy and Society.* 2 vols. Berkeley: University of California Press.

Wendt, Alexander. 1987. "The Agent-Structure Problem in International Relations Theory." *International Organization* 41 (3): 335–370.

———. 1994a. "Collective Identity Formation and the International State." *American Political Science Review* 88 (2): 384–396.

———. 1994b. Review of *Ideas and Foreign Policy,* edited by Judith Goldstein and Robert Keohane. *American Political Science Review* 88 (4): 1040–1041.

———. 1995. "Constructing International Politics." *International Security* 20 (1): 71–81.

———. 1999. *A Social Theory of International Politics.* Cambridge: Cambridge University Press.

———. 2003. "Why a World State Is Inevitable." *European Journal of International Relations* 9 (4): 491–542.

Weston, Burns. 1991. "Security Council Resolution 678 and Persian Gulf Decision Making: Precarious Legitimacy." *American Journal of International Law* 85 (3): 516–535.

Whitehead, Alfred North. 1928. *Symbolism: Its Meaning and Effect.* Cambridge: Cambridge University Press.

Williams, David. 1999. "Constructing the Economic Space: The World Bank and the Making of Homo Oeconomicus." *Millennium* 28 (1): 79–99.

Williams, Michael C. 1996. "Hobbes and International Relations: A Reconsideration." *International Organization* 50 (2): 213–236.

Williams, Michael C. 2005. *The Realist Tradition and the Limits of International Relations.* Cambridge: Cambridge University Press.

Williamson, Oliver E. 1985. *The Economic Institutions of Capitalism: Firms, Markets, and Relational Contracting.* New York: Free Press.

Wittgenstein, Ludwig. 1968. *Philosophical Investigations.* 3rd ed. New York: Macmillan.

Wolin, Sheldon. 1960. *Politics and Vision: Continuity and Innovation in Western Political Thought.* Boston: Little, Brown.

Wright, S. C., D. M. Taylor, and F. M. Moghaddam. 1990. "Responding to Membership in a Disadvantaged Group: From Acceptance to Collective Action." *Journal of Personality and Social Psychology* 58: 994–1003.

Wrong, Dennis H. 1961. "The Oversocialized Conception of Man in Modern Sociology." *American Sociological Review* 26 (2): 183–193.

Young, Oran. 1994. *International Governance: Protecting the Environment in a Stateless Society.* Ithaca: Cornell University Press.

Zedillo, Ernesto, ed. 2005. *Reforming the United Nations for Peace and Security.* New Haven: Yale Center for the Study of Globalization.

Zelditch, Morris, Jr. 2001. "Theories of Legitimacy." In John T. Jost and Brenda Major, eds., *The Psychology of Legitimacy: Emerging Perspectives on Ideology, Justice, and Intergroup Relations.* Cambridge: Cambridge University Press.